# American Scream

JONAH RASKIN

# American Scream

Allen Ginsberg's *Howl*
and the Making of the Beat Generation

UNIVERSITY OF CALIFORNIA PRESS
Berkeley   Los Angeles   London

University of California Press
Berkeley and Los Angeles, California

University of California Press, Ltd.
London, England

© 2004 by the Regents of the University of California


Library of Congress Cataloging-in-Publication Data
Raskin, Jonah, 1942–.
    American scream : Allen Ginsberg's Howl and the making of the Beat Generation / Jonah Raskin.
        p.    cm.
    Includes bibliographical references (p. ) and index.
    ISBN 0-520-24015-4 (pbk. : alk. paper)
    1. Ginsberg, Allen, 1926– Howl.   2. Literature and mental illness—United States—History—20th century.
3. Ginsberg, Allen, 1926—Knowledge—Psychology.
4. Ginsberg, Allen, 1926—Psychology.   5. Poetry—Psychological aspects.   6. Mental illness in literature.
7. Beat generation.   I. Title.
PS3513.I74H636 2004
811'.54—dc22                                    2003059527


Manufactured in the United States of America
10  09  08  07  06  05  04
10  9  8  7  6  5  4  3  2  1

The paper used in this publication is both acid-free and totally chlorine-free (TCF). It meets the minimum requirements of ANSI/NISO Z39.48-1992 (R 1997) (*Permanence of Paper*). ⊗

For R.F.

# Contents

# Acknowledgments

I would like to thank Bob Rosenthal and the Allen Ginsberg Trust for permission to quote from unpublished Ginsberg material at libraries across the United States. I also want to thank the Trust for permission to quote from the *Annotated Howl*, as well as from psychiatric reports obtained from the New York State Psychiatric Institute in Manhattan and from Langley Porter in San Francisco.

I would like to thank the libraries themselves for permission to quote from Ginsberg's letters, manuscripts, and journals. Unpublished material appears here courtesy of the Department of Special Collections, Stanford University Libraries; Rare Book and Manuscript Library, Columbia University; Fales Library, New York University; Bancroft Library, the University of California at Berkeley; Harry Ransom Humanities Research Center, the University of Texas at Austin; and the Berg Collection of English and American Literature, The New York Public Library Astor, Lenox, and Tilden Foundations.

I have quoted widely from Allen Ginsberg's poetry and wish to thank HarperCollins for permission to do so.

I also want to thank Northern Lights for permission to quote from Louis Ginsberg's poetry. In researching and writing this book I have had valuable commentary and help from Don Emblen, Robert Friedman, Bill Barich, Bob Coleman, Julie Allen, Tim Wandling, John Kunat, J. J. Wilson, Jack Ritchie, Allen Tobias, Nina Willdorf, Michael Covino, Bob Holman, David Bromige, Lawrence Ferlinghetti, Nancy J. Peters, Adam Raskin, Polly Armstrong, Aram Saroyan, Ilka Hartman, Paul Cohen, Chris Felver, Lee Perron, Louise Yelin, Gerald Nicosia, Peter Hale, Michael Schumacher, Bill Morgan, Dr. Philip Hicks, and Dr. Frederick Quitkin. At the University of California Press I want to thank Naomi Schneider; Sierra Filucci; Marilyn Schwartz; Nola Burger; Nancy Evans; Barbara Roos; and my copyeditor, Sue Carter, in Austin, Texas. At the proverbial last minute, several people came through brilliantly—John Natsoulas, Michael McClure, Pierrette Montroy, and Mike Morey.

*Allen Ginsberg's genius for public life should not obscure his genius as an artist or his study of his art.* —ROBERT PINSKY, 1997 U.S. POET LAUREATE

# Allen Ginsberg's Genius

### The Secret or Hermetic Tradition

In 1957, at the age of fifteen, I bought for seventy-five cents a copy of the City Lights paperback edition of *Howl and Other Poems* with the trademark black-and-white cover. It was the first book of poetry I ever bought, and it made me feel as cool as anyone in my high school. *Howl* was underground poetry, outlawed poetry. Ginsberg made it seem as though it was cool to be a teen and that teens, not adults, knew what was cool. To those of us— I wasn't the only teenage beatnik in suburbia—who owned a copy, *Howl* conferred a strange power. Reading it brought initiation into a secret society. It bound us together and gave us a sense of identity as members of a new generation that had come of age in the wake of World War II and the atomic bomb, a generation that lived in the shadow of nuclear apocalypse. There was something wonderfully subversive about *Howl*, something the poet had hidden in the body of the poem because it was too dangerous to say openly, something we had to uncover and decode.

Ginsberg didn't want to be too easily understood. As he himself would explain, *Howl* was meant to appeal "to the secret or hermetic tradition of art." Of course, as a teenager I didn't know there was a secret tradition of art. It was Ginsberg who introduced me to it and prompted me to pursue it.

### The Cold War and Literary Creativity

Years later, I met Ginsberg in Manhattan, along with his longtime lover and fellow poet, Peter Orlovsky, and Gregory Corso, the author of *Gasoline*. In the 1980s and 1990s, I interviewed Ginsberg several times in New York and in California. In 1985, after having listened to him on record albums for years, I first heard him read his poetry live. It was at College of Marin, just north of San Francisco. After the reading, we talked about the Cold War and American culture, a subject with which he had been preoccupied ever since the mid-1940s—and a subject that had more than academic interest now that Ronald Reagan was president. Indeed, he had been writing new, angry political poems, like "Birdbrain!" and "Capitol Air," that were inspired by the global crisis between East and West, communism and capitalism. "Oh, yes, the Cold War has returned with Reagan," Ginsberg said. "But it's not like the Cold War of the 1940s and 1950s. The CIA doesn't do the dirty work anymore, the corporations do." He complained—as he had complained many times before—about the role of the CIA in creating "a middle stratum of intellectuals and writers to be anti-Communist, to keep a lid on genuine creativity."

"Kerouac was a writer of genius," he said. "For years, he was prevented from being published by the middle-brow intellectuals that the CIA had created. They had already rejected William Carlos Williams and they rejected Kerouac, too." Perhaps no major twentieth-century American poet had a more conspiratorial frame of mind than Ginsberg did; and arguably his sense of conspiracy inspired him to write some of his best poetry, including *Howl*, in which scholars support wars, radios read minds, and America has turned into a fascist state. There was often more than a grain of truth in Ginsberg's conspiratorial vision. Granted, there is no evidence that the CIA was directly or indirectly responsible for Kerouac's rejections by American publishers for half a decade. But as Frances Stonor Saunders shows in *The Cultural Cold War: The CIA and the World of Arts and Letters* (1999), the CIA did engage in covert operations with American writers and intellectuals to win the hearts and minds of people all over the world, much as Ginsberg claimed. The CIA funded magazines such as *Encounter* and established organizations such as the Congress for Cultural Freedom to combat radicalism, subvert dissent, and make America seem like the only friend to freedom. The agency sent American writers and teachers to conferences to confront intellectuals and artists from the Soviet Union and the Eastern bloc countries.

Who were the CIA-sponsored intellectuals? I asked Ginsberg when we talked in Marin in 1985. Lionel Trilling, Norman Podhoretz, and Mary McCarthy, he replied. In his eyes they contributed to the unhealthy climate of the Cold War as much as the cultural commissars behind the Iron Curtain did. There were few American intellectuals he did admire. At Columbia in the 1940s, he insisted, Raymond Weaver—the man who discovered the manuscript of Herman Melville's masterpiece *Billy Budd*—was the only professor who had integrity. Ginsberg said that he and

Kerouac, who was briefly a student there, had received their real education from men like Herbert Huncke, a hustler and drug addict they'd met in Times Square. "We got the bottom-up vision of society," he said. "We saw wealth and power from the point of view of down-and-out people on the street. That's what the Beat Generation was about—being down-and-out, and about having a sense of beatitude, too." When I asked him why he hadn't been silenced by the climate of the Cold War and the anti-communist crusaders—in fact, he had gone on writing all through the late 1940s and early 1950s—he said that he had never been intimidated and never felt afraid. "Kerouac and I had a zany view of the world," he said. "We had a W. C. Fields view of J. Edgar Hoover. Even in the mid-1940s we couldn't take him seriously." Indeed, in *Howl* there is a kind of W. C. Fields view of the FBI; J. Edgar Hoover's FBI agents are figures of absurd comedy. The poet turns the tables and talks about investigating the investigators.

"Nineteen forty-eight was the crucial postwar year," Ginsberg explained. "It was the turning point. Of course the atom bomb had already gone off in 1945, and Kerouac and Burroughs and I had talked about it, but the psychological fallout from the bomb—the consciousness—didn't really hit until 1948. There was the splitting of the atom, and the splitting of the old structures in society and also a sense of the inner world splitting up and coming apart." Like many other writers around the world, Ginsberg turned the atom bomb into an all-inclusive metaphor. Everywhere he looked he saw apocalypse and atomization. Everything had been blown up. And almost everywhere he looked he saw the Cold War. He was thinking of the Cold War when he wrote his 1956 poem "America," he said. "I was playing on the phrase 'Cold War' when I wrote, 'America when will we end the human war?'"

In the 1980s, the Cold War was still very much alive for Ginsberg, both abroad and at home. He was distressed about the neo-conservatism of the Reagan era, the administration's attack on radical and avant-garde artists, and the critical reception of his *Collected Poems*. He seemed to feel that his own work had been ignored or attacked because of the right-wing climate of the country. "Most reviewers didn't seem to actually read the book," he said. "They didn't see the growth, the maturity of my work. They were stuck in the past—with *Howl* and *Kaddish*, which they admitted are good, but they mostly argued that I was in decline." The fact that he couldn't read *Howl* and "America" on prime-time TV infuriated him. "I still can't go on CBS or NBC and say, 'Go fuck yourself with your atom bomb,'" he complained. "America still doesn't understand. America is still trapped."

### Quarrel with Yourself

In April 1986, Ginsberg spent two days at Sonoma State University. I was his host; I guided him, chauffeured him, saw to it that he was well fed and had a place to sleep. At an afternoon workshop for students, he insisted that he aimed for "candor, accurate candor, total candor" in his poetry. He never meant to "shock the bourgeoisie," he insisted. When someone asked, "What about the time you took off your clothes in public?" he said, "That was natural! That was spontaneous! Whitman didn't mean to shock and I don't either!"

Though he revised *Howl*, and though his revisions improved

his poem significantly, he was unwilling to acknowledge the importance of revision in his own work. "The first thoughts are the best thoughts," he argued. "Recycled thoughts deny freshness. Register your thoughts when you have them, or when you first notice them. Cultivate the habit of noticing your mind and registering your own mind, too. Don't wait to be discovered. Discover yourself. Publish your own work and circulate your work."

Whitman influenced his work, he said, though he also acknowledged William Butler Yeats's role in shaping his poetry: "Yeats was right when he said that 'out of our quarrels with others we make rhetoric. Out of our quarrels with ourselves we make poetry.'" He added, "Quarrel with yourself. Your quarrels with yourself often make the best poems. Tell yourself your own secrets, and reveal yourself. The purpose of art is to provide relief from your own paranoia and the paranoia of others. You write to relieve the pain of others, to free them from the self-doubt generated by a society in which everyone is conniving and manipulating."

After his informal remarks, Ginsberg gave the students a series of writing exercises. Using the seminal phrase "hydrogen jukebox" as a model, he invited the young poets in the room to join seemingly unrelated words and create phrases that might offer a new, startling vision of the world. Like most good teachers, he praised the students when they read their work. "Apple-cart bloodbath," "suitcase bingo," and "windowshade midget"—to name just a few—were among his favorites.

That evening in the Commons, Ginsberg smiled, shook hands, and introduced himself to students and faculty members. All day long he had been worried about the microphones and the tape recorders—he insisted that we record him on reel-to-reel tapes—and just before he was to perform he requested one final sound check. The stage had been arranged like a living room. There was a coffee table, a vase filled with flowers, a pot of tea already mixed with honey, a few ceramic cups—everything placed in accord with his precise instructions. A few minutes after 8 P.M. the audience—mostly students—craned their necks, eager for the event to begin. Professor David Bromige, a Canadian-born poet who had known and admired Ginsberg for decades, took the podium and introduced him as "Sir Allen," a comment that brought a smile to Ginsberg's face.

Suddenly he was on stage, a bundle of intensely focused energy. Pumping his right foot and squeezing his little red harmonium with both hands, he began to sing "Airplane Blues," which chronicles his ongoing sexual attraction to young men—and his declining sexual powers at sixty. Like many of the poems Ginsberg read that night at Sonoma State University, "Airplane Blues" would be published, with major revisions, in *White Shroud: Poems, 1980–1985*.

"White Shroud"—the title poem in that volume—moved the audience more than any other poem that evening. That wasn't surprising, since it describes in vivid detail a haunting dream in which Naomi Ginsberg, the poet's mother, appears alive and well in the Bronx—though she died in 1957. In the 1980s, he seemed to be as haunted by his mother as he'd ever been. Despite his politeness and willingness to please one and all at Sonoma, I had the feeling that he was increasingly a lonely figure—a poet who had wanted glory and now felt trapped by it.

When he died a decade later, I attended the memorial service at Temple Emanu-El in San Francisco. Rabbi Peretz-Wolf Pursan told the crowd that his own congregation had opposed a tribute to Ginsberg. In death he was still controversial. Andrew Shilling spoke of Ginsberg's "long karmic connection to San Francisco." Lawrence Ferlinghetti read a poem he'd written entitled "Allen Ginsberg Dying." "I'll always remember Allen's voice," he said. "I think I'll remember his voice more than anything else." Michael McClure said he loved Ginsberg "for bringing the mercies of enlightened Buddhism to poetry." Gary Snyder said he learned from Ginsberg "the power of sharing poetry with friends and not just reading it in the privacy of one's room." Joanne Kyger said that Ginsberg had "widened the area of consciousness" and that she admired him for his "freedom of language, political honesty, and spontaneous mind." Robert Haas lauded Ginsberg for using "his fame to help his friends," and Nancy J. Peters praised him for "opening the door of poetry to so many people around the world." San Francisco clearly loved Allen Ginsberg. Elsewhere, though, his reputation seemed to be tarnished. *Howl* was frequently dismissed. For David Remnick, the editor of the *New Yorker*, Ginsberg's great poem was *Kaddish*, not *Howl*. In the *New York Times Book Review*, Charles McGrath depicted Ginsberg as a "cultural busybody" and an "inspired yenta." For McGrath "his most enduring contribution to our culture" wasn't *Howl* or *Kaddish*, "but the way . . . he transformed the American avant-garde, and the angry alienation of the Beats, into something altogether more cheerful and benign." For me *Howl* has always been Allen Ginsberg's masterpiece—a horrifying, funny, surreal, and prophetic poem. So I set out to write this book about *Howl*. I reread all the poems, went to libraries, read the unpublished letters and manuscripts, and talked to Ginsberg's friends and acquaintances, including Ginsberg's therapist in 1955 and 1956, when he was writing *Howl*. Ginsberg had acknowledged Dr. Philip Hicks's pivotal role in his development as a poet; Dr. Hicks "gave me the authority, so to speak, to be myself," Ginsberg told Jane Kramer. But Dr. Hicks himself had never talked about his patient. Now that he was retired and Ginsberg was dead, he was ready to share his memories. "Allen brought his poems to therapy and read them," Dr. Hicks said. "He brought *Howl* for me to read when it was still in manuscript." Ginsberg had always insisted that he never received help from anyone while writing the first draft of *Howl.* Dr. Hicks said that his patient worked on his poem while in therapy and that therapy helped make it possible for him to write *Howl.* He added, "Allen had rigid ideas of who he was supposed to be; he thought that he was supposed to be heterosexual. During one session he mentioned his homosexuality and I said something like 'So? What else is new?'" I also obtained confidential medical reports on Ginsberg from the New York State Psychiatric Institute and from Langley Porter in San Francisco, reports that reveal for the first time Ginsberg's experience as a patient and a poet inside a mental hospital, and as an outpatient in therapy.

### A Short History of *Howl*

In a way, Ginsberg never let go of *Howl.* Year after year, he returned to it, continually adding to the mythology of the poem as a spontaneous work that brought him and the world out of the closet of a repressive society. In 1956, he told the poet and critic Richard Eberhart that his intention in writing *Howl* was to liberate readers from their "false . . . self-deprecating image" of themselves and to persuade them that they were "angels." In 1965, when Tom Clark interviewed him for the *Paris Review*, he insisted that *Howl*, and especially the last section of the poem, was "really an homage to art." In 1974, he told Allen Young, who interviewed him for *Gay Sunshine*, that *Howl* was a literal "coming out of the closet" and an "acknowledgement of the basic reality of homosexual joy." In 1975, two decades after he first sat down to write *Howl*, he explained—this was among his biggest literary bombshells—that it was "really about my mother." In 1986, when Harper and Row published the original draft facsimile edition of *Howl*—modeled after T. S. Eliot's facsimile edition of *The Waste Land*—Ginsberg explained that his poem was meant to be an "emotional time bomb that would continue exploding . . . [the] military-industrial-nationalistic complex." For Ginsberg *Howl* was a magic mirror. Whenever he peered into it he saw another side, another aspect. Readers around the world, too, brought their own cultures and histories to *Howl*, reading it in the context of their own lives. Indeed, how we read *Howl* and interpret it today is in part the legacy of its legendary status from Prague to Peking, Barcelona to Budapest.

By the time that Ginsberg died in 1997, *Howl and Other Poems* had sold over eight hundred thousand copies. It had been translated into at least twenty-four languages, including Spanish, Polish, Dutch, Japanese, Chinese, Hungarian, and Italian—and it was one of the best-known American poems in the world. It had played a significant part in changing poetry in America—by making it more personal, more confessional, and more akin to the performance arts. *Howl* also played a small part in changing the world itself by collapsing cultural boundaries at the height of the Cold War and by encouraging cultural rebellion around the world—from San Francisco to Havana, New York to Mexico City.

Ironically, the very fame that *Howl* brought to Ginsberg may also have caused his exclusion from the elite company of feted American poets. He received honors and grants, but the top literary prizes eluded him. Ginsberg was not shy about promoting himself or his poem; he did not honor the prescribed mold for poet behavior, which did not include tooting one's own horn. Perhaps if he had gone on writing and perfecting the formal poetry he wrote in the 1940s, he might have won a Pulitzer Prize or become poet laureate. When he strayed from his original course and wrote *Howl*—with its wildness and exuberance—he set himself apart from the respectable crowd of poets. Many of his own Columbia classmates and teachers felt that he'd turned against them and the education he'd received at college. By writing and publishing *Howl*, he committed an act of cultural treason.

Adrienne Rich—the author of *Diving into the Wreck* (1973) and *On Lies, Secrets and Silence* (1979)—observed that American poetry often emerges from the "point of stress in our society." She also noted that the "stress in itself creates a search for language in which to probe and unravel what is going on here." *Howl* emerged from the fissures in American society after World War II, as well as from the fault lines in the author's own secret, volatile life. In his best poetry, Ginsberg dove into the wreck of himself and of the world around him to salvage himself and something worth saving of the world at large. In the act of writing *Howl*, he discovered the very language he needed—a language of the everyday and of Judgment Day—a language of the mundane and the apocalyptic.

"The artist is extremely lucky who is presented with the worst possible ordeal which will not actually kill him," the poet John Berryman wrote. The Pulitzer Prize–winner in poetry for *77 Dream Songs*, Berryman suffered from depression before taking his own life in 1972. When he wrote about suffering and death, he knew whereof he spoke. Similarly, Ginsberg came close to suicide repeatedly in the decade before he wrote *Howl*. He wrote about death, dying, and suicide again and again. It was death—the death of so many members of his own generation and the spiritual death of a mechanized world—that inspired him to create his best work. Fellow poet Kenneth Koch once asked him, "What do you have to have, or to be, to start with, in order to leave yourself open to produce good poetry?" Ginsberg replied, "A little glimpse of death. And the looseness and tolerance that [it] brings." When he wrote *Howl*—his autobiographical/mythological poem—he found the tolerance and the looseness he needed in order to create an American masterpiece.

### Do I Contradict Myself?

In *American Scream* I have tried to explain what it was like for Ginsberg to write *Howl*—how he felt, what he was thinking, why he wrote it, and who influenced him. Ginsberg's journals, which he kept from 1937 until his death in 1997, provide a clear record of his evolution as a poet and of the genesis of his poems. A storehouse of images and ideas, they are the seedbed from which many of his poems spring. Another key to understanding the man and the poet is to acknowledge the importance of his journey to San Francisco, where he began to write *Howl*. I have tried to show what happened to him in the Bay Area that made it possible for him to find a place in America, both as a poet and as a homosexual.

Madness is another central theme in Ginsberg's life and poetry, and I have described Ginsberg's complex and often contra-

dictory ideas and feelings about it. Along with nakedness and se-
crecy, madness is at the heart of his work, and especially at the
heart of *Howl*. And, while this book is primarily about *Howl*, I
have also written about poems that Ginsberg wrote immediately
before and immediately after *Howl*, including "A Strange New
Cottage in Berkeley" and "Sunflower Sutra," because they help
us understand both Ginsberg and *Howl*. Ginsberg's relationships
with Kerouac and Burroughs form another primary focus in this
book. Their story has been told before in books about the Beats,
but no one has explored how Kerouac and Burroughs helped to
shape *Howl* and the extent to which *Howl* tells their story as well
as Ginsberg's. The time that Ginsberg, Kerouac, and Burroughs
actually spent together was brief indeed—a few months here and
a few months there. It was not, however, the exact hours that
they spent together that matter most, but rather the intensity of
their initial experience together in New York when the United
States was at war and when they were young aspiring writers—
linked by dreams and ambitions. Then and there, Ginsberg, Ker-
ouac, and Burroughs bonded as few American writers have ever
bonded before or since.

Theirs was literally a friendship hammered out in letters and
in novels and poems, and across great distances. For decades they
corresponded with one another, extending the dialogue about
language, art, and the role of the artist that they started in New
York during World War II. *Howl* stands as a testament to Allen's
friendships and to his male friends—Jack Kerouac, William
Burroughs, Neal Cassady, and Carl Solomon. It is perhaps *the*
quintessential twentieth-century American poem to celebrate
male comradeship and male bonding in the spirit of Walt Whit-
man and Herman Melville, and not surprisingly Kerouac and

Burroughs recognized the genius of *Howl* from the moment they read the poem in typescript. That largely underappreciated story of literary friendship and literary influence is a thread that runs through *American Scream.*

Likewise, little attention has been paid to the influence of T. S. Eliot on Ginsberg's work. Ginsberg read Eliot, of course, and his approach to poetry was shaped by Eliot's ideas about tradition and the individual talent and about the form and the language of poetry. As Cynthia Ozick observed, "Ginsberg's 'Howl,' the single poem most representative of the break with Eliot, may owe as much, thematically, to 'The Waste Land' as it does to the bardic Whitman or to the opening of the era of anything goes. Ginsberg belongs to the generation that knew Eliot as sanctified, and, despite every irruption into indiscipline, Eliot continues in Ginsberg's ear." It was part of Ginsberg's genius as a poet that he could borrow from both Eliot and Whitman, fusing them to make something new.

Near the end of *Song of Myself,* Walt Whitman wrote, "Do I contradict myself? / Very well then I contradict myself, / (I am large, I contain multitudes.)" Ginsberg had a special affinity for those lines, and he frequently quoted them, especially when he wrote about *Howl,* his poem of immense contradictions. *Howl* is explosive—as befitting a poem for the atomic age—and yet it's also symmetrical. It's carefully crafted, expertly shaped. The poet and critic William Everson allowed that *Howl* was like a "scream from a paddy wagon," but he also noted that "even a scream has structure." Ginsberg himself suggested that the poem was a kind of scream. "I occasionally scream with exasperation (or giggles)," he wrote. "All this can hardly be called incoherence except by oververbal madmen who depend on longwinded defenses of their own bad prose for a livelihood."

*Howl* is a work of synthesis that fuses disparate elements in Ginsberg's own contradictory life: the sacred and the profane, the prophetic and the self-promoting. *Howl* synthesizes his early years with his parents, his college years at Columbia under the tutelage of Lionel Trilling, his hipster days in New York, and his life on the road in the 1940s and 1950s. *Howl* was also born at a particular time and place. To understand the poem, it helps to understand America and the Cold War—and the underground culture of San Francisco. "Almost all times of crisis," Octavio Paz wrote, "are fertile in great poets." Like *The Waste Land, Howl* was born of crisis; like *The Waste Land*, it is a "historical product, the fruit of a time and a place."

Sayulita, Mexico

# CHAPTER ONE

# Poetickall Bomshell

### A Person Named Allen Ginsberg

In September 1955, Gary Snyder—then a twenty-five-year-old unpublished poet and graduate student—wrote to his friend and fellow poet Philip Whalen in Oregon to say that he had been backpacking in the Sierras for ten days and that he'd thoroughly enjoyed the isolation of the outdoors. Now, he was living in a small cottage in Berkeley, he said, baking his own bread and studying Japanese. Moreover, he was preparing to read, with several other poets, at a place called the Six Gallery, perhaps the leading showcase for young artists in San Francisco. (In 1955 the Six Gallery exhibited the innovative work of Jay DeFeo, Fred Martin, and Richard Diebenkorn.) Whalen was in on the "deal," Snyder wrote. He had pulled a few strings and made all the necessary arrangements and was delighted to report that they'd share the stage together after so many years of writing poetry together. Then, too, Snyder was delighted to tell Whalen that his poems had been well received by the San Francisco literary underground. They had even reached a "certain subterranean celebration," Snyder wrote, thanks to Kenneth Rexroth, the Bay Area's bohemian impresario and veteran poet. Whalen had better "come as soon as possible" and join the festivities, Snyder urged. The reading at the Six Gallery, which was scheduled for the first Friday in October, was not to be missed.

Rexroth himself would be the master of ceremonies and Philip Lamantia, a successful young poet who was born in San Francisco in 1927 to an Italian American family, was to be the featured performer. André Breton, the French surrealist, had published Lamantia's work in 1943, and *Erotic Poems*, Lamantia's first book, had been published in Berkeley, with its small but lively poetry scene. Also on the program, Snyder added almost as an afterthought, was "a person named Allen Ginsberg," whom he had recently met and was just getting to know. Snyder had not read widely in Ginsberg's work—Ginsberg had almost no published work to read. But he was familiar with a letter that Ginsberg had written to William Carlos Williams, the grand old man of American poetry, a letter that Williams had thought well enough of to include in his long poem *Paterson*. Ginsberg was largely unknown and yet had a certain cachet among the poets in the West because he was a friend and disciple of Williams. Williams had even written a letter of introduction for Ginsberg before he left the East Coast, and that letter had gained him access to Rexroth's salon, where artists met anarchists, workers met intellectuals, and there were plenty of literary fireworks.

Snyder predicted that the Six Gallery reading would be a "poetickall bomshell"—his liberties with the spelling of the words were meant to be playful. Snyder proved to be prophetic. The Six

Gallery reading turned out to be a big bombshell in the world of poetry, and in the world at large, a world that was preoccupied with atomic bombs, hydrogen bombs, blonde bombshells, and the classified secrets of the bomb—almost everything *but* poetical bombs.

**Under Wraps**

The Six Gallery reading was a direct and deliberate response to the culture of the bomb and to American power and wealth. To understand the cultural and political significance of the reading, it might be helpful to look at the United States in the era after World War II, an era that profoundly shaped Ginsberg and the Beat writers. Like *On the Road* and *Naked Lunch, Howl* was a product of the Cold War. During World War II, American writers were, on the whole, enthusiastic about the global battle to defeat fascism. Most novelists, poets, and playwrights were patriotic and optimistic. Some worked directly for the government at agencies like the Office of Strategic Information. Others wrote literature that celebrated American democracy. Allen Ginsberg was only seventeen in 1943, but he cast himself as the voice of his generation, and in high school wrote poetry that looked forward to the defeat of the Axis powers and the birth of a better world.

When the war ended in 1945, there was a sense of euphoria and liberation among writers and intellectuals as well as in the population as a whole. The troops came home. Families were reunited. Overt U.S. government censorship ended. The promise of peace and prosperity at home instilled an infectious sense that a new day was dawning. The euphoria was short-lived, however. In the aftermath of the war, citizens began to realize that the bombs dropped on Hiroshima and Nagasaki not only had ended the war but also had ushered in a new and frightening era. The horrors of the German concentration camps were revealed. The Iron Curtain descended on Europe and the Cold War began. As Americans became more aware of the dark side of the postwar era, and the dark side of humanity, too, the mood in America shifted and writers reflected it. It was the era of the noir novel and film noir.

Behind the calm exterior, the house beautiful and the happy family, there was anxiety, paranoia, and restlessness. In fiction, poetry, and the theater, writers described, in darkly pessimistic works—Norman Mailer's *The Naked and the Dead*, Arthur Miller's *The Death of a Salesman*, and Robert Lowell's *Lord Weary's Castle*, to name just a few—the end of the American dream, the fissures in American society, and collective apprehension about the future. At the same time the mass media and the White House promulgated the idea that America was a near-perfect society— the apogee of historical progress—threatened by evil communism and all its agents.

Nineteen forty-eight was, as Ginsberg noted, a pivotal year. Tennessee Williams wrote, in an essay entitled "On the Art of Being a True Non-Conformist"—published in November 1948, just after Truman defeated Dewey for the presidency—that "reactionary opinion descends like a ton of bricks on the head of any artist who speaks out against the current of prescribed ideas." He added, "We are all under wraps of one kind or another, trembling before the specter of investigating committees." Williams had achieved success with *The Glass Menagerie* (1944) and *A Streetcar Named Desire* (1947), but now he felt like an outcast in his own country, which seemed to be turning totalitarian at home even as it battled totalitarian nations abroad. Norman

Mailer, who published his antiwar novel *The Naked and the Dead* in 1948, observed sadly that war was an obscenity and that government officials "were leading us into war again."

World War II, and the war economy generated by the Cold War and the Korean War, created a new class of American millionaires—a "Babylonian plutocracy," Tennessee Williams called it. A small circle of writers enjoyed financial success, but most had to struggle just to survive. The American elite was "grossly affluent," Williams noted, and it "should have exhibited a bit more concern for the fate of its young artists." In the midst of unprecedented prosperity, American culture turned increasingly commercial, and writers turned increasingly to conformity. After an extensive visit to the United States, the British author Stephen Spender wrote in 1949 that authors like Henry Miller and Kenneth Rexroth were the "last remnants of a race of independent writers." At the same time, Spender noted, American writers were often isolated and, unlike European writers, deprived of a sustaining cultural community.

The U.S. government—from the State Department to Congress—regarded writers as dangerous. Hollywood directors and screenwriters were jailed. Irish poet Dylan Thomas was investigated by the FBI and begrudgingly issued a visa; Arthur Miller was denied a passport and not allowed to leave the United States for years. Dashiell Hammett, the author of *The Maltese Falcon* and *The Thin Man*, was sent to prison for refusing to knuckle under to investigators and to name names. In academia and in the leading literary magazines of the day, teachers and critics warned against innovation and radicalism. W. H. Auden— a British-born poet who had become a naturalized American citizen in 1946—urged caution. It was not the time for "revolutionary artists" or "significant novelty in artistic style," he wrote in 1951. Before any new literary works could be written there would have to be a "cultural revolution," he insisted. While Auden was dubious about any future cultural revolution, Tennessee Williams looked forward to it. In 1948 he anticipated the day when young people would discard "conservative business suits," let their "hair grow long . . . make wild gestures, fight, shout and fall downstairs!" That day would be "brave and honest," he predicted.

It took nearly a decade for the brave Beat Generation to flower in this hostile cultural environment. From the late 1940s to the mid-1950s, the Beats were under wraps. Ginsberg was closer to T. S. Eliot and to W. H. Auden than he was to William Carlos Williams and Walt Whitman. William Burroughs published his autobiography *Junky* under the pseudonym William Lee because books that accurately described the drug world were taboo. Granted, Kerouac went on writing in his own inimitable style, but from 1950 to 1955 almost no one would publish his work. Gradually, the underground scene spread and matured. In the mid-1950s, all over the United States, young artists felt the need to experiment, rebel, and turn to bohemia. Sylvia Plath, who was only twenty-two and a Smith College student in 1954, wrote, "I need to practice a certain healthy bohemianism . . . to swing away from the gray-clad . . . clock-regulated, responsible . . . economical, practical girl."

### Healthy Bohemianism

The 1955 Six Gallery reading was bohemianism at its best. It was something "brave and honest"—to borrow Tennessee Williams's

phrase—in the midst of a society that seemed cowardly and in-
sincere, and it marked the start of the cultural revolution that
would sweep across America in the 1960s. Indeed, the Six Gallery
reading helped create the conditions for both the San Francisco
protests against the House Un-American Activities Committee
in 1960 and the Free Speech Movement at Berkeley in 1964. The
Six Gallery reading was living proof that the First Amendment
hadn't been destroyed by McCarthyism and the committees that
investigated artists, playwrights, Hollywood directors, and TV
screenwriters. In America in the twentieth century, there was no
public poetry reading that was a bigger bombshell than the Six
Gallery reading. As Snyder himself noted in 1999, "That event
launched all of us. It launched Allen Ginsberg, of course, and Phil
Whalen and Michael McClure and Jack Kerouac. After the Six
Gallery, poetry readings became regular cultural events not only
in this country but all over the world." Poetry came out of the
closet at the Six Gallery, and off the printed page.

Nearly a half-century after the reading, Michael McClure
looked back and described it as a personal turning point. "I was
twenty-two years old," he said in 2003. "The reading was an ini-
tiating event. Then and there, I set my belief in poetry as a truth-
ful and adventurous art. It was important, I realized, to stand
up in front of an audience and not write ivory tower quatrains
that would gather dust in books." Half a century later, the read-
ing also looked and felt like a liberating social, political, and cul-
tural event. "If there had not been a Six Gallery reading, there
would not have been an ongoing Beat Generation," McClure
said. Ginsberg's brave new poem carved out a decisively different
territory. "*Howl* spoke for so many of us in a time of McCarthy-
ism and grim, stark, cold war silence," McClure observed. "It was

as though Allen drew a line in the sand." From McClure's point of view, Allen manifested his "socialism" at the Six Gallery reading night. Snyder manifested his "Buddhist anarchism," while Phil Whalen manifested his "gentleness of consciousness and conscience." That night, McClure himself manifested what he calls his own "biological and anti-political anarchist stance."

In October 1955, Allen Ginsberg had almost no published work to his name—except for a dozen or so poems that had appeared in his college literary magazine, a few book reviews in *Newsweek* and the *New York Herald Tribune*, and a playful poem about sex entitled "Song: Fie My Fum" that he had written with Kerouac and that had been published in *Neurotica*, the notorious magazine edited by Jay Landesman. Kerouac had a bit more to show for his literary efforts. Six months before the Six Gallery reading, in April 1955, he published, under the pseudonym "Jean-Louis," a work of fiction entitled "Jazz of the Beat Generation" from a novel in progress he called *The Beat Generation*. Eventually that novel would be published as *On the Road*. Five years earlier, in 1950, he had published, under the name Jack Kerouac, a novel entitled *The Town and the City*. Now, it was nearly forgotten; Kerouac was not widely known in Berkeley or San Francisco. At the Six Gallery almost no one knew him except for Ginsberg, Cassady, Rexroth, and a handful of local poets, including Robert Duncan. But by the end of the evening the crowd knew a great deal about Kerouac. As he himself noted in *The Dharma Bums* (1958), "I was the one who got things jumping." He was Ginsberg's co-conspirator, the essential link between the performers on stage and the people in the audience. It was Kerouac who helped break down the barriers.

The Six Gallery reading was—to borrow from Gary Snyder's

letter to Phil Whalen—a "subterranean celebration." It was a gathering of underground poets and writers from the East Coast (Kerouac, Ginsberg, Ferlinghetti) and from the West Coast (Snyder, Whalen, Lamantia). It was a festival of cross-continental and cross-cultural pollination. East met West. The urban poets who had been shaped by the culture of New York—the epicenter of American arts and letters in the 1940s and 1950s—met and mingled with their contemporaries who had been shaped by the culture on the western edge of the continent. The Six Gallery reading was also a pivotal moment when the subterranean world of dissident, nonconformist American writers defied the chilly climate of the Cold War and came out into the open. The voices that had been ignored, dismissed, and repressed came to the surface and began to be heard by the culture at large. Even the *New York Times* noticed and sent a reporter to cover the cultural explosion.

It was no accident that the Six Gallery reading took place in San Francisco in 1955—and no accident that Ginsberg wrote *Howl* in San Francisco, either. San Francisco, with its spectacular location on the Pacific Ocean and its exuberant recklessness, had long been a hotbed of bohemian activity. And there was something about the city that encouraged poets and novelists to draw creative work from their innermost depths. "San Francisco is a mad city— inhabited for the most part by perfectly insane people," Rudyard Kipling exclaimed. Frank Norris noted, "Things can happen in San Francisco . . . there is an indefinable air." And John Steinbeck observed, "I felt I owned the city as much as it owned me." In the 1950s, Kerouac felt much the same way. "San Francisco . . . always gives you the courage of your convictions," he wrote. For Kerouac, as for Kipling, it was a mad city with mad people, and he loved it for its madness. "The only people for me are the mad ones, the ones who are mad to live, mad to talk, mad to be saved," he wrote in *On the Road*. San Francisco gave Kerouac the courage to write *San Francisco Blues*, his first book of poetry, and he praised the city to Allen Ginsberg, who experienced it as a kind of creative irritant that stirred up his worst nightmares and darkest memories.

San Francisco was a long way from the political and cultural establishment in Washington, D.C., and New York City, and that geographical distance engendered a sense of freedom that wasn't found elsewhere in the United States in the era of the Cold War. It was an era, E. L. Doctorow noted in *Jack London, Hemingway and the Constitution*, that was dominated by an "ideology of fear" and by "sworn oaths of loyalty, blacklists, and public rituals of confession and repentance." In San Francisco, the "ideology of fear" didn't exert as powerful a force as it did in many other American cities. Anarchists, socialists, communists, pacifists, and Wobblies took part in the political and cultural life of San Francisco, giving it a distinctly left-leaning character. There had been a general strike in San Francisco in 1934, which for many citizens was still a vivid memory and an inspiration, especially to the members of the International Longshoremen's Union. In the mid-1950s, Tillie Olsen was beginning to write again in San Francisco, after years of silence; her stories, including "I Stand Here Ironing," would be published in *Tell Me a Riddle*. Alexander Saxton, the proletarian novelist, was also writing about the power of art to create a sense of community, in his novel *Bright Web in the Darkness*. The Mattachine Society, the first American gay organization, had a strong though initially secret presence in San Francisco. Henry Hay, society founder and an influential San Francisco citizen, was a communist as well as a homosexual.

If the city provided a sanctuary for American bohemians and radicals, so too 1955 offered a respite from the rigidities of the Cold War. In 1955, McCarthyism as a political phenomenon had not run its course, but Senator Joseph McCarthy had been censured by his colleagues in the Senate and he was no longer the powerful demagogue he had been. In 1954 the televised Army-McCarthy hearings had exposed him as a bully and a lout. Liberals and radicals alike breathed a sigh of relief. The military-industrial complex, as President Dwight David Eisenhower called it in 1960, was as powerful as ever, but the Korean War was over, and the nation was at peace—relative peace—for the first time since 1950. Moreover, the country was in flux. In the South the civil rights movement was beginning to take shape and gather momentum. In 1954, the U.S. Supreme Court had ruled racial segregation in schools unconstitutional, and that landmark ruling spurred church leaders, activists, and radicals to demand freedom and equality for American blacks. Chicago teenager Emmett Till was brutally murdered in Mississippi in 1955, and that same year his courageous mother, Mamie Till, spoke on television and described to the world the horrors of southern racism and the brutality of segregation. America was beginning to wake up.

There were visible cracks in the culture of the Cold War and sounds of liberation in rock'n'roll, in Hollywood movies like *Rebel without a Cause*, and in plays like Arthur Miller's *A View from the Bridge* and Tennessee Williams's *Cat on a Hot Tin Roof*. There were popular novels like Sloan Wilson's *The Man in the Gray Flannel Suit* that presented a critical perspective on American corporate culture, and there was provocative and innovative fiction like Vladimir Nabokov's *Lolita*, first published in Paris. In baseball, the Brooklyn Dodgers defeated the New York Yankees in the 1955 World Series, an upset that showed Americans that the raggle-taggle team of bums could defeat the seemingly all-powerful machine and the men in pinstriped uniforms.

In San Francisco, at least, society was ripe for cultural break-throughs like the Six Gallery reading. And the event happened in large part because Ginsberg made it a reality. Wally Hedrick—a painter and a veteran of the Korean War—approached Ginsberg in the summer of 1955 and asked him to organize a poetry read-ing at the Six Gallery—a "run down second rate experimental art gallery" at 3119 Fillmore Street in San Francisco. At first, Gins-berg refused. He didn't know enough local poets, he said, and he didn't feel that there was enough worthwhile Bay Area poetry to warrant a reading. But once he'd written a rough draft of *Howl*, he changed his "fucking mind," as he put it. A reading would pro-vide an occasion both for his birth as a poet and for the birth of the Beat Generation, which had been slowly germinating for years. Ginsberg learned that there was a tradition of poetry read-ings in San Francisco and in Berkeley where poets like Jack Spicer rejected the academic critics of poetry and embraced pop-ular American entertainers and singers. "There is more of Or-pheus in Sophie Tucker than in R. P. Blackmur," Spicer pro-claimed. In the spirit of Sophie Tucker, Spicer enlivened the literary scene with readings featuring himself, Robert Duncan, Robin Blaser, and Philip Lamantia.

Ginsberg liked the idea of being an outsider, a New Yorker, carrying on a local tradition. But the reading at the Six Gallery would be different from any other Bay Area poetry reading. It would be bigger and wilder and far more public. Everything would be allowed. Nothing would be sacred, not even poetry itself. Ginsberg set the date and time for the Six Gallery reading: October 7, 1955, at 8 P.M. His idea—and Jack Kerouac's too—was to drink a lot of red wine, have fun, and act amateurish and goofy. On a more serious note, Ginsberg explained that the reading was meant to "defy the system of academic poetry, official reviews, New York publishing machinery, national sobriety and generally-accepted standards to good taste."

### Six Poets at Six Gallery

Having worked in New York and in San Francisco in marketing and advertising, and having worked as a literary agent for both Burroughs and Kerouac in the early 1950s, Ginsberg knew how to promote and sell a product, plan an event, and publicize an idea. With a minimal budget, he managed to squeeze out maximum marketing impact. He was a gadfly, energizing and stimulating the literary scene. His little cottage on Milvia Street in Berkeley—where he lived with Kerouac and entertained the likes of Gary Snyder and Philip Whalen—served as the headquarters for the event and for the local poetry industry. The cottage was a beehive of activity, with constant comings and goings and conversations at all times of the day and night.

Colorful signs about the event were posted in North Beach cafes and bars. About a hundred postcards with a catchy slogan—"6 poets at 6 Gallery"—were mailed to poetry aficionados in town. "A remarkable collection of angels on one stage reading their poetry," the postcard read. There would be no admission charge for the "charming event," Ginsberg wrote, but the organizers would take up a "small collection for wine." The post-card also announced that the poets would read "sharp new straightforward writing."

Ginsberg selected Kenneth Rexroth as the master of cere-monies. At fifty, Rexroth belonged to an older generation, but he was the perfect MC for the event. An anarchist and a bohemian, he also had an air of respectability. He'd been published by New Directions and he was the host of a popular radio program on KPFA, the listener-sponsored station in Berkeley. Rexroth's job was to set the mood for the evening and to introduce the poets, none of whom, with the exception of Lamantia, were native to San Francisco. Many of the notable local poets—Robert Dun-can, Jack Spicer, and Robin Blaser—were not included in the program, and so the gala event at the Six Gallery was a cultural snub of sorts to the poets who thought they embodied the best of Bay Area poetry. The outsiders were taking over.

Ginsberg was understandably anxious about the cultural event that he was organizing. For weeks ahead of time he was appre-hensive about his own imminent appearance on stage to read what he called the "first scraps" of a long poem to a largely un-known audience in a city he thought of as foreign. But he wasn't going it alone; he had a community, and he had Kerouac, his old-est and closest friend, to support him and give him a sense of self-confidence. At Milvia Street, on the day of the big event, he put on his best clothes—a charcoal gray suit, white shirt, and a tie. Then he and Kerouac took the bus together to San Francisco. There they were met by Lawrence Ferlinghetti, who drove them in his vintage Aston Martin to the Six Gallery. They were exu-berant as they arrived at 3119 Fillmore Street. They were brash and swaggering and they were ready to crown themselves the reigning American poets. There was a sense of anticipation in the air. By eight o'clock the room was packed with North Beach bohemians and San Francisco State English teachers, as well as Ginsberg's loyal friends and lovers: Peter Orlovsky, Neal Cassady, and Natalie Jackson.

The Six Gallery reading was a radical departure for everyone—the members of the audience as well as the performers on stage. "This was no ordinary poetry reading," Ginsberg and his fellow New York poet Gregory Corso wrote in the essay "The Literary Revolution in America." There was nothing academic about the event and nothing refined about the behavior of the poets themselves, though the reading began on a note of formality. At first, the members of the audience were "rather stiff," Kerouac observed, but they were gradually transformed into wild participants. Kerouac collected dimes and quarters and bought gallons of cheap California burgundy. He passed the wine around the room, encouraging everyone to "glug a slug from the jug"—including the poets themselves. "They got drunk, the audience got drunk, all that was missing was the orgy," Ginsberg and Corso noted. The orgy would come later.

Rexroth's job as the master of ceremonies was to maintain a semblance of order. That wasn't easy—not with an intoxicated audience and intoxicated poets, and especially with Kerouac at the back of the room uttering "little wows and yesses of approval and even whole sentences of comment with nobody's invitation." Rexroth was dressed for the part of impresario; he wore a pinstripe suit and a bow tie. He welcomed the audience and talked about San Francisco as an oasis of cultural freedom in a country of conformity, one of his favorite topics. As the evening unfolded over the next several hours, he introduced each poet in turn: Philip

Lamantia, Michael McClure, Philip Whalen, Allen Ginsberg, and Gary Snyder. The young men who read together at the Six Gallery could hardly be called a school of poets or a literary circle, though almost all of them admired William Carlos Williams and almost all of them were in rebellion against the stodgy academic poetry of the day, with its emphasis on ambiguity, irony, symbolism, and formalism. The poets came from very different geographical and aesthetic directions: from the backwoods of the Pacific Northwest and from the boroughs of Manhattan; from French surrealism and from American imagism. Moreover, they would go in different directions—Snyder would depart for Japan and life in a Buddhist monastery, while Ginsberg was bound for Los Angeles, New York, and the bohemian life on the Left Bank of Paris.

What they had in common was a profound love of poetry, a belief in the vitality and integrity of their own work, and a deep discontent with the militarism and materialism of American civilization. They were all spiritual seekers of one sort or another, and they all were willing to take personal risks—to experiment not only with poetry but with politics, drugs, and sex. And, though they ascribed to very different ideas about death and rebirth, nature and civilization, they were bound together by a love of ancient myths and a penchant for transforming those myths to create new myths about the world. The historic reading at the Six Gallery provided the participants themselves with all the drama and excitement they needed to assert a grand cultural myth about the rebirth of poetry—the "Poetry Renaissance," as it came to be called—in San Francisco in 1955.

In the lofty language of Ginsberg and Corso, the "reading was such a violent and beautiful expression of their revolutionary individuality (a quality bypassed in American poetry since the formulations of Whitman), conducted with such surprising abandon and delight by the poets themselves, and presenting such a high mass of beautiful unanticipated poetry, that the audience, expecting some Bohemian stupidity, was left stunned, and the poets were left with the realization that they were fated to make a permanent change in the literary firmament of the States." It was as though Dionysus had come back from the dead, and as though art and religion were united again. And that was precisely what Ginsberg wanted—a return, as he put it, "to the original religious shamanistic prophetic priestly Bardic magic!"

Soon after 8 P.M. Lamantia began to read the work of John Hoffman, a fellow surrealist poet and friend who had recently died in Mexico. Lamantia declined to read his own poems, and in Kerouac's eyes that personal gesture was an "elegy in itself to the memory of a dead young poet." It also set the tone for the rest of the evening. Death was everywhere and so was life, and that night poetry celebrated both life and death. Michael McClure, who had recently arrived in San Francisco from Kansas, read "For the Death of 100 Whales"—a short, angry poem inspired by a *Time* magazine story about seventy-nine American GIs with machine guns who slaughtered a pack of whales. Philip Whalen, who was born and raised in Portland, Oregon, read—in a tone of "mock seriousness"—"'Plus Ça Change . . . ,'" which captured the sense of alienation and loneliness he saw as characteristic of the time. People wouldn't look at one another or touch one another, Whalen noted in his poem. At 11 P.M.—after a brief intermission—it was Ginsberg's turn. Wally Hedrick remembers that Ginsberg was in the bathroom, which faced the main room. Suddenly, the door opened and there he was sitting nonchalantly on the toilet. After pulling up his trousers, he made his way to the stage and began to read Part I of *Howl* in a "small and intensely lucid voice." At that point, Part III did not exist at all, and Part II was only beginning to take shape. But no one felt cheated or left hanging; Part I seemed like a complete work in itself.

"Scores of people stood around in the darkened gallery straining to hear every word," Kerouac wrote. After several hours of drinking cheap red wine, Ginsberg was drunk, but as he read he became increasingly sober, and as he gathered momentum he was surprised by his own "strange ecstatic intensity." He developed a deeper sense of his own identity than he had ever had before. He thought of himself, he said, as a rabbi reading rhythmically to a congregation. Indeed, there was something of the Old Testament prophet about him. In the process of reading the poem, he found himself forging a new identity as a public poet sharing his private thoughts and feelings with eager, admiring listeners. *Howl* made Allen Ginsberg. The poem created the poet. The audience was transformed too—indifferent spectators becoming energetic participants. "Everyone was yelling 'Go! Go! Go!'" Kerouac wrote. No one had ever been at a poetry reading that was so emotional and so cathartic, not even the veteran Kenneth Rexroth.

By the end of his performance, Ginsberg was in tears, and Rexroth was "wiping his tears in gladness." The ending of *Howl* provided an emotional climax, but the evening wasn't over yet. Gary Snyder, who was wearing jeans, his beard neatly trimmed, read from *Myths and Texts*, a long work in progress, and the five-part poem "Berry Feast," which celebrates the rituals and myths of the Native Americans of Oregon, particularly Coyote, their mythological trickster/hero. But Ginsberg was clearly the hero of the evening. Appropriately enough, Kerouac was among the first to congratulate him on his success. *Howl* would make him famous all over San Francisco, Kerouac observed. Rexroth was certain that the poem would make him famous all across America. "This poem will make you famous from bridge to bridge," he exclaimed. After the reading, Ginsberg and Kerouac, along with Neal Cassady, Natalie Jackson, and Peter Orlovksy, drove to Nam Yuen in Chinatown "for a big fabulous dinner." Then they went to The Place, a bohemian haunt in North Beach, where they drank, talked, and began to create the legend of the Six Gallery reading.

### The Greatest Poet in America

Lawrence Ferlinghetti, who had attended the reading but had not been invited to join the revelers afterward, was full of praise for Ginsberg. Ferlinghetti was an accomplished poet—his first book, *Pictures of the Gone World*, appeared in 1955—but Ginsberg thought of him in part as a "square bookstore owner." Indeed, he operated City Lights Books on Columbus Avenue in North Beach. The day after the reading, Ferlinghetti sent Ginsberg a telegram at his cottage on Milvia Street. He wrote, "I greet you at the beginning of a great career. When do I get the manuscript?" The significance of Ferlinghetti's words were not lost on Ginsberg. One hundred years earlier, in July 1855, Ralph Waldo Emerson had written Walt Whitman to praise *Leaves of Grass* as the "most extraordinary piece of wit and wisdom that America has yet contributed." In his letter to Whitman, Emerson exclaimed, "I greet you at the beginning of a great career, which yet must have had a long foreground somewhere." Ginsberg was familiar with the celebrated letter; he had just read Gay Wilson Allen's biography of Whitman, and he had also been rereading *Leaves of Grass*. Now, for the first time in his life he felt unequivocal in his enthusiasm about Whitman. He was "better than Pound & Eliot & Williams," he insisted. As a high school boy, he thought that *Leaves of Grass*, though great literature, was flawed because of the poet's own homosexuality. Now that he felt more accepting of his homosexuality, he was less ambivalent about Whitman. And, for a poet who wanted to define himself in opposition to the literary establishment, Whitman was a near-perfect poet to adopt as a cultural hero. As late as 1955, Whitman was still largely untaught in college poetry classes and still largely unappreciated in academic circles, though he had a solid reputation in the nonconformist world.

And clearly there were similarities between Whitman and Ginsberg. Like Whitman, Ginsberg had a "long foreground"—a relatively long period before he emerged as a poet in his own right. Like Whitman he wrote long poems with long, prose-like lines and long catalogues of things and people and events. Like Whitman, he wrote for America and about America, and like Whitman he sang about himself in the first person. Neither Whitman nor Ginsberg extinguished his personality in his poetry. Whitman had his "barbaric yawp," which he sounded "over the roofs of the world," and Ginsberg had his animal howl, which he sounded "across the tops of / cities." Both poets created striking public personae and myths about themselves. Both were self-dramatizing, and both were poseurs and promoters.

Unlike Whitman, however, Ginsberg had a deep abiding sense of evil, and unlike Whitman he saw the city as the modern inferno. His world was darker than Whitman's. Ginsberg

seemed as innately pessimistic as Whitman was innately opti-
mistic. Moreover, unlike Whitman, Ginsberg often did not like
or trust the masses, nor did he believe wholeheartedly in the
efficacy of American democracy. As he knew full well, the masses
could be manipulated by demagogues like Senator Joseph Mc-
Carthy, and democracy could be subverted by military leaders
like General Douglas MacArthur. At the start of *Leaves of Grass*,
Whitman wrote, "One's-Self I sing, a simple separate per-
son, / Yet utter the word Democratic, the word En-Masse." Allen
Ginsberg sang of himself, but for the most part he did not con-
sistently "utter the word Democratic." On the contrary, he often
sang about the fall of Whitman's America, the fall of American
democracy, and the degradation of the masses. A sense of doom
and disaster informs *Howl*.

Unlike the writers of the American Renaissance of the
1850s—Whitman, Emerson—the writers of the San Francisco
Poetry Renaissance of the 1950s did not have a deep, abiding
faith in American democracy. Neither did Ginsberg's closest
friends, especially Kerouac and Burroughs. "Democracy is can-
cerous," Burroughs wrote in *Naked Lunch*. "America is not a
young land: it is old and dirty and evil." Kerouac was less cynical
than Burroughs, though he too felt that America was in decline
and that its best days had come and gone. Again and again in *On
the Road*, he writes about "the end of America," the "dregs of
America," the "washed-out bottom of America," and the "whole
mad thing, the ragged promised land, the fantastic end of Amer-
ica." Granted, when Sal Paradise, Kerouac's narrator, first arrives
in California it looks "green and wondrous," but before long he
writes of the "end of the continent sadness," and "the loneliness
of San Francisco." For Kerouac, the country's newness, its bright

hope, was a fast fading memory. By the 1950s, the nation, as well as its art and culture, was in decline.

Michael McClure, the youngest of the poets to read at the Six Gallery on October 7, expressed a sense of hope more clearly and strongly than any of the others, though he also expressed a sense of sadness and despair. For McClure, America on the eve of the Six Gallery reading was "locked in the Cold War." The whole country "had the feeling of martial law," and "there was no way, even in San Francisco, to escape the pressure of the war culture," he wrote. When Ginsberg read *Howl*, McClure said, he and his contemporaries stood "cheering and wondering." They understood that "a barrier had been broken, that a human voice and body had been hurled against the harsh walls of America, and its supporting armies and navies and academies and institutions and ownership systems and power-support bases." Of course, if you thought that everything was right with America, and that everything was going your way, you weren't likely to praise *Howl*. It helped to feel, as McClure felt, that you were living under martial law, that America was an occupied country and that you belonged to the underground. From that perspective, Ginsberg looked and sounded like a defiant poet surfacing from below, prepared to change the world.

Despite his sense of despair and his ingrained gloominess, he wanted to be cheerful, even joyful, and to believe that utopia was possible. Even before the reading, he observed in his journal that there was a "primary good of this here civilization . . . the primary good . . . of individual suffering & conscience & creation." Lionel Trilling, his mentor at Columbia College in the 1940s, had never recognized that goodness, he noted angrily, and now Ginsberg wanted to emphasize it. He wanted to see what Whitman had seen, but in a new way—to forge a vision about America that would reflect the realities of the twentieth century. He seemed to think that if Whitman had been alive in 1955 he might have written *Howl*. In his own peculiar way, Ginsberg did care profoundly about American democracy. Tellingly, as a young man in the 1940s he insisted that poets like Carl Sandburg, who revealed the flaws of America, were performing a democratic duty. The task of the poet of democracy wasn't only or simply to speak well of the society, or to simply praise the masses. Now, in the 1950s, he saw it as his democratic duty to show the country that it had strayed from its democratic path. He would rescue the nation from the edge of the precipice. That too would be an act of poetic patriotism.

"The solitary and haunted individual is now the mass," he wrote in his journal, as though describing himself, and he suggested that the poet—again thinking of himself—"who will speak for his own wild naked mind will also speak for the mass." There was a genuine sense of patriotism in that perspective. Optimism didn't come to Ginsberg easily, but he tried. When readers pointed out that *Howl* was dark and despairing, he would allow that the "surface" of the poem was "littered" with "rusty machinery & suicides," but he insisted that at a deeper level the poem was "energetic & healthy & rather affirmative & compassionate." And so it was. Beneath the weighty images of death and the waste land, there was a sense of joy, holiness, and freedom. In the mid-1970s, in the midst of the counterculture he had helped to create, he promised to rewrite *Howl*. Now that he was a hippie minstrel and a Pied Piper for the generation that advocated peace and love he would alter *Howl*, he said, so that it might reflect the euphoria of the hippies. He would include a "positive redemptive catalogue," he said, and he would begin his poem with the upbeat line, "I saw the best minds of my generation turned on by music." Of course, *Howl* lacked a long, affirmative, Whitmanesque catalogue. Ginsberg's utopian vision was shrouded in 1955. Still, the Six Gallery reading and the enthusiastic reception to *Howl*—including Ferlinghetti's invitation to publish the book—gave Ginsberg more self-confidence and more of a sense of joy and pride than he had ever had in his whole life. As a boy, he had predicted that he would grow up to "be a genius." Now, he felt he was that genius. In his journal in April 1956—six months after the Six Gallery reading—he exclaimed, "God! How great to be great like Hart Crane! To realize in one life all the longing for real glory." Ginsberg, who had been reading Philip Horton's *Hart Crane: The Life of an American Poet*, felt that he had arrived. In that same journal entry, he wrote, "I am the greatest poet in America." And then, seemingly aware of and embarrassed by his own enormous ego and his intense competition with others, especially Kerouac, he added in a characteristic spirit of generosity, "Let Jack be greater."

# CHAPTER TWO

# Family Business

**Poets Are Born**

His parents, Naomi and Louis Ginsberg, named him Irwin Allen at his birth in Newark, New Jersey, in 1926. Twenty-nine years later, in San Francisco in 1955—when he began to write *Howl*— he liked to think that he was in a cosmos of his own creation. In fact, he was still very much connected to his parents. Wasn't Naomi a madwoman, and wasn't *Howl* about madness? Didn't Louis write apocalyptic poetry, and wasn't *Howl* an apocalyptic poem, too? His parents haunted him in the months just before he wrote *Howl*—they appeared in his dreams, and he wrote about them in his journals and unpublished poems from that period. Moreover, they provided the germinating seeds for *Howl*— madness, nakedness, and secrecy.

Naomi Ginsberg—"the madwoman in the attic," as she's come to be known—dominates the pages of Ginsberg's biographies. Barry Miles, for example, calls her the single most important person in Allen's life. Yet Louis was no less influential.

Naomi and Louis were two equally potent superpowers engaged in a kind of brinksmanship, with Allen caught in the middle. Both could make him feel small and insignificant, and he had to fight back with his own brand of verbal pyrotechnics to survive their onslaught.

Few poets have quarreled with their parents as intensely as Ginsberg quarreled with his, and few young men have turned those quarrels into poems as remarkable as *Howl* and *Kaddish*. His quarrels were with himself as much as they were with Naomi and Louis, and in the quarrels with himself he expanded the possibilities not only for himself, but for American poetry, as he pushed against the limits of literary caution and conservatism that characterized the times. If ever there was a poet in rebellion against his own parents it was Allen Ginsberg. And yet if ever there was a dutiful poet it was also Allen Ginsberg. The son carried on the family heritage even as he railed against it.

For years, Allen complained that his father was an old-fashioned lyrical poet, a rhyming poet who couldn't stop making clever puns. When he introduced Louis to Jack Kerouac and their mutual friends at college in the 1940s, he introduced him as a high school teacher. *There* was a bit of revenge. He concealed his poet-father, burying him beneath a myth of mediocrity. Kerouac heard Allen tell the legend of the Ginsberg clan so often he could tell it himself, as though he were part of the family, and indeed he almost was. "What can I say?" Kerouac asked rhetorically when the novelist John Clellon Holmes urged him to describe what he knew about a young poet named Allen Ginsberg, whom he was making into the hero of his New York bohemian novel *Go*. "His mother was a Communist who went mad," Jack explained. "His father [is] a schoolteacher.... He is justifying his mother by playing madman. His father represents hateful sanity." Repeatedly, Allen Ginsberg turned his father into the all-controlling authority figure, and repeatedly he took on the persona of the madman. It was his favorite role—the role he played when he wrote *Howl* and when he read *Howl* in public. He was the modern mad poet, speaking for all the madmen and the madwomen the world over.

In 1955 in San Francisco—where he let his madness go naked in public for the first time in his life—he told himself that he would never show *Howl* to Louis, since Louis would disapprove. Then, as though to prove himself right, he sent the manuscript to Louis and waited for the inevitable rebuke. On February 29, 1956, Louis wrote from Paterson, New Jersey, to Allen in San Francisco—where much to his delight he had become the "local poet-hero" in the wake of the Six Gallery reading. Louis's letter from the other side of America shocked Allen and pleased him, too. "It's a wild, rhapsodic, explosive outpouring with good figures of speech flashing by in its volcanic rushing," Louis gushed, as though he'd been infected by his son's raucous rhythms. "It's a hot geyser of emotion suddenly released in wild abandon from subterranean depths of your being."

No one knew Allen's "subterranean depths" better than Louis—not even William Burroughs, who became his surrogate father and self-appointed Reichian analyst, or any of his other surrogate fathers, from Lionel Trilling to William Carlos Williams. No one scrutinized Allen's poetry more thoroughly than Louis—not Jack Kerouac, his surrogate older brother, and certainly not Naomi, his mad mother. When he sent Naomi a copy of *Howl* in 1956 at Pilgrim State Hospital, where she was a patient, she deferred to Louis's judgment. When it came to poetry, father really did know best, Naomi insisted, even though by then Louis had divorced Naomi and remarried. "Do tell me what father thinks of it," she wrote, and for emphasis she added, "Now what does *he* think of it!"

And, if Louis scrutinized Allen's poetry more closely than anyone else, so too did Allen read Louis's poetry more closely than anyone else. Despite their antagonism, they were one another's best readers, best critics, best teachers, and best friends. The more Allen distanced himself from Louis geographically, the more Louis haunted him, and never more so than when he sat down to write *Howl*, a continent away from his father. Louis's ghost hovered above Allen's desk in San Francisco, and so did the ghost of Naomi, though he was too busy rebelling against them to notice how much he owed to them.

In 1956, when Louis and Naomi read *Howl* for the first time, they had both known Allen intimately for nearly thirty years— from the moment he was born. Naomi was often oblivious of her son's comings and goings, but Louis monitored his journeys— from Manhattan to Denver to Houston, to Dakar to Manhattan to Mexico City to San Francisco. For the most part, Louis raised Allen and his older son, Eugene, as a single parent. All through the 1930s and 1940s, Naomi moved in and out of mental institutions, rarely providing the mothering that Allen and Eugene needed, and the companionship and love that Louis craved. A "Russian émigré"—as Allen described her (he had no ordinary immigrant mother)—Naomi Levy came to the United States after the abortive Russian Revolution of 1905. He told her story again and again—how she joined the Communist Party in America, married a young poet, and went crazy.

In fact, almost immediately after her wedding ceremony in

1919 Naomi suffered the first of a series of mental breakdowns that disrupted her life and traumatized her husband and sons. "My mother got a nervous breakdown," Allen wrote in 1937, at the age of eleven, the year he began to keep a journal. He was terrified that Naomi might soon die; she seemed to be in that much pain. But he discovered that was not the case, much to his relief. "Her sickness is only mental . . . she has no chance of dying," he wrote in his journal. Even as a child he was thinking about death and about dying—his lifelong literary preoccupations. And he was also already thinking about the mind and the body. He thought of Naomi's body and his own body, too—how beautiful and yet how grotesque. As a child he saw the dark shadow that Greystone—the New Jersey mental hospital—cast on Naomi's body; he empathized with her and railed against everything and everyone, including his father, who seemed to conspire against her. "Mommy came home . . . Is fat, lost her girlish laughter and figure," he wrote in his journal after her release from Greystone. "I don't blame her for her condition." If any individual was to blame for Mommy's condition it was Louis. "Lou should have known better," he complained. Louis might have saved her from Greystone and her doctors. Louis might have given her back her laughter and her youth, Allen felt. In fact, there was little if anything that Louis could have done. Naomi was a paranoid schizophrenic who saw enemies everywhere: President Roosevelt conspired against her; Nazi spies stalked her; her mother-in-law planned to assassinate her; or so she insisted. The whole industrial world aimed to destroy her. That story line was essential to Allen Ginsberg's myth about his mother—the myth that infuses *Howl*. His mother—and all the innocent, idealistic young men and women of the world—had "human individuality and non-mechanical organic charm," he wrote. Like them, Naomi clashed head on with "modern, mechanical, scientific robot government." Moloch murdered Naomi with madness, and Moloch would murder him with madness, too, unless he could slay the monster with the sword of poetry.

As a boy, Allen was curious about the mystery of madness. As an adult, he invested it with social and political significance. "A lot of madness begins with a grand universal insight, the insight that there is more in the world than subways and offices," he wrote. Naomi was an American Sybil. "She had a great grasp of the transient and irrational nature of the modern capitalist world and a clear idea of the brainwashing that was going on in this country," he explained. "She was no madder than me or my father or . . . for that matter . . . Roosevelt himself." From Allen's point of view, Naomi was a utopian dreamer driven mad by the insanity of the modern world. There was something fragile about her, something too pure for a world at war, a world wracked by poverty and pain. "She / reads the Bible, thinks beautiful thoughts all day," he wrote in *Kaddish*. Naomi was immensely creative—an artist, folksinger, and storyteller—and yet she never fulfilled her own creativity. To Allen, his mother's own individual tragedy seemed emblematic of the larger generational tragedy that befell so many immigrant women from Europe who found the madhouse at the end of the American dream.

Even in her madness, or perhaps especially in her madness, Naomi seemed poetic. "I saw God / . . . He was a lonely old man with a white/beard," she told Allen. "When we die we become an onion, a cabbage a carrot, / or a squash, a vegetable." He remembered her words and included them years later in *Kaddish*. He wished that he, too, might see God and the world as his

mother saw them. Then he might become a mad poet, a vision-
ary poet. Naomi had Russian soul. Louis had American practi-
cality. For years, Allen preferred Naomi's Russian soul to Louis's
American practicality.

Occasionally, Naomi seemed like a real mother and not a mad-
woman, and in *Kaddish* Allen described one long-anticipated
homecoming in the early 1940s. "I waited for that day," he wrote.
"My mother again to cook &—play the / piano—sing at man-
dolin." Increasingly, those occasions were uncommon, and in-
creasingly he remembered things he did not want to remember—
Naomi's nakedness and Louis's nakedness, too. Years later Louis
urged Allen not to write about the nakedness of the Ginsbergs—
and especially not about his own secret sex life with women when
Naomi was locked up in Greystone. "Take out . . . references to
'my affair.' It's too embarrassing and will prove troublesome to
me," he wrote to Allen after reading *Kaddish* in manuscript. Allen
obliged. Some secrets had better be kept secret.

But he also argued fiercely with Louis, especially when it came
to the passage in *Kaddish* about the "beard about the vagina"—his
mother's "beard." "It's bad taste and offends my sensibility,"
Louis wrote. "Too obscene." Allen had a clear answer. A great
many boys saw their mother's naked bodies, he claimed. His ex-
perience was "an archetypal experience & nothing to be ashamed
of." There were other images and other memories, however, that
he chose not to remember, or at least not to include in *Kaddish*.

On one occasion in June 1937 Naomi tried to commit suicide,
an event that must have terrified Allen, and yet it appears in only
the briefest passage in his poetry. When he was eleven years old
he wrote in his journal, "My mother locked herself in the bath-
room early in the morning and my father had to break the glass

to get in . . . She also went back to the sanitarium." Louis had his own memories of Naomi's attempted suicide. "The boys stood there, shivering in their night clothes, panic in their eyes," he remembered. "What traumas, I thought, might sink into them and burrow into their psyches." Louis knew firsthand how harrowing Allen's childhood was. His biographers have often minimized the trauma and emphasized the sense of community and generosity in the Ginsberg family. For the most part, however, Allen seems to have experienced his childhood as a nightmare, and in his poetry he emphasized disharmony and dissonance.

There were many occasions when he "saw what he never should have seen," as Edith Ginsberg, his stepmother, put it. On at least one occasion, Naomi lay in bed naked, beckoning to him to make love to her, a scene he described at length in therapy at Langley Porter in San Francisco in 1955, when Dr. Hicks assured him that he wasn't crazy like his mother. There's no explicit description of his mother's attempt to seduce him in *Howl*, though in the first draft he wrote, "with his own mother finally fucked"—which might well be a reference to Naomi's invitation to have sex with her. Later, he revised the manuscript and expunged the words "own" and "fuck" and inserted six asterisks in the place of "fuck" so the text reads "with mother finally ******." But he couldn't expunge the inner wound, and in *Kaddish*, he returned to the traumatic seduction scene at length and in detail. "One time I thought she was trying to make me come lay her," he wrote. "Lay back on huge bed that filled most of the room, dress / up round her hips, big slash of hair / . . . ragged long lips between her legs—What, even, / smell of asshole? I was cold— later revolted a little, not much—seemed per- / haps a good idea to try—know the Monster of the Beginning Womb." For most of his life, the female body appeared repulsive to him and sex with women proved to be difficult, if not impossible. In his poetry he mythologized the vagina and the womb as dark, deadly places.

The story about his mother that he told and retold and that his biographers repeated, was the story about the day he took Naomi by bus, and on the advice of her doctor, to a convalescent home in Lakewood, New Jersey. "Ride 3 hours thru tunnels past all American industry, Bayonne preparing for World War II, tanks, gas fields, soda factories, dinners, locomotive roundhouse fortress," he wrote in *Kaddish*. The boy peers through the bus window at a rapidly shifting, surreal landscape where wartime and peacetime merge into one another. He might have chosen any New Jersey city, but Bayonne in France was the birthplace of the bayonet and fit with the imagery of war. The infernal industrial landscape of New Jersey—the ironically named Garden State— was stamped indelibly on his imagination and in *Howl* it appears as desolate, dirty, and lonely. Yet it appears as Zen-like, too. T. S. Eliot's wasteland grew in his boyhood backyard, the insane asylum rose up in his bedroom, and the war news from abroad invaded his youthful daydreams. By the time he was eleven—and until he was in his twenties—he read the *New York Times* and *PM*, the left-wing newspaper, and was shocked by the global horrors that were reported of dictators and death camps.

Like his parents, he was not religious—at thirteen he would not be barmitzvahed—but he was a Jew, and in the late 1930s and early 1940s, the world looked like a deadly place for Jews. Instinctively, he sided with the antifascist cause. "I'm an atheist and a combination of Jeffersonian Democrat-Socialist Communist," he wrote in his journal just before his fifteenth birthday—adding that he disapproved of Soviet dictatorship. He was astounded to learn that in Germany and in Italy political parties advocated "killing all the Jews." It was crazy, surreal, and terrifying. The horror of fascism became an everyday reality for Allen, and it haunted his imagination. "The world is now in turmoil," he noted. He followed the battles of the Spanish Civil War and complained in March 1938 that the "fascists are winning." He was anxious about the future, and by the spring of 1938 he knew it was only a matter of time before the world would be at war again.

Given the geopolitical and personal backdrop of Allen's early development, it's understandable that he grew up to write the poetry of personal crack-up and political catastrophe. Fissures were everywhere in his childhood and youth. His family was in crisis; capitalism was in crisis. And he was in crisis, too, about his own sexual identity. He was a child of the 1930s—breadlines, unemployment lines, poverty. Like Kerouac and Burroughs, he was profoundly shaped by the tremors that shook American society, but unlike them he was also influenced by the subculture of the American left.

As a boy, Allen adopted as heroes the martyrs of the radical movement in America, and as an adult he celebrated the martyrs of the global left—from Vladimir Mayakovsky to Che Guevara. In the 1930s, he revered Nicola Sacco and Bartolomeo Vanzetti—the Italian-born anarchists who were executed in Massachusetts in 1927—and he adored Eugene V. Debs, the Socialist Party's perennial presidential candidate, who was jailed for his opposition to World War I. Allen learned a great deal from Aunt Rose and Uncle Max, who appear in several poems—"America," *Kaddish*, and "To Aunt Rose," in which he describes the time he "stood on the toilet seat naked" and Aunt Rose saw his own "tender / and shamed first black curled hairs." He had poison ivy; she applied calamine lotion. "What were you thinking in secret heart then / knowing me a man already," he wondered. His own naked body and the body politic seemed inextricably linked. The toxin of fascism spread across Europe as poison ivy spread across his limbs. It was as though his own body had been invaded. Later, his poetry would spring from his own flesh and blood, as William Carlos Williams noted in his introduction to *Howl*. "It is the poet, Allen Ginsberg, who has gone, in his own body, through the horrifying experiences derived from life in these pages," he wrote. For a poet who was so much in his mind, he was also much in his body.

As a boy, Allen felt uncomfortable in his body and embarrassed by his mind. Many of his earliest poems are about the mind/body dichotomy, and in *Howl* he would write about the "best minds" of his generation as though those minds were somehow separate from the bodies of real people—and of bodies separate from minds. "I'm the smallest boy in class," he noted in 1938, when he was twelve. At ninety-five pounds he felt "fragile." He was also uneasy about his own "baser emotions," as he called them. He had been conscious of them from the age of seven. "I'm capable of almost anything," he wrote in his journal. His motto in grade school was, "Do what you want to when you want to," and he seems to have practiced what he preached. He was an exhibitionist and often took off his clothes, exposing himself to the world. He often slept in Louis's big bed, and when Louis was asleep he masturbated and fantasized about having sex with his father and his brother. In his own fantasy world, he was spanked, or he spanked others; sometimes in daydreams he turned other boys into "naked victims" and punished them.

## No Joy like Creative Activity

At times, Louis seemed oblivious of Allen's problems. He had his own financial and emotional troubles to worry about; he had borrowed two thousand dollars to publish a volume of his own verse, and he was in debt. At school, he was overworked; at home he was in distress about Naomi's madness and the collapse of their marriage. Still, he did his best to care for his wife and his two sons, and he tended to his own soul, too, and that meant writing poetry. "When I loved a woman who grew incurably psychotic, I was handicapped," he wrote. "Yet in my handicap I used the handcuffs as bracelets by letting my spirit feed in creative poetry." It was a lesson that Allen learned early in life: turn pain into poetry, or simply turn to poetry. Louis introduced him to verse and taught him how to read a poem. The point was to read between the lines, Louis explained. The world of poetry was infinite and it existed everywhere. You could lose yourself in a single poem—discover its meter, rhyme, metaphors, and similes.

Louis showed Allen how to perform poetry. Pacing back and forth in the living room in Paterson, and breathing deeply, he read aloud from the works of Milton, Wordsworth, Dickinson, and so many others. Allen listened enthralled. For the most part, Louis was cool, calm, collected, even when Naomi went mad, but when he read poetry he caught fire and revealed his own raw emotions. Allen caught his father's vocal fire. He watched Louis as he sat at his desk writing poetry, and he marveled at his father's power to make order out of chaos and metaphor out of madness. The world was a horrible place, and suffering was everywhere, Louis insisted, but there was always the ecstasy of poetry. "There is no joy like the joy of creative activity . . . of making articulate what is inarticulate and imprisoned in most people," he explained.

When he was a boy, his father's books were sacred to him. He delighted in *The Attic of the Past* (1920), which includes a whole section of poems *about* Naomi and *for* Naomi: "The Lover Thinks of the Beloved," "To Naomi," and "Song," in which he wrote, "You are the Spirit / And I am the Flute." Allen was moved by *The Everlasting Minute* (1937), which Louis dedicated to his wife, whose shadow seems to darken his poems. Long before Allen wrote about Naomi, Louis wrote about her; even Allen's brother, Eugene, wrote about Naomi before he did, most remarkably in a poem entitled "To My Mother" that was first published in the *New York Times* and later in his own volume of poetry, *Rites of Passage*. Naomi served as the muse for all the Ginsberg men. Edith Ginsberg, Louis's second wife, was nurturing, loving, and emotionally stable, but she rarely inspired poetry. Crazy women inspired Allen: his mother, Naomi; his surrogate mother, Joan Burroughs, who lived on the edge until her accidental death at the hands of her husband, William; and Natalie Jackson, who was lover to both Allen and Neal Cassady, and who committed suicide in late 1955, when Allen was in the midst of writing *Howl*. His muse—whether male or female—tended to be mad.

In 1970, when Allen wrote "Confrontation with Louis Ginsberg's Poems"—his introduction to *Mornings in Spring*, his father's third collection of poetry—he complained that Louis's work was an "anachronism" and "the outworn verse of previous century voices." In fact, Louis's work was often musty, sentimental, and sweet, the rhymes predictable, the lines on the page neat and tidy. Louis sometimes seemed to live in a fairy tale where there was always a happy ending. Allen noted that the city of Paterson—where his father lived and wrote almost all of his poems (he was known as "Paterson's Principal Poet")—was corrupt and crime infested. In Allen's view it was "a XX Century Mafia-Police-Bureaucracy-Race-War-Nightmare-TV-Squawk suburb," a microcosm of all American cities. For the most part, Louis ignored the crime, the Mafia, and the racism. As Allen pointed out, the lyrical mode his father adopted didn't seem sturdy enough to encompass the grim realities of Paterson in the twentieth century.

In his short poem "Buttercups," which Louis Untermeyer included in his popular anthology *Yesterday and Today* (1926), Louis wrote, "Buttercups, buttercups, / What do you hold? / Buttercups, buttercups, / Minting your gold." Neither worms nor blight appeared in Louis's flower poems, and there's no sweetness of decay either. Allen's own poems about flowers—"On Reading William Blake's 'The Sick Rose,'" for example, which ends with the question, "Is this the sickness that is Doom?"—were darker and more menacing than his father's. Allen's world was darker than his father's, though Louis did have a more shadowy side that emerged in many poems—"Ruined Houses," "In the Subway," and "Midnight"—poems that seem to derive from his sadness about Naomi's madness. And some of Louis's work exhibited real power and resiliency. As Allen himself pointed out, Louis could look as unflinchingly as he did at the hideousness of the human condition and the bestiality of the self.

### Planetary Catastrophe

Despite his grousing, Allen was also generous enough to recognize that his father's poetry offered a "contemporary prophetic glimmer of the planetary catastrophe." Like Allen, Louis was apocalyptic and paranoid. Like Allen, he imagined disaster, and like Allen he crafted poems to express his sense of impending disaster and doom. "My sons, watch out. This is a dangerous age," he wrote to Allen and Eugene in "My Sons, Watch Out." The poem continues, "Our history's trapped. Our century leaks disaster / . . . Fissions of men and atoms react faster." He was proud of his advice to Allen and Eugene, as he should have been. The atomic age *was* dangerous. In five major poems—"Ode to Machines," "The Revolt of the Machines," "The End of the World," "When Bombs on Barcelona Burst," and "Atomic"—Louis grappled with the horrors of the twentieth century. He grappled with war, nuclear disaster, and the madness of the machine age. Allen's "Moloch" is akin to Louis's "fierce Behemoths," who appear in "The Revolt of the Machines." The wild Behemoths unleash "their fury on the city." It is "slacked," "slain," "smeared into the plain!" and "Devoured by a maddened holocaust." For the most part, Louis managed to be optimistic, and he ended "The Revolt of the Machines" with the line "Peace on the wound of earth again!" Here, too, Louis influenced Allen. Even in his darkest poems—even in *Howl* and in *Kaddish*—he pointed a ray of light. In hell, he found paradise—like a good Blakean.

In hindsight, it seems inevitable that Allen would grow up and become a poet like his father. "I grew up in a poetry atmosphere," he observed near the end of his life. "Poetry . . . was a family business." He enjoyed the business, observing, "Would that all sons' fathers were poets!" His own burden was to make a unique home for himself in the world of poetry, and not accept ready-made the house of poetry that his father had built. As T. S. Eliot wrote in his benchmark essay "Tradition and the Individual Talent"

(1919), "Tradition . . . cannot be inherited, and if you want it you must obtain it by great labor." Understandably, Allen rejected the literary inheritance that his father offered freely. But in rejecting his father and exploring his own talent, he often echoed his father. As Eliot noted, "the most individual parts" of a poet's "work may be those in which the dead poets, his ancestors, assert their immortality most vigorously." In *Howl*, and precisely where he felt he was "most individual," his father's hand is hard at work.

### Better than Whitman

By the time he was fifteen, Allen Ginsberg believed that he was a literary genius and that one day he would become a famous writer. "If some future historian or biographer wants to know what the genius thought or did in his tender years, here it is," he wrote in his journal in May 1941. "I'll be a genius of some kind or other, probably in literature." His own boyhood genius is perhaps most apparent in an essay entitled "Walt Whitman and Carl Sandburg—Biography, Poetry, Criticism, Comparison," which he wrote for his high school English teacher Frances Durbin. It was an essay that he saved for his whole life, as though he couldn't bear to throw it away or destroy it, and yet he never discussed it, and it remained buried in his archives for decades.

After the publication of *Howl*, he rewrote his own literary history and insisted that he had always loved Whitman. But that wasn't exactly true; he didn't always love Whitman without reservation. In the early 1940s, he preferred Carl Sandburg to Walt Whitman, in part because he was confused about his own homosexuality. Moreover, by the populist political values of the Gins-

berg family, Sandburg seemed superior to Whitman. "The pre-
dominant characteristic of Carl Sandburg's poetry is the love for
the people, and Democracy," Allen wrote in his high school es-
say for Frances Durbin. He added, "Sandburg adds something
which, in my mind, takes his poetry above the level of Whit-
man's." Whitman's verse was "long winded," while Sandburg was
"shorter, often more poignant," and so he had the "edge" on
Whitman in "poetic expression" as well as in political perspec-
tive. Ginsberg noted that Whitman was a homosexual—he was
"born a 'freak,'" he wrote—and he suggested insightfully that
"we are fortunate in his abnormality, because it was the prime
factor in shaping the message of *Leaves of Grass*." Reading be-
tween the lines, one might say that Allen recognized that he, too,
was born a freak. Whitman helped him to recognize his own ab-
normality and to accept it, at least in part. But he was also
ashamed of his abnormality, and he felt that *Leaves of Grass* was
"very slightly tainted" by Whitman's abnormality. He was sad to
have to conclude that homosexuality marred Whitman's work.
Ginsberg was also troubled by Whitman's deliberately crafted
persona—his habit of calling himself Walt not Walter Whitman,
his manner of wearing "working man's clothes," and his habit of
posing in public with his hand resting casually on his hip. "While
it would be pleasant enough to be able to believe that these
Homeric gestures demonstrating his democracy were sincere
and spontaneous, apparently they were carefully cultivated," he
wrote. Whitman was a poseur, Allen noted; sincerity wasn't his
strong point. Still, he concluded that Whitman was a genuine lit-
erary genius. "While his style seems loose and spotty, it shows
careful planning," he wrote. Whitman's style was similar to Her-
man Melville's style, and it was "like the style of the verses of the

Bible, large magnificent strophes, building up to mighty climaxes, or like a massive Bach oratorio." A decade and a half later, when he wrote about *Howl*, he used nearly identical language to describe his own work, depicting *Howl* as Melvillean, biblical, and Bach-like. When he sat down to write *Howl*, he would write lines that he would describe as "large magnificent strophes." Thus *Howl* had origins in his high school experience of reading Whitman.

Though poetry was the Ginsberg family business, it looked like bad business to Allen. Louis couldn't make a living as a poet, and that seems to have made an indelible impression on his younger son. Money appears throughout Allen's poetry, including *Howl*, where one of the unnamed anonymous hipsters (perhaps Carl Solomon) burns money in a wastebasket in a dreary room. Money shows up in "Stanzas: Written at Night in Radio City" (1949), where it's part of the madness of modern society, and in "Paterson" (1949), too, where it drives people crazy. At the end of Ginsberg's life, money showed up in poems like "The Velocity of Money" (1986). Here the poet himself has made a fortune from his poetry. He's rich. Of course as a young man, he had no idea that writing poetry would lead to his financial success. That seemed unreal. At seventeen, Allen Ginsberg thought, albeit briefly, that he ought to try to fit in, get a job, and take part in American public life. In the early 1940s, he supported liberal Democratic candidates for public office, including New Jersey's pro-labor Congressman Gordon Canfield, and he wrote effusive letters to the *New York Times* and to local newspapers endorsing liberals and progressives and denouncing anti-communism. In 1943, he went to college, not to become a poet but a lawyer for organized labor. In many ways he was still back in the 1930s, an

era when lawyers like Clarence Darrow and Samuel Liebowitz—
who had defended the Scottsboro Boys—were cultural icons,
and a boy from a left-wing family could dream of following in
their footsteps. But that would change almost as soon as he en-
tered Columbia and met William Burroughs and Lucien Carr,
cynics about the working class, socialism, and crusading lawyers.

# CHAPTER THREE

# Trilling-esque
# Sense of "Civilization"

## The Culture Clash at Columbia

In the mid-1950s American poets rarely howled, screamed, ranted, or raved. They composed themselves and then composed odes and sonnets, or, if they happened to be innovative, like Jack Kerouac, they composed the blues—as in *San Francisco Blues* (1954). Animals and savages howled. Of course, *Howl* was carefully composed, as the poet Denise Levertov and others pointed out, but Ginsberg wanted readers to think of his poem as the distillation of "ten years' animal screams"—the screams of a madman. Ginsberg conceived of *Howl* as a call to arms and a cultural weapon in the war against academic poetry, the literary criticism of the day, and the American poetry establishment. If you were reared on the poetry of Allen Tate and John Crowe Ransom, and if Cleanth Brooks and Robert Penn Warren's *Understanding Poetry* was your bible in the 1950s, then *Howl* looked and sounded uncouth. For James Dickey, who reviewed *Howl* in the *Sewanee Review*, Ginsberg's poem was the work of an "American adolescent" and a meaningless diatribe. As far as he was concerned, Ginsberg was "the perfect inhabitant, if not the very founder of Babel." It wasn't only in the *Sewanee Review* that *Howl* provoked heated debate about poets, poetry, and the idea of civilization itself. In almost every major literary publication, *Howl* incited controversy—perhaps more than Ginsberg himself could handle, though he seemed to thrive on it. On the eve of the publication of *Howl*, he described his poem as a weapon against highbrow culture and the formal education he'd received as a student at Columbia College from 1943 to 1948. In *Howl*, he told Richard Eberhart, the poet, critic, and contributor to the *New York Times Book Review*, he was "leaping *out* of a preconceived notion of social 'values,' following my own heart's instincts—*allowing* myself to follow my own heart's instincts." Moreover, he was "overturning any notion of propriety, moral 'value,' superficial 'maturity' [and] Trilling-esque sense of 'civilization.'"

Trilling was of course Lionel Trilling, the famed Columbia professor and Allen's intellectual mentor in the mid-1940s. A radical in the 1930s, Trilling turned into a mandarin intellectual in the 1940s. "Allen holds you in great esteem and places great value on your dicta," Louis Ginsberg wrote to Trilling in 1945. A great many Americans with a modicum of culture held Professor Trilling in great esteem all through the 1940s and 1950s. A mainstay at the Book of the Month Club, Trilling was the author of *Matthew Arnold* (1938), an intellectual biography; *The Middle of the Journey* (1947), a political novel; and several collections of provocative essays, including *The Liberal Imagination* (1950) and *The Opposing Self* (1955). At Columbia, Trilling seemed synonymous with civilization itself, and as a teacher and a critic, he argued that civilization was synonymous with upper-class British civilization as expressed at Oxford and Cambridge by men like Matthew Arnold and E. M. Forster. Ginsberg had no use for Matthew Arnold—or any of the Victorian poets, with the exception of a few poems by Alfred, Lord Tennyson, Queen Victoria's poet laureate. Nor did he have much use for English novelists of manners and morals like E. M. Forster. Still, as an undergraduate at Columbia, he tried to conform to "Trilling-esque 'civilization,'" and that meant rejecting or at least squelching the radical political values of his own family and the left-wing culture in which he'd been reared. He did his very best to be a scholar and a gentleman in the mold of the college, and in many ways he's as much a product of Columbia as the poet John Hollander and the critic Norman Podhoretz, two classmates who would condemn *Howl* in the late 1950s. At Columbia in the 1940s Allen studied diligently and dreamed about becoming an academic like Professor Trilling. Ginsberg read everything he could get his hands on—as though driven by an insatiable need for endless ideas and systems of thought, and as though his intelligence would die of hunger unless he went on feeding it books. "I read each book for a special purpose," he wrote in his journal. He took bits and pieces from each work he read and then arranged and rearranged them in a gigantic, ever-expanding jigsaw puzzle of the mind. In *Howl* he alludes to his college reading in the line "who studied Plotinus Poe St. John of the Cross." In the original manuscript version there's a much longer list. It includes Karl Marx, Oswald Spengler, Antonin Artaud, Jean Genet, Arthur Rimbaud, Thomas Wolfe, Louis-Ferdinand Céline, Marcel Proust, Walt Whitman, and Buddha. And that wasn't all. A glance at his college papers and journals reveals that he read and reflected on Aristotle, Thomas Hobbes, John Locke, Jean Jacques

Rousseau, John Stuart Mill, Denis Diderot, Tom Paine, Edmund Burke, V. I. Lenin, Dante, Goethe, Dickens, Dostoyevsky, Rainer Maria Rilke, William Butler Yeats, T. S. Eliot, Hart Crane, Maxim Gorky, Leo Tolstoy, and many others.

In the 1940s, Ginsberg also rebelled against the idea of civilization that Columbia tried to impose on him and his fellow undergraduates. He certainly wandered far from the curriculum and read books he wasn't encouraged to read. On his bed table there was pulp fiction like *Butterfield 8*, by John O'Hara, and noir novels by James M. Cain and Raymond Chandler, as well as Superman and Batman comic books, which he described to Trilling, who had never read or even heard of them. In the 1940s in Manhattan Ginsberg identified with the wild young barbarians and the savages, as he liked to think of them—Jack Kerouac, William Burroughs, Herbert Huncke, and Lucien Carr. He, too, was a young savage, though he kept one foot in the fold of civilization. Allen and Columbia College were a difficult fit, though exactly how difficult, he didn't say until the mid-1960s. "The whole syndrome of shutdown and provincialism extended to the academy," he explained to Jane Kramer. "Like, at Columbia, Whitman was hardly taught and was considered like a creep. Shelley was a creep too. John Crowe Ransom and Allen Tate were like the supreme literary touchstones . . . The only poet at the school was [Mark] Van Doren, and even he was writing in a classical style." (Curiously, Ginsberg omitted mention of Trilling in his diatribe on Columbia, though he mentioned most of his other teachers.) Perhaps he might have felt more at home if he had attended Black Mountain College, the experimental liberal arts school in North Carolina where the poet and critic Charles Olson served as chancellor, where Robert Creeley and

Denise Levertov were students, and where poetry reigned su-
preme. It certainly didn't reign supreme at Columbia in the
1940s. It was the novel that reigned supreme, and it was Lionel
Trilling who had crowned it the king of all genres.

In 1943, when he began his education at Columbia, Allen was
a budding young homosexual from a left-wing Jewish family, and
in 1943—and all through the 1940s—Columbia did not take
kindly to budding young homosexuals from left-wing Jewish fam-
ilies. Radicalism was out of fashion with the faculty in the 1940s.
A decade earlier, in 1930, Trilling had written that the "salvation
of American art lies not in a greater rapprochement with the en-
vironment but in its becoming more subversive and dangerous to
the social order." By the time Ginsberg entered Columbia, Trill-
ing had changed his tune, and so had most of his colleagues.
They had started out as radicals in the 1930s and now were mak-
ing peace with the American social order. Homosexuality had
never been in fashion at Columbia, and anti-Semitism lurked just
beneath the polite surface of college life. Lionel Trilling was the
first Jew to become a full professor in the English Department,
and he became a professor in part because he effaced his Jewish
identity. The "more he studied the Jewish identity the more he
recoiled from it," one biographer noted. He recoiled from his
radical past and made it his mission to dismantle Marxism and
promote Freudianism. "I want to learn Marxism . . . because
I think we cannot teach our best students—mostly Marxist—
until we know a great deal more than they do about their reli-
gious conversions," he told colleague Jacques Barzun, who also
served as one of Ginsberg's mentors.

Trilling made it his business to challenge students like Allen
Ginsberg, who came to college imbued with burning ideas about

human progress and the perfectibility of man. The young ideal-istic Ginsberg and the middle-aged, disillusioned ex-radical Trilling were perfect foils for one another. In the course of their ongoing debates, discussions, and correspondence, Ginsberg forged his own identity as a poet and an intellectual. And through his encounters with Ginsberg—who was his student and who often came to his apartment and whose troubled life he knew firsthand—Trilling came increasingly to understand the role of adversarial cultures in American society. It seems likely that Ginsberg reminded Trilling of what he had been like as a young student. And there was a great deal about Ginsberg he could admire. Even at twenty, Ginsberg was more knowledge-able about modern poetry than Trilling. As odd as it may seem, Trilling hadn't read Rimbaud—or Enid Starkie's groundbreak-ing biography of Rimbaud—until Ginsberg introduced him to his work, and he hadn't appreciated William Butler Yeats's work until Ginsberg sang his praises.

For Trilling, left-wing politics and literature were antithetical. In 1945, he noted in his journal that the "liberal progressive has not produced a single writer that it itself respects and reads with interest." He also observed that "when a man does begin to court the liberal-democratic ideal, it is either a sign or the beginning of spiritual collapse in his work." From 1945 to 1950, he exhausted his thesis about liberalism and literature in a series of essays published in *The Liberal Imagination*. The "liberal ideology," he noted, has not produced "a single writer who commands our real literary admiration." (As Trilling's biographer Stephen Tanner pointed out, "liberalism" was his code word for Marxism and communism.) Moreover, Trilling insisted that the major literary figures of the twentieth century—his list included Marcel

Proust, James Joyce, D. H. Lawrence, T. S. Eliot, Franz Kafka, Rainer Maria Rilke, and André Gide—were all "indifferent" to liberal ideas and values. Despite all his learning and erudition, dozens of twentieth-century writers—Mayakovsky, Brecht, Virginia Woolf, Neruda, Sandburg, Simone de Beauvoir, Langston Hughes, and Richard Wright—who had embraced liberal and left causes (and sometimes abandoned them, too) escaped his scrutiny.

When Allen arrived at Columbia in 1943, he was convinced that Carl Sandburg and Walt Whitman were the greatest of American writers and that American democracy was the envy of the world. He soon discovered that neither Whitman nor Sandburg was taught at Columbia and that grassroots democracy wasn't much respected by the leading intellectuals on campus, either. In 1943 and 1944, Ginsberg switched ideological sides— or at least gave that impression. He devoured Rilke, Joyce, Eliot, Proust, Mann, and Kafka, emerging as "Trilling-esque." He could identify with the characters in modern fiction and poetry—Stephen Dedalus, J. Alfred Prufrock, Swann, Hans Castorp, and K.—and he used them to justify his own lifestyle. If you teach *The Magic Mountain*, *Ulysses*, *The Waste Land*, and *The Trial*, you'll get students like me, he seemed to say, students who belonged to the "adversarial culture," as Trilling called it.

Ginsberg read everything Kafka wrote, and he wrote more college papers about Kafka than about any other single writer. On the one hand, he could adopt a Marxist perspective and disapprove of Kafka "because he was decadent." On the other hand, he could be a modernist and admit that he read Kafka's *The Castle* "with a mad secret delight." As for *The Trial*, it truly belonged at the heart of modern literature, he argued, because its "madness . . . is really something new—perhaps a basic cosmic description, even atomic maybe." Again and again in the 1940s, he identified himself as a character in a Kafka novel. The world as he came to know it was Kafkaesque. From his point of view, Columbia itself was Kafkaesque—it was an absurd, irrational world of bureaucratic college deans. Like Kafka's anti-heroes, Ginsberg felt that he was on trial and in a state of perpetual punishment.

### Madmen and Artists

In the 1940s, Ginsberg had all sorts of teachers in addition to his Columbia teachers. Most of his unofficial teachers were at war with Columbia and with academia. Ginsberg would describe them in the opening line of *Howl* as the "best minds of my generation destroyed by madness." Kerouac was at the center of the circle of "madmen and artists"—as he called it—that provided his countercultural education. (More than a decade before he wrote *Howl* he was enthralled by "madmen.") To Ginsberg, Kerouac was a real live hero as well as the king of the madmen. Jack had attended Columbia briefly on a football scholarship and then dropped out in 1941 because "he couldn't take the Philistinism of Lou Little, the piggish priggishness of the football players, and the restrictions of academic life," Allen explained to his brother, Eugene. In 1942, Jack served as a merchant seaman and in 1943 he joined the U.S. Navy, but he ended up in a "Navy Madhouse" and was "discharged as psychoneurotic." By 1944 he was back in Manhattan, where he met Ginsberg, Burroughs, and Carr and married his first wife, Edith Parker. All through World War II he was writing, whether at sea or on land. Kerouac's madness was inspiring to Ginsberg; it made him an authentic misfit in a world of imposters and hypocrites. That Kerouac had been in a mad-house, like Ginsberg's mother, endeared him to Ginsberg, too. So did Kerouac's literary aspirations. Like so many other young men of his generation—from Gore Vidal and James Jones to Norman Mailer and William Styron, all of whom had served in World War II—Kerouac wanted to write the great American novel. In the late 1940s, he was working on a big novel in which Ginsberg would appear as a character preoccupied with madness and nuclear disaster.

William Burroughs, who also belonged to Ginsberg's circle of Manhattan madmen and artists, had graduated from Harvard in the late 1930s, where he studied English literature. He had gone on to explore the world of petty crime and heroin addiction in Chicago and New York. Like Kerouac, Burroughs hadn't served in World War II, and like Kerouac he'd been in a madhouse—briefly he was a patient at Bellevue Hospital in Manhattan, where he was diagnosed as paranoid schizophrenic. Lucien Carr, the third member of the group, had attempted suicide in 1943 and had been a patient at Cook County Hospital in Chicago. After flunking out of one school after another, he ended up at Columbia in 1944, where Allen met him and fell in love with him. In Allen's sophomore year he began to write a novel about Lucien and homosexuality that landed him in big trouble at school and at home. Writing about homosexuality was unacceptable at Columbia, and unacceptable to Louis. "Allen, as classwork, is writing a novel whose hero is a fictionalized Lucien Carr, a twisted eccentric," Louis complained. "He is making clever but false verbal rationalizations that the immoralist's way of life (à la Gide, I think) is a valid one . . . He seeks to philosophize abnormality into normality."

On the night of August 14, 1944, on the Upper West Side of Manhattan, Lucien Carr murdered David Kammerer, a schoolteacher from St. Louis who had come to New York hoping to become Carr's lover. The story has been told repeatedly by Beat biographers. What has not been told is how the Kammerer/Carr incident shaped Ginsberg—how it taught him, at the age of nineteen, about the persecution of homosexuals in America. Indeed, as he learned, it was dangerous to be a homosexual, certainly as dangerous as being a communist. As Ginsberg knew, Kammerer pursued Carr relentlessly for years, until finally Carr stabbed him and dumped his body in the Hudson River. Kerouac helped dispose of the murder weapon—a knife. Burroughs insisted that Carr surrender to the police—which he did. The story became front-page news in New York and promptly became a crucial chapter in the Beat Generation's book of its own legends. Kerouac and Burroughs were both arrested and held as material witnesses. Everyone in the know conspired to keep Carr's bisexuality a secret. He didn't discuss it with the police and neither did Kerouac, Burroughs, Ginsberg, or his girlfriend, Celine Young. Everyone insisted that Carr was an innocent, clean-cut kid who had been stalked by a predatory homosexual and that he had defended his own honor. The police bought the story and so did the press. Indicted and found guilty of manslaughter, Carr was sentenced to a term of one to twenty years at the Elmira Reformatory. Ginsberg hovered in the wings, absorbed, taking notes. To his brother, Eugene, he wrote that Carr would probably serve less than two years. (In fact he was released in 1946.) Allen added emphatically that it was "what I call getting away with murder!" To Ginsberg, the lesson seemed to be that if you concealed your homosexuality, anything was possible, even homicide. So the perfect crime à la André Gide was possible after all.

In his novel *The Vanity of Duluoz* (1968), Kerouac noted that Allen wanted "to be in on it all the way . . . like the old litterature [*sic*] in [Dostoyevsky's] The Possessed." The reference to Dostoyevsky is precise and accurate; Ginsberg was reading *The Possessed, The Brothers Karamazov, Crime and Punishment, Notes from the Underground,* and *The Idiot.* He seemed to be living in one Dostoyevsky novel or another, as the underground man, Raskolnikov, Prince Myshkin, or as one of the Karamazov brothers— Ivan, Alyosha, or Dmitri. What's more, Allen hoped to emulate Dostoyevsky—to use the Carr case to write an American version of *Crime and Punishment.* "I think I'll start a novel on the affair," he told Eugene in 1944. "There is much detail and significance that would make a brilliant if pessimistic novel." Only a fragment of that novel survives. In those pages, Carr appears as the narcissistic, cynical Claude de Maubri, who tries to wean Ginsberg of his left-wing ideas, while Ginsberg appears as the altruistic, idealistic Goldstein, who fights to hold on to them. In what is probably the best scene, the two characters engage in verbal sparring. "My multitudes," Goldstein shouts. Claude replies, "Your rabble," to which Goldstein adds, "underdog," and Claude says, "Herd." Later, Claude takes a shower and Goldstein notices that he "rubbed the soap reflectively over his genitalia." Still later, they visit Claude's mother's apartment, which the author describes as "the womb." Later, the two characters discuss the "phallic symbol" in a painting they admire. In a climactic scene that takes place in the men's room of a Greenwich Village bar, Goldstein accidentally drops his fountain pen into the urinal and Claude retrieves it from "the yellow water."

As a high school student in Paterson in the early 1940s, Allen Ginsberg wanted to organize the working class, vanquish fascism, and change the world. Now, in the mid-1940s, he had moved beyond Marx, Marxism, trade unions, and union organizers. All politics, whether of the left or of the right, was empty and meaningless, he insisted. Political extremists were one and the same. "There is only one man who can be more deadly a bore than a Communist," he wrote in 1944. "That is the man who once was a Communist and is sorry for it." (In the 1940s, the Columbia campus climate was in large measure created by ex-communists and Trotskyites from the 1930s. Ginsberg had little if any tolerance for those political persuasions.) Now, crime and criminals appealed to him. "A criminal is more interesting, certainly a more valuable member of a community than a banker or a priest or a grocery store owner," he wrote his brother, Eugene—who would graduate from law school and make a career of defending criminals. Allen preferred to associate with, and to aid and abet, common criminals—street hustlers, drug addicts, pickpockets, burglars, thieves, and con artists whom he met in and around Times Square, where he spent as much if not more time than he did in the classroom. The criminal, he told Eugene, was a "marvelous experiment in moral freedom," adding that "civilization is doomed . . . the western world is in decline."

Now, thanks to the mentoring of William Burroughs, he was reading Oswald Spengler's *Decline of the West*, and suddenly he became a Spenglerian. He couldn't say enough to express his awe and admiration for Spengler; he was a "great prophetic poet," Ginsberg wrote. *Decline of the West* was a "tremendous book in two fat volumes, with titles of ponderous power and chapter headings almost cabalistic in their imagery." The fall of the whole of western civilization was inevitable, Allen insisted. Doom was only a matter of time. Now, in the time that remained before the inevitable apocalypse, he wanted to take drugs, have visions, and experiment with sex. He wanted to live like Arthur Rimbaud, who had broken new literary ground for poets, Ginsberg explained, by smoking hashish in the "back alleys of Paris," rediscovering "Western magics," the "Alchemy of the Verb," and by his "long reasoned derangement of the senses."

No wonder Louis Ginsberg barely recognized his son after a year or so in New York in the mid-1940s. "Where is your former, fine zeal for a liberal progressive, democratic society?" he asked, and he urged Allen to consider that "the homosexual and the insane person is a menace to himself and to society." In the heart of wartime New York and away from his father's "Polonius-like tirades," as Allen called them, the idea of becoming a left-wing lawyer evaporated. Art took the place of law. It was as though he'd experienced a conversion from Marxism to romanticism, from left-wing politics to the art of the individual, and indeed art became his religion, as it had been for the nineteenth-century romantic poets he was studying at Columbia. "Whee! Out of the cracked and bleeding heart, I fashion—Art," he wrote in his journal in 1943, as though he was intoxicated by the idea of making art from his own wounds. The idea of becoming a famous poet was too seductive to give up for the glory of the labor movement. "In our day poetry is the last remaining messenger from Heaven," he wrote in a college essay about Dante. Elsewhere he noted, "The poet is the creature with the highest and most complete consciousness of all things about him." He could no more defuse the impulse to write poetry than he could defuse his sexual attraction to men, though he tried. His poetry and his homosexuality were inextricably linked; they both went to the core of his being.

In 1943, as a college freshman—and a virgin—he wasn't certain what literary gestures and styles he would adopt, and what identity as a homosexual, if any, he would carve out for himself. Still, almost as soon as he arrived at Columbia, he began to explore, albeit secretly, his own repressed homosexuality, often with men who were ostensibly heterosexual. He explored it with men who thought of themselves as great lovers, like Lucien Carr, who had exotic girlfriends like Celine Young and who drew a curtain around his secret love for other men. Like them, Ginsberg became a secret homosexual, a homosexual who masked his homosexuality and used the code of homosexuals to communicate with like-minded individuals in the great sexual underground of New York during World War II. He found homosexuals in the college dorms, in bars and cafes in Greenwich Village; he learned that there was a thriving culture of homosexuality all across the city. He read the literature on the subject—both fiction and nonfiction—and he studied obscure books about sex like Clifford Howard's *Sex Worship* (1902), which kindled his imagination and prompted him to think about the "phallus" and about his own penis. No wonder he was writing novels and poems about phallic symbols, from fountain pens to saxophones. In his journal, he recorded Clifford Howard's intriguing idea that the phallus was "the embodiment of creative power," and he gradually developed his own mythology about the phallus as the font of creativity. Sex and sexuality became the subtext of his fiction and his poetry; almost all his symbols were sexual symbols, he explained to Kerouac. At eighteen, Ginsberg fell in love with Kerouac and wrote love poems and love stories about him, including the unpublished "The Bloodsong." Here Kerouac appears as Bill Ducasse, a young writer eager to write a novel about his love for American places—from Lowell, his hometown, to far-off Hollywood. Ginsberg appears as Leon Bleistein, a deracinated Jewish intellectual from provincial New Jersey who turns his back, much to Bill Ducasse's disapproval, on his hometown. While Ducasse wants to write about America, Bleistein wants to write a philosophical novel about Europe and the whole of the western world. In "The Bloodsong" he quarrels with himself, even as he quarrels with Kerouac, about what direction to take as a poet.

In the mid-1940s, Allen Ginsberg wrote dozens of love poems, most of them unpublished, though a few surfaced in the college literary magazine. He seriously considered taking a pseudonym and writing poems about his own hidden homosexuality—much as William Burroughs would take a pseudonym to write about his heroin addiction. But hiding behind a pen name wasn't Allen's style. Years later, he would explain that in the mid-1940s he felt like a hypocrite because he kept his homosexuality under wraps. His compulsion to reveal himself slowly gathered momentum. At Columbia, he concealed almost all of his poems—and his identity as a poet—from his father, but Louis, the ever-vigilant inspector of his son's private life, soon found out about Allen's underground existence. When his son's college friends inadvertently gave him away—Louis was visiting campus—and revealed that he was a poet, Louis took him aside and delivered a sermon. "I don't want you to write poetry only because Eugene and I write," he said. "If you write poetry I want you to do so only because you have an inner compulsion." Allen replied, "I do feel I must write." He was compelled to write poetry, he insisted, and if writing poetry meant being abnormal, so be it. As it turned out, being a "geek," as he called it, exerted a powerful appeal. The great nineteenth-century poets were social misfits—so his own professors told him. Now they were read and studied in college English classes. Samuel Taylor Coleridge, Edgar Allen Poe, Charles Baudelaire, and Arthur Rimbaud had experimented with drugs and sex. The English romantics had been social revolutionaries in their time, and revolution had inspired them to write poetry. Percy Shelley had been expelled from college for writing about atheism, but later came to be seen as an inspiration and role model.

Becoming a poet gave Allen license to take on personae, and that too was appealing. He could perform alchemy on himself. All through the 1940s, he experimented with a whole series of identities. He adopted several pen names, including Allen Renard, the Frenchman; Edgar Allen Ginsberg, the literary descendant of Edgar Allan Poe; and Leon Bleistein, the cosmopolitan Jew (he borrowed this name from T. S. Eliot's poem, "Burbank with a Baedeker: Bleistein with a Cigar"). Kerouac gave him an assortment of names and identities too, including Irwin Garden (from the Garden State) and Carlo Marx (the romantic Marxist), though he urged Kerouac to call him by his real name. In *The Town and the City*, Kerouac's roman à clef, Ginsberg appears as Leon Levinsky. Wearing a "Paisley scarf and dark-rimmed glasses," he smokes cigarettes "with the aid of a long red cigarette holder" and carries "two slim volumes under his arm, the works of Rimbaud and Auden."

Semester after semester, Allen Ginsberg lived a volatile as well as a double life. In March 1945—shortly before his nineteenth birthday and in the waning days of World War II—it all exploded. In the dust on his dorm window, he traced two crude drawings—one of a phallus and testicles, the other of a skull and crossbones. He also traced two provocative phrases—"Fuck the Jews" and "Butler has no balls"—which were tantamount to a declaration of war on the college and a declaration of his own independence, too. In *Howl*, the incident is mythologized in the line "who were expelled from the academies for crazy & publishing obscene odes / on the windows of the skull." The Butler who had "no balls" was Nicholas Murray Butler, the eighty-three-year-old president of Columbia University and a powerful figure in American public life—a staunch Republican and a pillar of New York society. Describing him as a man without his manhood struck Allen's teachers and classmates as an act of madness. "Fuck the Jews" seemed crazy, too, especially to Lionel Trilling and his wife, Diana, who discussed Ginsberg's eccentric behavior with their colleagues and with Dean Nicholas McKnight, who couldn't understand why a Jewish boy might write such an obviously anti-Semitic remark. Trilling couldn't explain it either. Both McKnight and Trilling might have understood Ginsberg's state of mind in 1945—his bitterness and anger—if they had read two of his unpublished poems, "A Violent Ballad for the Inferior Races" and "Times Square, April 28, 1945." In "A Violent Ballad," which he wrote in February 1945, just a month before he traced the obscenities in the dust on his dorm window, he took on, oddly enough, the persona of a Nazi military officer. The Nazi narrator of the poem explains that he has spent the war years lashing Jews and hanging blacks. "There's a gibbet for the nigger and a whip for the Jew," he exclaims. In the grim ending to the poem, the Nazi narrator realizes that the fascist cause has been defeated and that "there is nothing we can do / but hang ourselves."

In the second poem, "Times Square, April 28, 1945," the narrator is a bitter young man who looks back at the war and the "ruins of mad nations." When he peers into the future, he sees nothing but "the scaffold of America," where the heroes will "be hung to their death / By the umbilical cord of the nations." When Ginsberg thought about America after World War II he was cynical and embittered. "Reaction rather than reform," he predicted. "Each howl of the jackals of reaction is important and significant—showing as it does the wild and barbarous country our road is leading us to." (This seems to have been the first time he used the word "howl.")

In the winter of 1945, after he was expelled from Columbia, he enlisted in the U.S. Maritime Service and began his career as a sailor, intrepid traveler, and peripatetic poet. Voyaging became a way of life, and a source of inspiration, too. At Sheepshead Bay in Brooklyn, he tried to take on the persona of the average American male and blend in with the crew. His paisley scarf was gone and so were his dark-rimmed glasses, along with the slim volumes of Auden and Rimbaud he had carried with him on campus. Now, he wore a T-shirt that revealed his arms and shoulders— he was also bodybuilding. Now he smoked a cigarette without the benefit of a long red cigarette holder, and now he looked like he might be able to handle himself in a fight. That's how he appears in the black-and-white photos that he took of himself in the merchant marine in 1945 with his very first camera.

To play the role of the average American male, Ginsberg not only dressed the part, he also talked the part, and that meant becoming a sexist and a racist, though of course he didn't use those terms. "They keep telling me about their women," he wrote of the sailors. "This sex talk is a real pistol. So I tell them about this cunt Joan Adams I used to live with, and how she laid me in the afternoon. My language is usually restrained; when I want to be 'regular' I use a slight southern accent and talk about Denver & St. Louis and curse the niggers." Joan Adams was none other than William Burroughs's wife, and Allen's primary mother figure, as he called her—though as a Benzedrine addict and a patient at Bellevue Hospital she was more of a crazy hipster than a nurturing mother figure.

Ginsberg explained to Kerouac that though he used words like "cunt" and "niggers," he "failed to maintain the mask of the 'regular guy.'" On one occasion, the sailors found him reading Hart Crane's poetry, and they thought he was a poet himself. On another occasion, he received a postcard, in French, from Kerouac, which was additional cause for suspicion about his identity. Hart Crane wasn't the only author whose work he was reading. He loved Thomas Mann's *The Magic Mountain*—he identified with the novel's hero, Hans Castorp—and *War and Peace* excited him, too, though he liked Dostoyevsky more than Tolstoy. The merchant marine gave him time to reflect on the contradictions in his own personality, as well as his contradictory feelings about his Columbia College education. From his bunk bed, he spent hours writing letters to Jack Kerouac and Lionel Trilling. He and Jack had much in common, Ginsberg observed, but he also wanted Kerouac to understand how far apart they were from one another. Jack was French Canadian and working class; his parents were anti-Semitic and anti-communist and never would befriend Louis and Naomi Ginsberg. Allen wanted Jack to remember that he was a Jew and an outcast. "I am alien to your natural grace," he wrote. "I am in exile from myself." He added, "You are an American more completely than I, more fully a child of nature and all that is of the grace of the earth . . . I am not a child of nature, I am ugly and imperfect."

Ginsberg's letters to Trilling were far less personal. Indeed, they read like term papers. Again and again he wrote about Arthur Rimbaud—how Rimbaud offers an "all-inclusive indictment of the state of civilization" and "crystallizes and compresses all of the works of Rousseau, Baudelaire, Joyce, Mann, Eliot, Auden." From his point of view, Rimbaud was the quintessential anti-bourgeoisie hero, the poet who went beyond the romantic poets of the nineteenth century and even beyond the modern poets of the twentieth century. What he didn't say to Trilling was that Rimbaud had written almost all of his work by the time he was nineteen. He was the quintessential adolescent literary genius and an inspiration to Ginsberg, who was then nineteen. And he was bisexual, too. Rimbaud had seduced the poet Paul Verlaine away from his wife and children.

Ginsberg didn't spell out everything for Trilling, but he didn't disguise his enthusiasm for Rimbaud, either. "*Season in Hell* seems to me the most individually expressive poetry I have run across," he wrote to Trilling. "To me it is pretty clearly the work of genius." Trilling couldn't disagree more. He had his own ideas about civilization, and he would never make room for Rimbaud on his reading lists for students. Ginsberg was permanently altered by his reading of Rimbaud. "Unscrew the locks from the doors! / Unscrew the doors themselves from their jambs!"—

those lines from Whitman serve as the epigraph to *Howl*. He might have used instead a few lines from *A Season in Hell:* "Misfortune was my God. I laid myself down in the mud. I dried myself in the air of crime. I played sly tricks on madness." Rimbaud reinforced Ginsberg's ideas about crime, madness, and youth, becoming his poster boy and role model for years to come.

# CHAPTER FOUR

# Juvenescent Savagery

## Native Sons, Exiled Sons

In the merchant marine in 1945, Ginsberg became more worldly and self-confident, and for years he wore his experience at sea and among sailors as a badge of honor. A decade later, when he published *Howl* and had to furnish Ferlinghetti with an autobiographical sketch, he proudly included his time in the merchant marine—along with his days at Columbia College and his nights in Times Square.

The time he spent at Sheepshead Bay also allowed him to do penance and to show Columbia that he was worthy of reinstatement to the college. (Finishing his education always remained his goal.) He also underwent therapy with Dr. Hans Wassing, who, odd as it may seem, had been his mother's therapist and who concluded that unlike Naomi, Allen was sane. Moreover, Dr. Wassing attested to Allen's sanity in a letter he wrote to Columbia. (Allen boasted to Trilling that he wrote the letter himself, and that Wassing merely signed it.) In any case, the letter persuaded the authorities to allow him to return to the college. By the winter of 1946, he was back on the Upper West Side taking classes again. Now he was in fact calmer and more poised, and his writing took on a new warmth and humanity. Surely, his warmest writing of that time was "Boba's Birthday," an autobiographical account of a birthday party for his grandmother on his father's side of the family that was published in the *Columbia Review*. "Boba's Birthday" suggests that he was drifting away from Trilling's and toward Kerouac's idea of civilization. He was certainly moving closer to his own people and to his own heritage. He was becoming a Jewish-American author. "Boba's Birthday" takes place in New Jersey, and all the characters are members of his family. Ginsberg doesn't once use the word "Jew" or "Jewish," and he doesn't broadcast his Jewish roots, either. Still, "Boba's Birthday" is thoroughly Jewish, from the description of the gefilte fish to the miniature portraits of his Jewish relatives. There's Solomon Katz, Uncle Max, and Boba herself, whose steps are as "faltering as her tongue in a language she had never mastered, broken as the sentences of English she tried to write in Adult School." Ginsberg's "Boba" is a sweet and loving portrait of a woman, and the first tentative exploration of the world of his ancestors that he would describe at length in *Kaddish* a decade later.

Still, if he began to feel less exiled from himself as a Jew and from his own Jewish family, he still identified with exiled authors, not native sons, and especially with T. S. Eliot and W. H. Auden, the leading 1940s emissaries of Anglo-American culture. In a review of Auden's poem *For the Time Being* for the *Columbia Review* entitled ". . . This Is the Abomination," Ginsberg noted that it was "one of the few great works of poetry of our time, rivaled only by Eliot's last book of poetry and his plays." Ginsberg's "review" wasn't really a review at all. It was an essay about his own outlook on the contemporary world and the first clear sign that he was developing his own worldview—his own Weltanschauung; he'd learned that much German reading Spengler. The essay ". . . This Is the Abomination" has been ignored by Ginsberg scholars, though it is a key work that reflects the growth of the poet's mind and that situates the birth of the Beat Generation in the social, political, and cultural context of its time—in the atomic age. Perhaps Ginsberg did not want it to be discussed since it glorifies the savage and the primitive.

"It is the kind of book that reviews the reviewer," Ginsberg noted of Auden's *For the Time Being*. He insisted that modernity could not be understood by recourse to historical facts, economic theories, or the "bestial rages of moralists, pedants and returning veterans." A comprehensive explanation of the modern condition might be provided, he suggested, through the "application of psychoanalytic-anthropology." Burroughs had said much the same thing; hearing it from Auden made it all the more appealing.

"What Auden attempts to do is to strip men to their private Calibans," Ginsberg wrote. Once men were stripped down to their dark Caliban selves, they were revealed to be "physically helpless, ethically confused, intuitionally perverted, frightened, weak, inconsistent." What's more, modern men were "a serious menace to society." As for society itself, Ginsberg argued, it was "one of complete anarchy, violent chaos, sado-masochistic barroom confusion and clinical hysteria." It seemed clear that "the body politic suffers from creeping death." America's social problems were obvious in suburbia, where one could see "the fetishistic accumulation of mechanical knick-knacks," and in big cities, too, where "megalopolitan mayors are continually trying to crusade against natural instincts." The birth of the nuclear age had magnified every problem, every neurosis and human fear. "The awful consummation of this holocaust of hysterical irresponsibility is the Atom Bomb," he asserted. It was his first literary effort to make sense of the nuclear age, and he despaired about the "hysterical irresponsibility" concerning the Bomb. Still, he saw a solution to the problem, and it wasn't going to come from proletarians or from the Communist Party, as his mother believed. What modern man needed was "Orphic creativeness, juvenescent savagery, primitive abandon." Moreover, Ginsberg argued, there were signs of hope in the midst of doom and signs of creativity in the midst of the destruction. "All our healthiest citizens are at this moment turning into hipsters, hopheads, and poets," he proclaimed. Was he thinking of Jack Kerouac and William Burroughs? Probably. And he probably thought that he too was a healthy citizen; he was writing poetry, taking drugs—heroin and marijuana—and he'd become a hipster, at least part of the time.

On campus again in 1946 he served as an assistant editor on the *Columbia Review* and wrote poems with great passion— "Spring Song" and "Spleen," for example, publishing them with a sense of pride. By the end of the year, he would receive the literary recognition and the acclaim he sorely needed, and by 1947, he would win two of the most coveted awards on campus for poetry—the Philolexian Prize and the George Edmund Woodbury Prize. He was famous from Hamilton Hall to the West End Bar on Broadway. After his time in the merchant marine, he returned to the classroom with renewed enthusiasm. English 63, English literature in the seventeenth century, exerted a powerful influence on his own thinking and his own work. Ever since 1943, he'd been reading widely in T. S. Eliot's poetry, especially *The Waste Land* and *The Four Quartets*. Now Eliot's essay "The Metaphysical Poets" provided him with a rich body of intriguing ideas that he tested and incorporated into his own work. The seventeenth-century poets had vitality of language, Eliot said; their best work was achieved by a "telescoping of images" and by "amalgamating disparate experience." Now, the challenge of poetry for Ginsberg was to telescope images and form new artistic wholes from the fragments of modern life.

Further, Eliot's essay on the seventeenth-century poets gave him the license he needed to write a poetry of complexity. "It appears likely that poets in our civilization, as it exists at present, must be *difficult*," Eliot proclaimed. "The poet must become more and more comprehensive, more allusive, more indirect, in order to force, to dislocate if necessary, language into new meaning." Between 1946 and 1949, Ginsberg's poetry became richer and more complex, increasingly reflecting Eliot's influence, as many of his classmates noticed. In "A Night in the Village," one of his first poems to be published in the *Jester-Review* (under the pen name Edgar Allen Ginsberg in 1944), he described, in predictable rhyme and with predictable images, his experiences in a Greenwich Village bar. "I smiled to my comrades two: / we found a door and entered through; / We stumbled to a smokey brawl." In "Hart Crane," which was published in the *Columbia Review* in November 1946, he entwined diverse sources—ancient Greek myth, Crane's life and poetry, and his own personal experience in the merchant marine—to create a complex poem about poets and their mothers, art and autobiography. And there were more comprehensive and allusive poems to come.

In 1946 Ginsberg wrote—for the *Passaic Valley Examiner*—

the first of several essays that he would write over the next few decades on William Carlos Williams, who was then sixty-three years old, still writing poetry, and still practicing medicine. In many ways, Williams represented everything that Ginsberg was rejecting at Columbia in the 1940s, and not surprisingly the review in the *Passaic Valley Examiner* was sharply critical of Williams and even patronizing—and Ginsberg later apologized to Williams. Unlike Eliot and Auden, Williams was a poet of the American provinces, not a cosmopolitan poet. "The poet who lives locally," he wrote, "is the agent and maker of all culture." Unlike Eliot and Auden, he wrote poems in the American idiom, and his work was far less difficult and obscure than *The Waste Land* and *The Double Man*. As late as 1946, with the Cold War quickly escalating and Soviet-American relations deteriorating, Williams was still writing poems that were sympathetic to the Russians. In the poem "Russia," for example, he invited his Russian brothers to become his comrades and, in the spirit of Walt Whitman, to loaf together and defy the threat of nuclear annihilation.

Nineteen forty-six was also the year Ginsberg met Neal Cassady, consummate lover and adventurer. Cassady appeared to be as comfortable in his body as Allen was alien in his, and Allen was drawn to his wildness and fell in love with him. Cassady was born in Denver in 1926, the same year as Allen, but he grew up poor, the son of an alcoholic father who took him hitchhiking at an early age and a derelict mother who lived among ex-convicts, prostitutes, and jazz musicians. In *The First Third*, his frenetic autobiography, Cassady boasted that he was sexually active even as a boy; by the time he was a teenager, he was a Henry Miller in the making and he was "doing it on golf courses, roofs, parks, cemeteries . . . snow banks, schools and schoolyards, hotel bathrooms." Cassady also loved to cover great distances at great speeds, all across America in fast cars—for the sake of speed itself, as Burroughs observed. Cassady was "The Mover, compulsive, dedicated, ready to sacrifice family, friends, even his very car itself to the necessity of moving from one place to another," Burroughs explained to Ginsberg. "Wife and child may starve, friends exist only to exploit for gas money . . . Neal must move." Allen was not blind to the dark side—the Caliban side—of his friend and lover from Denver. He knew Neal intimately: in bed, at the steering wheel of his car, and with his wives and girlfriends. He concluded that Neal buried his neuroses in promiscuity. His own neuroses, he explained, were buried in poetry. They were both escaping from painful experience. Cassady and Ginsberg brought out the Calibans in one another, and in that sense they were well matched, as Kerouac noted in *On the Road*, where Neal Cassady is Dean Moriarty and Allen Ginsberg is Carlo Marx. "A tremendous thing happened when Dean met Carlo Marx," Kerouac wrote in his opening chapter. "Two keen minds that they are, they took to each other at the drop of a hat. Two piercing eyes glanced into two piercing eyes—the holy con-man with the shining mind, and the sorrowful poetic con-man with the dark mind that is Carlo Marx."

What Kerouac declined to describe in *On the Road*—despite his insistence on candor—was the homosexual relationship between Ginsberg and Cassady, and the sexual games they played, in which Ginsberg was the sex slave and Cassady the sex master. Cassady described his own obsessive heterosexuality—though not his homosexuality—in *The First Third*. "I ripped into her like a maniac and she loved it," he wrote of one sexual encounter. What he wanted, most of all, he proclaimed, was "to have a cunt to love & suck, one that is so perfect you can't resist raising your tired body above it to spend all the pure feeling you've left into the hole." In an age when sexual relations between men and women, and even between husband and wife, were rigorously and strictly prescribed by state law, Cassady appeared to be a sexual outlaw, and Ginsberg thought that the Cassadys of the world might invigorate decadent, sexless American society. In Ginsberg's mythology, Neal was the embodiment of the kind of "Orphic creativeness, juvenescent savagery, primitive abandon" that he described in his review of Auden's *For the Time Being*.

Neal was also just plain brutal. He inflicted cruel and unusual punishment—both physical and mental—on Ginsberg, though Allen was no simple victim. Servitude in bed would serve him well as a creative artist—or so he believed. Indeed, he turned the agony of their relationship into the ecstasy of art. If he was sexually abused, he would be inspired to write poetry, or so he felt. When Cassady abandoned him, Ginsberg wallowed in self-pity. "You know you are the only one who gave me love that I wanted and never had," he explained in a letter that he described as pure vomit. "I am lonely, Neal, alone, and always am frightened. I need someone to love me and kiss me and sleep with me." In desperation, he wrote, "What must I do for you to get you back? I will do anything."

For the most part, Ginsberg was candid in his letters to Neal, as well as in his letters to his friends and his father—who tolerated Kerouac and Burroughs but regarded Cassady as a menace to his son and to society. "Exorcise Neal," Louis urged his son. Allen could no more expunge Neal from his life than he could expunge him from his poetry, and Neal appeared, albeit in disguise, repeatedly in poems like "Oedipus Eddie"—the first section of

"The Denver Doldrums," which is subtitled "Suicide Waltzes for the Denver Birds." The "Denver Birds" were his own suicidal friends, including Kerouac and Cassady. In the poems from the mid- to late 1940s, Ginsberg was mostly in hiding. His own naked self—most of all, his homosexuality—seemed so shocking and so antithetical to social norms that he kept it hidden. It was abhorrent to his own father and terrifying to the conventional part of himself. His only recourse was to smuggle it into his poems, so he disguised his naked self, camouflaged it, and buried it.

### Secret Poet, Secret Language

In the half decade from 1945 to 1950, Ginsberg cultivated the art and the craft of the symbolist poet. His work was carefully encoded, and his principal symbols were largely private and mostly indecipherable—unless the poet himself cracked the code for the reader. "Art is a secret language," he explained to Lionel Trilling in 1948. "The poems I write are my own reflections of my own state and the state of the cosmos, and are written in a secret language." He added that all art—and his poetry in particular—was a secret only to those who weren't members of the cognoscenti. "To the wise it is direct and inevitable fact speech," he explained. "The secret is within, not outside, and to be learned," he told Trilling. "So it is not a secret language really." Kerouac understood Ginsberg's poems; he was part of the cabal. He had the key to the code, and in *On the Road*, he revealed Allen's literary secrets to the world. The nightingale who appears in "The Denver Doldrums" is really Allen's own mother, Kerouac explained to his readers. Ginsberg couldn't reasonably expect that even astute editors of poetry magazines would understand his secret language. In the mid-1940s, few readers grasped what he was trying to say in his poetry. Louis Ginsberg read "The Denver Doldrums" and felt baffled: his son was writing poetry as opaque as that of T. S. Eliot. Robert Giroux, then an editor at Harcourt Brace, read and rejected "The Denver Doldrums"—as well as the whole series of related poems that Ginsberg entitled *A Book of Doldrums*—because they were too obscure. Even Allen was mystified by his own poems. He confessed that when he looked back at them only months after he had written them, he found them indecipherable. His own symbols were so oblique that he forgot the meanings he had assigned.

In 1947, he visited William and Joan Burroughs in Texas, and, after the birth of their son, he wrote a poem in their honor that he sometimes called "Birthday Ode" and sometimes "Surrealist Ode." The main symbols here, as in "The Denver Doldrums," are birds: "cruel pigeons," "little vultures," and an "immortal Nightingale" who is "my mind's first vision, / Image of love pleading for love alone"—a stand-in for Naomi. In the preface to the poem, Ginsberg describes Burroughs as a "skeptical genius of failure," and his wife as "self-annihilating." He explains that the saxophone that appears in the poem is a symbol of "mature passion and vigor, and . . . evil and knowledge." What's most illuminating about the preface is Ginsberg's confession that he hopes that the new-born child—Bill and Joan's son—will not grow up to become a homosexual. "Part VII," he explains, "is a lamentation against the possibility of homosexuality."

The failure of his relationship with Neal Cassady plunged him into a state of despair. To his father, he disclosed that he felt "irritation & ennui & floating anxiety & constant self-lacerating introspection." To Kerouac, he wrote, "I am insane" and "I think my mind is crumbling just like crackers." He added, "I can see you reading this and telling me coldly to stop posing." In part, his insanity was a pose, though he also knew that he was deeply troubled and needed psychiatric help. In a letter to Wilhelm Reich, the German-born psychiatrist who was living in the United States, he begged for help. His mother, he explained to Reich, had "suffered a series of nervous breakdowns" and had been locked up for several years. He was an English major at Columbia and poetry was "his major intellectual interest." He "used narcotics pretty extensively," and he was "on the periphery of criminal circles in New York," he explained. And, he told Reich, he suffered from "the normal Oedipal entanglement." He had been homosexual for as long as he could remember, and in his relationships with women he was impotent. Moreover, much of the time he was depressed, saddled with a sense of guilt and a feeling of sordidness about himself. He had undergone psychoanalysis with a friend—Ginsberg didn't mention Burroughs by name— and that experience had left him "washed up on the shore of my neuroses with a number of my defenses broken" and with "nothing to replace the lost armor."

To pay for psychoanalysis, and to escape from his own sorrowful state, he sailed on a steamer to Dakar in West Africa, hoping to find a native boy who would satisfy his sexual fantasies. It seems inevitable that Ginsberg would have followed the arc of Rimbaud's experience and travel to Africa. Once again, his college education was delayed, and yet his voyage to Africa also seemed a vital part of that education. For years he had been writing about voyages in his college essays; there was a long essay in which he analyzed Rimbaud's *The Drunken Boat*, Shelley's *Alastor*, and Baudelaire's *The Voyage*, and another long essay on Coleridge's

"The Rime of the Ancient Mariner." He'd also been writing poems about voyages and voyagers. There was "The Last Voyage," in which he suggested that voyaging was perilous and potentially self-destructive since it took the traveler to the end of the night and the end of the world. And there was *The Character of the Happy Warrior*, which was also entitled *Death in Violence*—an anti-epic dedicated to William Burroughs. (The phrase "Happy Warrior" was taken from William Wordsworth's poem of the same name. It shows how deeply immersed he was in nineteenth-century romanticism, despite his attempts to escape from it.) In the six-page preface to *The Character of the Happy Warrior*, Ginsberg boasted that he used "various anti-romantic devices developed for poetry by T. S. Eliot and W. H. Auden." Eliot argued that "poetry is not a turning loose of emotion, but an escape from emotion," and Ginsberg was laboring to escape from his emotions and his romanticism. The voyage was a symbol, he explained, and the voyager was symbolic of "the psychoanalyzed man." It was not the outer physical journey that concerned him most, but rather the inner, personal journey. The goal of the voyage was a "vision."

The one major poem that emerged from the voyage to Dakar was "Dakar Doldrums"—a secret love poem to Neal Cassady that reinvents the conventions of seventeenth-century metaphysical poetry, in which the male poet typically wrote about his love for a woman. "Love's gender was kept [in the] closet," Ginsberg wrote of his poems to Cassady. "Dakar Doldrums" shared first prize—along with John Hollander's poem "Desert Sequence"—in the Boar's Head competition at Columbia in 1948. In many ways it's the most polished of his poems from the 1940s as well as the culmination of his early poetry. Along with "A Further Proposal," "A Lover's Garden," and "Love Letter"—which were imitations of John Donne, Christopher Marlowe, and Andrew Marvell—"Dakar Doldrums" is included in the appendix to Ginsberg's *Collected Poems: 1947–1980*. Neal Cassady is never specifically named in the poem, but he is the "sweet soul" for whom the poet longs. He is the "near and dear and far apart in fate." The unnamed first-person narrator of the poem is Ginsberg himself. "I am a brutish agonist," he exclaims. "How mad my youth."

Ginsberg didn't begin to candidly describe his sexual relationship with Cassady until 1956, the year *Howl* was published. In "Many Loves" (1956), which begins with a line from Whitman—"Resolved to sing no songs henceforth but those of manly attachment"—he uses Neal Cassady's full name for the first time, and not merely his initials, "N.C.," as he does in *Howl*. In "Many Loves" he celebrates their tender lovemaking: "So gentle the man, so sweet the moment." Near the end of the poem, Ginsberg hints at the dark side of their sexuality—"I made my first mistake, and made him then and there my master." It wasn't until after Cassady's death in 1968 that Ginsberg described their sadomasochist relationship in the poem "Please Master." "Please master drive me thy vehicle," Ginsberg wrote. "Please master call me a dog, an ass beast, a wet asshole, / & fuck me more violent, my eyes hid with your palms round my skull." That perverse relationship with Cassady drove him all the way to Dakar; on the way home, he thought of suicide, but poetry held him back, saved him, as it saved him from suicide again and again.

After his misadventures in Africa, he returned to Paterson, New Jersey, and then to Columbia to finish his college education. He was bored during his last semester, but there was an experience at his apartment in East Harlem that seems to have changed his life and that he went on describing for the next forty years. One afternoon, while reading William Blake's poem "Ah! Sun-Flower" and smoking marijuana and masturbating, he experienced what he described, in his 1965 *Paris Review* interview, as an "auditory hallucination." Ever since high school, he had been reading and imitating Blake. Now he claimed that for the first time he actually heard Blake reading "Ah! Sun-Flower" aloud. A vision: this was a personal and poetic turning point.

What really happened that afternoon in Harlem in the summer of 1948 isn't clear. As the critic Paul Berman pointed out, "One of the peculiarities of this famous Beat epiphany is that Ginsberg, the least shy of all poets, has been reticent to write or at least to publish much about it, though he has been willing to discuss it with interviewers." Near the end of his life, Ginsberg even implied, in an interview with Jack Foley on radio station KPFA, that he'd made up the story. "I cooked it up, somehow," he said. There's no contemporaneous description in Ginsberg's journals—no recorded first thought—and over the years he related so many different stories, many of them contradictory, that it's impossible to separate fact from fantasy. Blake and Harlem in the summer of 1948 became one of the key legends in Ginsberg's legendary life, not only because of his own efforts, but because his friends aided and abetted him. In *Go*, John Clellon Holmes devotes a full chapter to the event. David Stofsky hears Blake's voice and wants to "leap blindly, thoughtlessly, into the vortex of that sound." Moreover, he wants to "howl as the animality within him erupted." Stofsky believes that he has had a rare vision; he decides that at last he knows what his "mad, forlorn mother . . . had tried to tell him." Now, he wants to tell everyone that he, too, has had a vision, that "God is *love!*" and that "the world *can* be redeemed."

The Harlem epiphany was a spur to his creativity; he wrote a series of poems about his vision and about Blake. The earliest poems include "Vision 1948," in which he describes "a vast machinery / descending" to earth, and "On Reading William Blake's 'The Sick Rose,'" which offers images of fire, fright, and "Doom" and sets the stage for the apocalyptic imagination that reached maturity in *Howl*. In 1958, a decade after his Blake vision, Ginsberg tried to recapture the experience in "The Lion for Real." Diana Trilling concluded that it was really about her husband. The lion was a symbol for Lionel Trilling, she insisted. Allen read Diana's account and replied that the lion was God, not Lionel Trilling. It was an unfortunate misunderstanding. Even astute literary critics like Diana Trilling could look silly hunting for symbols in poetry, he observed with a certain delight. By 1958, Ginsberg had all but given up on Lionel and Diana Trilling. He had tried to join them in the 1940s, tried to see the world as they did. Now he knew for sure that the Trillings didn't speak his language, share his symbols, or hear his distinct voice. In 1956 he sent a copy of *Howl and Other Poems* to Lionel. Perhaps he hoped that his former professor would finally recognize his genius and invite him to Columbia to teach or at least to talk to undergraduates, but that was not to be. Ginsberg and Trilling— the student and the teacher—were now worlds apart. They belonged to two different cultures. To Trilling, Ginsberg sounded "dull." He had no sense of music. He had no feeling for poetry, either. He didn't seem to have learned anything at all at Columbia about poetry or prose, or the literary tradition. He was practically uncivilized. "I don't like the poems at all," Trilling wrote of *Howl and Other Poems.* "There is no real voice here. As for the doctrinal element of the poems, apart from the fact that I of course reject it, it seems to me that I heard it very long ago and that you give it to me in all its orthodoxy, with nothing new added."

Trilling's rebuke notwithstanding, Columbia was kinder to Ginsberg than Ginsberg was to Columbia. After the publication of *Howl,* Ginsberg gave his papers to Columbia. Then, in the 1980s, he changed his mind and sold his archive to Stanford for 1 million dollars. Columbia didn't seem to hold that against him. When he died, *Columbia College Today,* the alumni magazine, published a cover story about him by the poet and critic David Lehman. "He was an autodidact to the end," Lehman wrote. "His life was his greatest poem and he was its hero." Eventually Trilling changed his mind about Ginsberg's work and included two of his poems, "A Supermarket in California" and "To Aunt Rose," in his comprehensive anthology *The Experience of Literature,* which was published in 1967 and used widely as a textbook. Ever since Ginsberg wrote *Howl* in the mid-1950s, he had wanted to be included in the canon, and now he was. Of course, he was delighted that it was none other than Trilling who made a place for him. The inclusion and validation was exhilarating to Ginsberg. He had stayed true to himself and his own practice of poetry, and the academic world had seen fit to bend and sway and become more open. The adversarial culture had made its way into mainstream culture.

# CHAPTER FIVE

# Just like
# Russia

## The Lower Depths

Madness was much on Ginsberg's mind in 1948—the year of his graduation from college, his hallucinations in Harlem, and his obsession with Paul Cézanne. At the Museum of Modern Art in Manhattan, he looked, with the aid of marijuana, at Cézanne's paintings—the *The Card Players* and the *Rocks at Garonne*—and saw "sinister symbols." He looked at Cézanne's life and saw a "big secret mystic" who "didn't know if he was crazy or not." Everywhere he looked he seemed to see himself, and everywhere he looked he saw madness. So did his Beat brothers. Madness was the Beat badge of honor in a world gone insane with bombs and dictators, terror and tyranny. In the midst of the madness of 1948, Ginsberg was still recommending writers antithetical to liberalism and liberals, and now his favorite writer was Louis-Ferdinand Céline—the French novelist, veteran of World War I, doctor, anti-Semite, and anti-communist. Céline was a "mad author" who had taken on a "weird mask," Ginsberg wrote in a review of *Death on the Installment Plan*, the 1936 novel that had been reissued by New Directions and that he reviewed for *Halcyon* in the spring of 1948. Céline's novel was a "megalopolitan odyssey of deracinated lower class life," Ginsberg wrote. What's more it was "really insane." There were no terms more superlative than "insanity" and "madness" in his critical vocabulary, though he also admired Céline for his ability to wallow in "filthy horrors" and to describe dispassionately—and without a program for reforming anything or anyone—"the dangerousness of modern life."

Ginsberg's own life was becoming increasingly precarious, increasingly dangerous. He lived in a third-floor, cold-water, thirteen-dollar-a month apartment at 1401 York Avenue in Manhattan that he had inherited from his friend Walter Adams. A Columbia College poet now fled to Paris, Adams would become yet another friend who attempted suicide. Ginsberg reconnected with Herbert Huncke, whom he had met during World War II and who struck him as the quintessential New York hipster. A petty thief, drug addict, hustler, convict, jazz aficionado, and sometime author, Huncke seemed to have stepped out of the sordid subterranean world of Céline's *Death on the Installment Plan* or Gorky's *Lower Depths*, which Ginsberg was also reading. Once again, he collapsed the boundaries between life and literature, between real-life human beings and fictional characters. Huncke seemed as real as any of Céline's or Gorky's troubled souls from the underground of urban life.

Born in 1915 to middle-class, Jewish parents, Huncke dropped out of high school and went on the road as a young man. He arrived in New York in 1939, haunting Times Square and serving as a splendid subject for Dr. Alfred Kinsey, who was studying the sexual habits of the American male. Huncke provided information about deviant sex and sexuality, not only to Kinsey but also to Ginsberg. Throughout the 1940s, he wandered in and out of Allen's world, enlarging and disrupting it. In Allen's romantic imagination, Huncke was a diabolical angel who offered further evidence that the criminal was a far more interesting type than a banker or a grocer. Released in 1948 from Riker's Island, where he'd served time for possession of marijuana, he descended on Ginsberg's York Avenue apartment and began to strip his host of everything he owned—suits, jackets, ties, and books, which he sold or pawned to buy drugs. Ginsberg didn't appreciate the theft, but what could he do? Huncke was a junky, and to be a junky in America, Allen believed, was to be persecuted by the authorities. There was no way he could have Huncke arrested. Huncke was an artist and he was writing brilliant autobiographical stories—"Suicide," "Dancing in Prison," and "Song of Self," and his insights amazed Ginsberg. The sound of his own name filled him with "a sense of disgust," Huncke wrote in one sketch, adding that he was "at last slipping into an insanity from which there is no escape." Ginsberg knew what he meant. He read Huncke's work and described it as "wondrous personal prose." He aspired to write like Huncke—in his journal he even copied phrases he found in Huncke's notebook—and came to love him "like an older brother, a mother, a whole family."

Like Huncke, Ginsberg felt he was slipping into an inescapable kind of insanity—an insanity he longed for. "I really will go mad and that's what I half hope for," he wrote Kerouac. The winter of 1948 was a nightmare; he felt cold and lacking in creativity. He felt, too, that he was "losing control" of himself and his own life. To Kerouac, he confessed that he wanted to die but lacked the willpower to take his life. He was "haunting queer bars" in Greenwich Village, becoming "more actively queer," and feeling more ambivalent about his queerness. One night he found himself "in the most bestial of postures" with a man from South America. He felt sordid—a kind of American untouchable. Despite his suicidal despair, he had moments of clarity about himself and his work. His poetry was far too symbolic, he concluded. His passion was often "artificial," and he usually spoke "thru other men's voices" and not through his own. Sad to say, he was merely a ventriloquist and only a dreamer. "I have let abstract ideas . . . carry me away . . . till they are out of control and have no real meaning," he explained. Now he knew what he wanted. His goal as a poet was to make his writing an authentic reflection of himself—to "find a style, a form and a language wholly suited to what I really think." *Howl* was still years away, but he was on the road to it.

### A Hostile Time

Ginsberg's predicament as a young poet was unique, but he certainly wasn't the only young poet to feel at odds with the world. The poet Robert Creeley—who was born in 1926 and who met Allen in San Francisco just as he was beginning to write *Howl*— noted that the "forties were a hostile time" for young American poets. In many ways it was a wonderful time for young novelists— Norman Mailer, Irwin Shaw, and Gore Vidal, for example. But poets were less fortunate. It was an especially unfriendly time for poets—like Creeley and Ginsberg—who rallied to Ezra Pound's cry to "make it new" and who found themselves inhibited by the academic emphasis on ambiguity, irony, symbolism, and formalism. Even T. S. Eliot, who had been an avant-garde poet in the 1920s, was against the avant-garde now. "We cannot, in literature, any more than in the rest of life, live in a perpetual state of revolution," Eliot observed in New York in 1947. "If every generation of poets made it their task to bring poetic diction up to date with the spoken language, poetry would fail in one of its most important obligations." Eliot's insistence on the preservation of poetic diction put Ginsberg in an impossible bind. On the one hand, he wanted to extend Eliot's tradition, and in the 1940s, he was imitating Eliot in his own poetry. On the other hand, he was eager to break from Eliot's tradition and write in the hipster argot used by Neal Cassady and Herbert Huncke—to bring words like "dig" and "Daddio" into his poetry. He wanted to write the way Dizzy Gillespie played the trumpet—"so shrill and high"—the way Charles Parker played the saxophone, with "passion and vigor," and the way he'd heard Lester Young "blow" at the Apollo in Harlem in 1948. The only real encouragement to write like Parker and Young came from Kerouac, but Kerouac's career wasn't going anywhere fast. Sometimes it seemed to him that he and Jack were crazy to want to write like jazz musicians.

For the most part, Ginsberg adhered to Eliot's injunction to preserve the English language. It hurt him, but he resisted the impulse to bring poetic diction up to date. Moreover, the voices of dead poets—like Blake and Eliot—still dominated his own voice. Tradition counted more than his own individual talent, and in 1949 he noted, "The clearest expression of what I have in mind is in Blake & Eliot." His goal was admirable, though difficult, and no one else encouraged him. Again and again, his own instincts put him at odds with established ideas about poets and poetry. Again and again, he found himself at odds with his

hero W. H. Auden. "No more movements. No more mani-
festoes. Every poet stands alone . . . and joins nobody, least of all
his contemporary brother poets," Auden proclaimed in the late
1940s, though as a student at Oxford two decades earlier he'd
been a movement poet—a Marxist and an antifascist.

Ginsberg wanted to join his contemporary brother poets and
create a secret society of poets. He wanted to issue manifestoes,
too, and start a cultural movement that would rival the avant-
garde movements of the 1920s. In fact, Ginsberg and his friends
had a name for it—the "New Vision." It was predicated on "the
death of square morality," the "belief in creativity," and "the rise
of a second religiousness." The established American poets and
critics of the 1940s didn't encourage religiosity, nor did they en-
courage hallucinations and derangement à la Rimbaud. In the
late 1940s, the poet and critic Karl Shapiro argued against "vi-
sion or madness" and insisted that what was essential was the
"knowledge of form." Ginsberg wanted form, too, but he wanted
vision and madness as well—the form of madness, the form of
the visionary. It had been done in the nineteenth century. Why
couldn't it be done again?

In many ways, Ginsberg wanted poetry to reach a wide audi-
ence. But as the poet and critic Selden Rodman observed in
1949, the contemporary poet spoke mostly to other poets, not to
the people, as Shakespeare, Dante, and Goethe had done. In the
nineteenth century, Rodman complained, Blake and Coleridge
had chosen to "limit their audience, if not to poets, then at most
connoisseurs of poetry." Twentieth-century poets, like Auden,
had continued to widen the gap between poets and the public, he
wrote. Auden's poetry "seemed to be written in code—a code
that could be properly understood only by fellow-subversives,"

Rodman noted. Ginsberg liked the idea of writing in code and in secret for his fellow subterraneans, but he also liked the idea of writing open secrets that everyone could understand. He wanted to make poetry popular again and turn poets into heroes for the whole human race.

The poet and critic Muriel Rukeyser pointed out in 1949 in *The Life of Poetry* that poetry was suspect after World War II, and Ginsberg knew that she was right—that poetry was hated in America. "The resistance to poetry is an active force in American life," Rukeyser wrote. "Poetry is foreign to us, we do not let it enter our daily lives." Further, she noted that in America, poets weren't regarded as "real men." "Poetry as an art is sexually suspect," she noted. "Almost any man will say that it is effeminate." In the eyes of his society—even at Columbia—Allen Ginsberg was "sexually suspect." He was also a failure—in his own eyes. He looked back at his life and remembered that in his boyhood he had "wanted to be a great influential poet." Now he was no closer to that dream than he had been at fifteen. In the late 1940s, he felt that he was even more of a nobody; now he had nothing: no book, no career as a poet—not even his youth and innocence. "I haven't even got a platform, no sense of dignity—or hope of anything," he complained in his journal. "A reader would be impatient with me now. He wants rightly to be entertained."

Herbert Huncke entertained him, but it was a depressing kind of entertainment, and little by little Ginsberg became a spectator in his own downfall. For months, Huncke and his confederates in crime—Jack Melodia and Priscilla Arminger—used Allen's York Avenue apartment to store their stolen goods (jewelry and furs), and once again Allen saw the makings for a novel about crime and criminals. But, he was using Benzedrine, heroin, and marijuana—which Burroughs shipped from Texas—and his own judgment was impaired. Moreover, his habit of "mythologizing" Huncke for literary purposes took him further and further away from the dangerous reality that was unfolding before him. Afraid that the police would raid his apartment and find his journals and his love letters to other men, he asked Kerouac to hide them. Jack refused. When his brother, Eugene, offered a safe haven at his house on Long Island, Allen set off with his papers in a stolen sedan packed with stolen goods. Melodia, who was on parole and without a driver's license, drove the car. The plan was doomed to failure from the start.

The events that unfolded that day became another key part of Beat mythology and were told repeatedly for decades. Aaron Latham has even argued that Ginsberg's joy ride—and the arrest that followed—was the decisive event in his life, the moment when he was initiated into the company of the Beats. And yet neither the joy ride nor the arrest led to any significant poetry. They were but the prelude to Ginsberg's time in the New York State Psychiatric Institute, which did transform him and which provided material for all kinds of poems, including *Howl*. Still, there was real drama in the journey from Manhattan to Long Island. Melodia drove the wrong way on a one-way street in Queens, and when a policeman tried to stop him, he fled from the scene. At sixty-five miles an hour, the car spun out of control, turned over, and landed upside down. Ginsberg was not seriously injured, but his glasses were broken, his papers scattered, and he was left "crazed and confused."

By subway he returned in a panic to his apartment, and soon thereafter the police arrived and found the stolen property. Now, Ginsberg took on the persona of Raskolnikov in Dostoyevsky's

*Crime and Punishment:* he confessed his crimes and practically begged for punishment. Asked if he used marijuana, he said yes. Asked if he was queer, he would not speak, but nodded his head up and down to indicate that he *was* a homosexual. His father lived in Paterson, New Jersey, he said. His mother was a mental patient at Pilgrim State Hospital. As for himself, he had a B.A. from Columbia and had "tied-in" with the gang to obtain the realistic details he needed for a story he was writing. There were huge gaps in his tale, of course, but he managed to get across the essentials: his crazy mother, his provincial New Jersey father, and his own aspirations as a writer. The chase, the car crash, and the stolen goods made the papers—the *New York Times,* the *New York Herald Tribune,* and the *New York Daily News.* All over the city, Ginsberg was news; it looked like he might go on trial and serve time in prison, but his friends, family, and professors—including Lionel Trilling, Mark Van Doren, and Jacques Barzun—came to his rescue.

For his lawyer, Ilo Orleans, who was also a poet and a friend of his father, he wrote a long autobiographical essay entitled "The Fall," in which he recounted the frenetic, chaotic experience of his whole life. He had used heroin and marijuana for years, he explained, and now he wanted to give them up. He had been in a rage against his father his whole life, and now he felt like "a shit." For years, he had idealized William Burroughs and allowed him to act as his "father confessor." Now, he saw through Burroughs, he said. He wanted to rescue Burroughs and persuade him to "stop fiddling around with drugs and romanticized quasi-underworld activity." For years he had seen himself, he confessed, as a literary character in a Kafka novel. Now he wanted to escape from the Kafkaesque world he had created and to become as normal as the people in a Norman Rockwell painting. "I am sick," he proclaimed. What he wanted most of all was "to be cured," and to be "stable, serene, secure, happy, working . . . and married." Whether he believed it or not, it was a compelling story.

Huncke, Melodia, and Arminger were indicted by a grand jury, but no criminal charges were brought against Ginsberg. Jacques Barzun wrote a strong letter of support stating that Allen was a promising intellectual and simply needed to control his unruly impulses. It was "mighty cricket" of them, Ginsberg told Kerouac. Instead of prison he would undergo therapy at the New York State Psychiatric Institute on West 168th Street in Manhattan. He had acted like a madman and now he would be treated like one. "The punishment literally fitted the crime," he wrote in his journal. But he wasn't treated like a menace to society or to himself. He was not thrown into a padded cell or placed in a straightjacket. He would even be allowed to leave the hospital on weekends, provided that a family member or friend took responsibility for his well-being and safety. It was the best of all possible worlds. Like his mother, he would experience the madhouse from the inside, and like his father he would be able to turn personal sorrow into poetry.

### The Madhouse

On June 15, 1949, just two weeks before he was admitted to the New York State Psychiatric Institute as a patient, Ginsberg wrote to Kerouac to explain that he was about to enter the "crazyhouse." In fact, he would never call the institution by its official name. Oddly enough it didn't seem to disturb him that he was about to enter a hospital for the insane; perhaps he felt a certain sense of validation and pride. To be a poet seemed to entail a certain madness. Of course there was a long tradition of mad poets that went back to the Greeks, then flowered with the nineteenth-century romantics and found expression again in the twentieth century. As Ginsberg knew, the poet Ezra Pound was a mental patient at St. Elizabeth's Hospital in Washington, D.C., in 1949. Many young poets, including Robert Lowell—who had won the Pulitzer Prize in 1946 for his book *Lord Weary's Castle*—made the pilgrimage to pay homage to Pound. (In the 1950s, of course, Robert Lowell, Sylvia Plath, and Anne Sexton would be mental patients at McLean's Hospital in Massachusetts. The madhouse seemed a required station of the cross for the American poet.)

Ginsberg's main concern in June 1949 was his poetry, not his impending treatment at the New York State Psychiatric Institute. He was still, unfortunately, writing allegory and symbolism, he complained. When he looked back at his own work in the decade that was coming to a close he observed, "I got so hung up on a series of words that I went around abstractly composing odes, one after another, until even now I can't tell them apart and what they mean." He still admired Blake's work, but increasingly he was coming to agree with Eliot that Blake wasn't a truly great poet. Blake "made up a lot of crazy symbols of his own which nobody understands," Ginsberg wrote. He was still attached to the idea that poetry spoke a secret language. His own work had "hidden invocations," he explained to Kerouac, and he wanted readers to look "under the surface" of his work. But he also wanted readers who were "themselves under the surface," who would understand intuitively what his poems meant. He went around and around in his own head, trying to create a theory of poetry that would justify the poetry he was writing.

Ginsberg spent nearly eight months at the New York State Psychiatric Institute, a time that he rarely if ever discussed publicly, though it shaped him as profoundly and as decisively as any other experience in his life. In fact, he used it to shape his own persona as a mad poet and to create the mythology of madness that infuses *Howl*. Near the beginning of his stay at the institute, he developed the idea of writing a novel in which "the hero is a madman." At the end of the 1940s, he was still hoping to become a novelist, and it was to the novel, not poetry, that he instinctively turned as a literary form. As a patient at the New York State Psychiatric Institute, he also developed the image of America as "a nation of madhouses"—and that image is at the heart of *Howl*. The anonymous hero of *Howl*—the "who" that appears throughout the first section and that has been "destroyed by madness"—is an archetypal madman: the "madman bum and angel." Then, too, in *Howl*, America is an "armed madhouse." It's a country of "madtowns," "visible madman doom," and "invincible madhouses!" Earlier in the 1940s, Ginsberg entertained the notion of America as a prison and a concentration camp, and though that metaphor expressed his anger and hostility, it didn't connect directly with his own personal experience. It didn't resonate. The madhouse metaphor obviously did; it enabled him to fuse his own persona as a madman with his mother's madness, and it infused his poetry with a powerful myth.

On July 3—just a few days after he entered the New York State Psychiatric Institute—Ginsberg wrote to Kerouac to tell him, "It is just like Russia." It probably did feel like Russia to him, or at least his idea of Russia. He certainly had less freedom than at any other time in his life. For years, he had been quarreling with Kerouac about Russia and America, communism and capitalism. Now, his own experience reinforced his idea that America was the land of the unfree, and as much of a dictatorship as Russia. Not surprisingly, Kerouac wasn't persuaded by his analogy. To compare America with Russia was a subversive idea during the Cold War. Nineteen forty-nine was the year of Alger Hiss's trial, which Ginsberg followed intently while he was a patient at the hospital and which shaped his own political education about the Cold War. Nineteen forty-nine was also the year of George Orwell's politically charged novel *Nineteen Eighty-Four*—which Ginsberg read and admired—and he was quick to see Big Brother in the hospital bureaucrats and psychiatrists, "machine men from the NKVD," he called them in a letter to Kerouac.

If the "madhouse" was Orwellian, it was also Kafkaesque, he explained. He was in a kind of penal colony in which the sadists wore white coats. "The doctors are in control and have the means to persuade even the most recalcitrant," he wrote ominously. Ginsberg ranted about the doctors; they were "seersucker liberals," "squares and ignoramuses," "social scientists and rat experimenters," and perhaps most of all, they were members of the "apoetic bourgeoisie." They didn't read, write, or enjoy poetry. What more could he say? Confinement five days a week, week after week, in the antiseptic environment of the institute was a spur to his imagination. He saw himself as Winston Smith, Orwell's hero, who writes his diary in secret, away from the watchful eyes of Big Brother and the secret police. For Allen, the agents of Big Brother were not only the doctors who read and censored his outgoing letters, but his own father, too, who from time to time read his secret journals and his private love letters. "Finish . . . my father is coming in," he wrote furiously one day when he was on leave from the hospital and at home in Paterson, and Louis happened to enter the room where he was writing. Father as Big Brother made his myth all the more appealing.

Ginsberg's idea that America was like Russia—and Russia like America—might have been taken as evidence that he was indeed insane. To Americans, whether they were Democrats or Republicans, America and Russia were polar opposites. America was free, Russia unfree, America democratic and Russia totalitarian. That was how it looked to most citizens and to their congressmen and senators in 1949. And Ginsberg was decidedly unlikely to win applause from the American Communist Party for suggesting that Russia was like America. To Communist Party members in the United States in 1949, Russia was a worker's paradise and the United States was an evil capitalist country of the rich by the rich for the rich. To Ginsberg—and to William Burroughs—the two nations had more in common than not. As a patient at the psychiatric institute, Allen made notes for a poem about the similarities, as he saw them, between the two rival powers. "The proletariat . . . the dye works, the mills, the smoke, the melancholy of the bus, the sadness of the long highway," he wrote. "The images of the Thirties, of depression and class consciousness." His America wasn't a classless society, as *Life* magazine insisted, and as American politicians and social scientists boasted. At the psychiatric institute, Ginsberg looked at America through Marxist eyes, and that, too, was unpopular in the heyday of McCarthyism, when government committees investigated government employees like Alger Hiss, as well as citizens in all walks of American life.

Three years later, in 1951, when the United States was fighting communism in Korea—a war Ginsberg did not support—he took the images and phrases he had recorded in his journal in 1949 and turned them into "A Poem on America." Not surprisingly, it begins "America is like Russia . . . / We have the proletariat too." Still later—in San Francisco in 1955—he returned to the idea that the two nations mirrored one another, but this time the mirror images were more menacing. In an early draft of Part II of *Howl* he wrote, "Moloch whose name is America / Moloch whose name is Russia . . . Moloch whose name is / Chicago and Moscow." Later, he removed those lines, making the Moloch section less overtly political, but his idea that the monster of war and tyranny could be found in both America and Russia came up again and again over the years—in interviews and in poems. "It seems to me that dogmatic cold-war types in the U.S. and the Socialist countries are mirror images of each other and are bent on world destruction," he exclaimed in 1965, the year he finally had a real taste of communist bureaucracy and was expelled from both Cuba and Czechoslovakia.

In 1969, after the police riot at the Democratic National Convention in Chicago and the Soviet military invasion of Czechoslovakia, he was even more convinced of the idea of two evil superpowers. Russia and America were both "police states," he said in 1969. "Both dig the same hot cold war." Communists and capitalists could change places and nothing would be different. And both countries were antagonistic to genuine poets and poetry. "Franco has murdered Lorca the fairy son of Whitman / just as Mayakovsky committed suicide to avoid Russia / Hart Crane distinguished Platonist committed suicide to cave in the wrong / America," he wrote in "Death to Van Gogh's

Ear!" The FBI and the KGB were one and the same; the Penta-
gon and the Kremlin equally abhorrent, he argued. "The com-
munists have nothing to offer but fat cheeks and eyeglasses
and / lying policemen / and the Capitalists proffer Napalm and
money in green suitcases to the / Naked," he wrote in 1965 in
"Kral Majales." There were continual variations on the theme,
and in his 1980 poem "Birdbrain!" he wrote, "Birdbrain runs the
World! / Birdbrain is the ultimate product of Capitalism / Bird-
brain chief bureaucrat of Russia." The ideas and the images for
these poems—and for many others with the same and with sim-
ilar themes—incubated in 1949 at the New York State Psychi-
atric Institute.

If Ginsberg's political perspective was altered by his time in
the "madhouse," so too was his artistic point of view. The New
York State Psychiatric Institute provided him—albeit uninten-
tionally—with an education in surrealism and contemporary
French literature. His mentor turned out to be Carl Solomon,
the man for whom *Howl* was initially written. (An early draft of
the poem was entitled *Howl for Carl Solomon*.) Solomon and Gins-
berg seemed to be cut from the same cultural and psychological
cloth. When they first met at the institute, Solomon extended his
hand and mumbled, "I'm Kirilov." Ginsberg had read *The Pos-
sessed* and was familiar with Kirilov, Dostoyevsky's suicidal ni-
hilist. Without missing a beat he replied, "I'm Myshkin," refer-
ring to the Christ-like hero in Dostoyevsky's *The Idiot*. From that
moment on, his life and Solomon's were inextricably entwined.
"The cadence of the surreal was never challenged," Solomon
wrote of their time together. "Not one of us would dare assume
responsibility for a breach of the unity which each hallucination
required." This story also became a Beat legend, but there's a

deeper, more complex story behind the legend of these two friends.

A Bronx-born Jewish intellectual, a bisexual, and a part-time communist, Dadaist, and existentialist, Solomon introduced Ginsberg to the work and the ideas of Jean Genet, Antonin Artaud, Jean-Paul Sartre, Henri Michaux, and Henry Miller, who, though American, lived and worked in Paris for much of his life. "Because of Solomon, I am reading in all the little magazines about the latest Frenchmen," Ginsberg wrote excitedly to Kerouac. It wasn't only or simply that Solomon had the books and the magazines—especially the latest issues of *Partisan Review*, which he devoured. What counted even more for Ginsberg was that Solomon had actually lived in Paris and immersed himself in the sea of contemporary French culture and politics. He heard Sartre lecture on Kafka, witnessed a reading by Artaud, and attended a Communist Party rally in Paris. Solomon was a hipster intellectual—a man with a brilliant mind who was also mad. Ginsberg was delighted by his unexpected encounter with Solomon, telling Kerouac rapturously that the institute offered "a perfect opportunity . . . for existentialist absurdity." Having lived in Paris among the existentialists, Solomon accepted Sartre's idea that it was crucial to reject both the United States and the Soviet Union, and he did his best to persuade Ginsberg to accept it too. In *What Is Literature?*—which appeared in France in 1947 and in an English translation in the United States in 1949—Sartre denounced the "statism and international bureaucracy" of the Russians and the "abstract capitalism" of the Americans. "The writer's duty," he wrote, "is to take sides against all injustices, wherever they may come from."

Solomon followed Sartre's lead, arguing "there is no room for an honest man on either side of the Iron Curtain." That notion shaped Ginsberg's thinking about America and Russia, too. Sartre argued for a "socialist Europe" and for democracy and peace. In 1949, Ginsberg favored socialism over capitalism. But the French writers who belonged to the Socialist Party and Communist Party were far less appealing to him than the writers—Artaud, Céline, and Genet—who belonged in madhouses and prisons and who seemed to extend the nineteenth-century literary tradition of his heroes Baudelaire and Rimbaud. Instinctively, he felt at home with Genet, not with Sartre. Genet's childhood seemed similar to Neal Cassady's, he wrote; and he described Genet affectionately as a "homosexual hipster" who wrote "huge apocalyptic novels." Richard Howard, poet, critic, and Columbia College classmate of Ginsberg's, remembered that in the late 1940s and early 1950s, Genet, Rimbaud, and Céline were their literary "masters"; their names were "on our lips at all times."

If Ginsberg's own letters and journals provide a portrait of his literary and political life at the institute, the medical reports by his doctors and nurses provide a psychological portrait. An hour or so a day, three days a week—for nearly thirty weeks—Allen Ginsberg told stories about himself, his friends, and his parents to nearly a dozen different psychiatrists, who took copious notes. In some of his comments to the doctors he seems to have made honest disclosures and at other times he seems to have tried to lead them on a false trail. He hid behind smoke screens and at the same time he was transparent. At an early age, he explained to his doctors, he was sexually attracted to both his father and to his brother. As a boy, a surgeon removed his appendix and he became afraid of castration. "It gave me a vagina," he told the doctors, perhaps consciously trying to provoke them or to tell them what he thought they wanted to hear. His mother was "batty," his brother "insecure," his father "patronizing." When he was ten years old, he said, he discovered that Louis was being unfaithful to Naomi and he felt personally betrayed. At college, he told them, he broke from his family and surrounded himself with homosexuals, drug addicts, and criminals. William Burroughs encouraged him to explore the underworld; Herbert Huncke provided him with ideas about crime and criminals. In 1948, he saw God, he said, and the universe itself blossomed like a rose. The way to "self-expression" was through "antisocial activity," he told his doctors—and yet he also explained that he was afraid of self-expression because he feared public exposure and ridicule as a homosexual.

According to the medical reports, Ginsberg spent much of his time with Carl Solomon. They played Ping-Pong and Monopoly, conversed in French, wrote letters to T. S. Eliot, and "laughed all over the ward." Ginsberg held court on the fifth floor. He wore a white suit—a "Palm Beach suit," in the words of his nurse—smoked cigarettes, and listened to recordings of Gustav Mahler and bebop. He wrote poetry, read his own poetry aloud, discussed the symbols in his work with his doctors, and perhaps most importantly, made recordings of himself reciting his own poems with bebop in the background. He listened, developing his voice, and increasingly he regarded poetry as an art to be performed in public. As part of his therapy, he painted pictures of phallic symbols and vagina symbols, of Adam and Eve, and of Christ on the cross. He signed one canvas, "Jesus Ginsberg," and he told one of his doctors that he was "being crucified by psychotherapy." Not surprisingly, the doctor observed that "he identifies with Christ" and "considers himself a Christ-like figure and he feels that he was sent to understand life and to save the rest of the world."

The image of himself as Christ on the cross is at the heart of "Paterson," the 1949 surrealistic poem that came bubbling to the surface in the wake of his therapy at the institute. In 1956, Ginsberg would boast that *Howl* was the first poem he'd written without a sense of fear. It's certainly the first *long*, fearless poem he wrote, but "Paterson," which he wrote in Paterson, New Jersey, in 1949, might be said to be his first genuinely fearless poem. It's clearly a forerunner of *Howl*, as is evident from lines like, "I would rather go mad, gone down the dark road to Mexico, heroin dripping / in my veins." No poem he had written so far was more autobiographical or more candid. In the first stanza of the poem, Ginsberg describes the dreary, suffocating world that he had known at home in Paterson and later in Manhattan: the "rooms papered with visions of money," the "employment bureaus," the "statistical cubicles," and the "cloakrooms of the smiling gods of psychiatry." In the second stanza, he imagines his own escape from those imprisoning rooms, and his visions and his voyages across America. The poem builds in intensity and by the second stanza, Ginsberg sounds hysterical. He pours out all his "thumbsucking / rage" and describes himself as an American Christ: "crowned with thorns in Galveston, nailed hand and foot in Los / Angeles, raised up to die in Denver," and "resurrected in 1958." (In 1958, he would indeed be resurrected from literary obscurity and find himself crowned the King of Beat poetry.)

"Paterson" would not be published until the early 1960s—in the volume *Empty Mirror*. Many of the poems he wrote in the 1940s and collected in *Book of Doldrums* would not be published for years. Some would remain unpublished. Near the end of his stay at the institute, Ginsberg sent the manuscript of *Book of Doldrums* to Robert Giroux. With Pound at St. Elizabeth's, he thought that a book from a young poet in a madhouse might be appealing; apparently not. He soon received a letter of rejection. One of the nurses noted in her log that Ginsberg was "disappointed in [the] news from the publisher." He had counted on Giroux accepting his work. But he was also happy to be leaving the institute—he was discharged on February 27, 1950—and he was happy, too, that Carl Solomon was getting married. "It's the best news I ever heard," he exclaimed. If Solomon was getting married, then surely he might also be happily married to a young woman. He told Kerouac that he was going to abandon his homosexuality and look for a wife. He was also going to get back to his own poetry, and with no place else to go he returned home to live with his father and with Louis's new wife, Edith Cohen, who accepted Allen as though he were her own son. Edith was a godsend, encouraging Allen as a poet and accepting his homosexuality. Years later, when *Howl* was favorably reviewed in the *New York Times*, she carried the clipping and read it proudly to one and all.

### An Unknown Young Poet

In March 1950, about a month after his discharge from the institute, Ginsberg attended a poetry reading by William Carlos Williams in Manhattan, and a few days later he wrote to Williams to introduce himself. "In spite of the grey secrecy of time and my own self-shuttering doubts in these youthful rainy days, I would like to make my presence in Paterson known to you," he wrote seductively. "I hope you will welcome this from me, an unknown young poet, to you, an unknown old poet, who live in the same rusty county of the world." He had studied poetry with Mark Van Doren, he explained, and he had won poetry prizes at Columbia for work he had done—not in imitation of Whitman—but of Hart Crane, Edwin Arlington Robinson, Allen Tate, and "old Englishmen." Ginsberg was "unknown," as he pointed out, but it wasn't fair or accurate to describe Williams as "unknown," though it was likely meant to be ingratiating. For forty years, Williams had been publishing poetry and, though he lived in New Jersey and wrote about local people and local places, he had a national reputation. He also had the admiration of established poets like Marianne Moore and Wallace Stevens, and of younger poets on the West Coast, including Gary Snyder, Lew Welch, and Philip Whalen, all of whom had been undergraduates together at Reed College. Williams would, of course, become Ginsberg's mentor, much to Louis Ginsberg's discomfort and distress. "I believe that Louie always felt hurt that Allen considered Dr. Williams more his mentor than his father was," his stepmother, Edith Ginsberg, observed. "He felt that Williams was sort of taking his place as a father figure."

In the winter of 1950, after therapy at the institute, Allen felt emotionally uncomfortable in the presence of his father. In his vulnerable state of mind, Louis couldn't help him grow as a writer; Williams could and did. Allen wanted to write Williams-like poems using the real language—the "actual talk rhythms"—of the everyday world, not the stilted language of the academic world. Moreover, he wanted to extricate himself from the tangle of abstract symbols and obscure symbolism and give himself over to self-expression. For decades, Williams had preached and had also practiced the kind of poetry that Allen Ginsberg wanted to write. "No ideas but in things," "no ideas besides the facts," and "things are symbols of themselves," Williams insisted. That was precisely the message that Ginsberg needed to hear and had been waiting to hear. Then, too, he was ready at long last to openly and proudly accept a liberal, politically engaged writer—a writer who believed in genuine democracy and who rejected both the bureaucracy of the Soviet Union and the crass capitalism of the United States. Williams had risen to the defense of Sacco and Vanzetti and attacked American injustice in "Impromptu: The Suckers," a poem that Ginsberg described as a "prophetic sort of anti-police-state radical rant." In 1948, Williams had proclaimed, "Absolute freedom is the artist's birthright," and "the past is our worst enemy." Now, in 1950, his words struck Allen as prophetic. After the madhouse, "absolute freedom" seemed more inviting than ever before.

# CHAPTER SIX

# Ladies, We Are Going through Hell

### Lost in His Own Head

As late as 1952, Ginsberg still thought of himself as a novelist in the making, and that isn't surprising since American novelists—not American poets—had real cachet in the early 1950s. So, in 1952, he prepared the outline for an autobiographical novel in which he was the hero. The novel—it never did have a title but it might have been called *My Metamorphosis*—was meant to begin in 1940. In the opening chapter the teenage hero would appear as "an introvert, an atheist, a Communist and a Jew." Later, he would aspire to become the president of the United States, and then in 1945 he would be reborn "a cocksucker," "hipster," and "totally apolitical Reichian." The heart of the novel would take place at the end of the 1940s and would tell the story of how a "hallucinating mystic" and would-be "saint" turned into a "dope fiend," "a despairing sinner," and a "criminal." After years of troubles, he would go to jail and then to the "bughouse" for psychoanalysis. But there would be a happy ending. After therapy, the hero would be mentally adjusted, or at least he would appear to be. He would "go out with girls," work as a literary agent, vote Democratic, and write poetry. That's exactly what Ginsberg did in 1952. He voted for the Democrats in the national elections, and not only dated women but also had sex with women for the first time in his life, much to his relief and to the relief of Louis. "I remember when I first got laid," he wrote in the 1955 poem "Transcription of Organ Music," which he wrote in Berkeley as he was revising *Howl*. He had already had sex, often with anonymous men he encountered on the street, but oddly enough he still considered himself a virgin. In his description of his first sexual encounter with a woman, he depicted himself as passive, and the woman as the initiating male. "H.[elen] P.[arker] graciously took my cherry," he explained. "Age 23, joyful, elevated in hope with the Father, the door to the womb was open to admit me if I wished to enter."

In 1952, he was also working as a literary agent trying to secure a publisher for Kerouac's *On the Road* and Burroughs's autobiographical novel *Junky*, which he described as an "archive of the underground" that provided a "relentless and perspicacious account of the characters that inhabit the junk world." He was also promoting his own work and actively seeking a publisher. In 1952, he gathered together several dozen mostly short poems, many of them about death and dying, including "In Death, Cannot Reach What Is Most Near," and "This Is about Death." He called the volume *Empty Mirror* as a way to express his own sense of emptiness, and he asked William Carlos Williams to write an introduction. Williams was happy to oblige. "This young Jewish boy," he wrote, "already not so young any more, has recognized something that has escaped most of the modern age, he has found that man is lost in the world of his own head." Allen was not eager to be known as a Jewish poet, and Williams's labeling of him as such did not help advance his career one iota. Still, Williams was insightful about Ginsberg's insights into the ways that modern man was a prisoner in the cage of his own head. Indeed, the cage of the modern mind is reflected in many of the poems in *Empty Mirror*—"Long Live the Spiderweb," "Two Boys Went into a Dream Diner," and "After All, What Else Is There to Say?" in which Ginsberg labels his madness feminine.

It took courage, or perhaps audacity, to ask Williams to recommend his work; at twenty-six Allen was still an unknown poet, and Williams was nationally famous. Everyone in the world of poetry knew his work—though it was largely out of fashion in the academic world of the 1950s, and Williams himself was a bit of a relic. An ex-friend of Ezra Pound, a steady foe of T. S. Eliot, and the author of a classic of cultural criticism, *In the American Grain* (1925), Williams seemed to belong to literary history rather than to the literary present. From an orthodox political point of view, he was politically suspect in 1952, when the United States was fighting communism in Korea, and Senator Joseph McCarthy was actively seeking out communists in Washington, D.C., and elsewhere.

The FBI began to keep a file on Williams as a subversive in 1930, and the bureau had continued to investigate him throughout the Great Depression and World War II. The investigations finally paid off for the FBI. In 1953, a year after he wrote the introduction to *Empty Mirror*, Williams was appointed as a Consultant in Poetry at the Library of Congress. FBI Director J. Edgar Hoover took immediate action and prevented him from assuming the post on the grounds that he was sympathetic to communism and communists. Hadn't he written a poem entitled "The Pink Church"? the FBI argued, and wasn't that proof enough that he was a communist sympathizer, if not a Red himself? The charges were ludicrous; so was the FBI's interpretation of Williams's poetry and his essays, in which he made it clear that he was no friend to communism and communists. In 1950, he observed, "Russia whose avowed intent has been to free the world of Capitalism . . . has turned out to be an empire seeker of the most reactionary sort."

To Ginsberg, the FBI investigation and persecution of Williams was yet another example of how America was like Russia. Like the USSR, the United States had its secret police and its dossiers on dissidents. Williams's story also showed Allen that America's best minds were being destroyed by the madness of America. In the early 1950s, Williams was physically and mentally unstable; in 1953, he entered Hillside Hospital in Queens, New York, for depression. Partially paralyzed because of a stroke and unable to write, he portrayed his eight months in the hospital as "unadulterated hell." To the young poet Robert Creeley and others, he complained about his "mental derangement." Like Ginsberg, he understood madness, and like Ginsberg he'd experienced life as a patient in a psychiatric hospital. He was "instinctively drawn" to Ginsberg, he told the poet Marianne Moore in 1952. Allen had a "clear, rigorous unrelenting mind" and he would "do outstanding work" if only he could survive. Survival was the key. In the early 1950s, as Williams knew, Ginsberg seemed hell-bent on self-destruction.

"I walk around aimlessly," Allen wrote in his journal. That image would show up years later in *Howl* when he wrote of hipsters "who wandered around and around." In the early 1950s, he was filled with a sense of self-hatred. When he looked into a mirror, he recoiled. "I don't like my own looks," he wrote in his journal, after peering into the mirror of a Manhattan bar. To his own eye, he appeared to be "an empty heel or a middle class con artist . . . lonely and personally sadistic . . . twisted and deformed, a cripple mental case." Somehow or other—perhaps because of his immense ego and perhaps because of his intense longing for fame—he survived and thrived.

In 1955, when Williams received the manuscript of *Howl*, he was both surprised and delighted to learn that Ginsberg had indeed survived. He was also overjoyed to be able to write yet another introduction for his friend. "I never thought he'd live to grow up and write a book of poems," Williams said. Ginsberg's "ability to survive, travel and go on writing astonishes me. That he has gone on developing and perfecting his art is no less amazing to me." In his introduction to *Empty Mirror*, Williams compared Ginsberg to Dante and noted that like Dante, Ginsberg was compelled "to see the truth, undressed." In his introduction to *Howl*, he again alluded to Dante and pointed out that Ginsberg had been "through hell." Readers who were about to read *Howl* were going to enter the author's hell, he noted. To ladies who had been reared on poetry about flowers, stars, and romantic love, he urged caution. "Hold back the edge of your gowns," he wrote. As Williams recognized, *Howl* offers a map of the inferno that Ginsberg inhabited in New York in the 1940s and 1950s. The city was hell, but it wasn't totally bleak. In his introduction, Williams did not suggest that readers who were about to read the poem abandon all hope. He found *Howl* remarkably inspiring. Granted, it was "a howl of defeat." And yet it was "not defeat at all." He said that "in spite of the most debasing experiences that life can offer a man, the spirit of love survives to ennoble our lives if we have the wit and the courage and the faith—and the art!"

### Like Baudelaire in His Damnation

In 1950, Allen's personal connection to Williams instilled in him a sense of hope and of great poetry to come. The sixty-seven-year-old Williams and the twenty-four-year-old Ginsberg were a happy couple—and an odd couple, too—as they roamed the back streets of Paterson, New Jersey. They poked their heads into smoky bars, observed the comings and goings of the city's poor, and talked about poets and poetry. With Williams's introduction to Ginsberg's *Empty Mirror*, it seemed that literary recognition would not be far off. But it was not to be. Even with Williams's endorsement, no editor would touch the book. The idyllic days in Paterson with Williams at his side proved to be a brief interlude in a long season of hell still to come. In his journals, Ginsberg poured out, with a sense of grandiosity, his despair, self-pity, and self-revulsion. "I feel like Baudelaire in his damnation," he wrote. "All of the time that's past has been horrible." The act of writing was itself "a prison," and he noted, "I may have to stop keeping journal." But he could not bring himself to that point. He was addicted to his journal—he was scribacious—and he was compelled "to put naked self down on paper." What he wanted most of all was to "tip my mitt," as he called it—to give himself away before he could suppress himself. Only then would he know himself deep down inside, he believed. For the first time since high school, he began to reconsider *Leaves of Grass*. He noted that Whitman "had put himself out in his book (as he never was able to do in the flesh)," and he began to think, albeit tentatively, of improving on Whitman by putting himself out as a "queer" in print and in the flesh.

Even in the depressing days of the Korean War, he managed to find solace and a few pleasures. In his apartment, he revisited, in memory, the "mysteries" of his childhood, as well as the "beauty of certain days and nights" with Lucien Carr, Neal Cassady, and William Burroughs. He ate peyote, listened to the pop singer Johnny Ray, whom he described enviously as "the agonist with the open heart," and he went to the movies to see *An American in Paris* and *Rashamon*. He was still reading voraciously and still keeping lists of everything he read. There was Conrad's *Heart of Darkness*, Herman Hesse's *Steppenwolf*, Djuna Barnes's *Nightwood*, Jean Genet's *The Miracle of the Rose*, Mickey Spillane's *One Lonely Night*, Paul Bowles's surprising best-seller *The Sheltering Sky*, and F. O. Matthiessen's *American Renaissance*, which encouraged him to see Kerouac as the successor to Melville and himself as the successor to Whitman. Later, he would see Gary Snyder as the successor to Henry David Thoreau. Burroughs didn't seem to have an obvious nineteenth-century counterpart unless it was Poe. Burroughs was a "spy from the future," Ginsberg astutely observed in his journal.

In the early 1950s, Ginsberg began to reflect on the 1940s, especially on the friends and acquaintances who had gone mad and had died. (They would reappear in various guises and incarnations in *Howl*.) He also came up with the idea of publishing a magazine that would be called *Crazy*, and that would be about his own insane friends. In his journal, he compiled a list of the madmen and the suicides. There was David Kammerer, Lucien Carr's would-be lover, "stabbed and aghast." There was Phil White, the heroin addict who committed suicide in prison—

"hanging in the Tombs labyrinth." And there was William Can-
nastra, a Harvard Law School graduate who died in a freak acci-
dent in the New York subway—"in the windows underground."
Again and again, when he went on the subway, Ginsberg thought
about committing suicide, and he thought too that he never
should have been born. He recorded his suicidal thoughts in his
journal, writing that he inhabited a living hell. His dearest, old-
est friends—Kerouac and Burroughs—were alive and in hells of
their own making, too.

Jack Kerouac's novel *The Town and the City* had been published
in 1950. Ginsberg raved about it and about Kerouac, too, to
everyone he encountered, from Williams to Trilling. He insisted
that Kerouac was a genius. "Jack is the greatest writer alive in
America of our age," he proclaimed. But no one else in America
seemed to agree with him. In Allen's estimation, Burroughs was
the next greatest writer in America, and he himself was the great-
est poet in America. Why publishers weren't begging for their
work in the early 1950s, he simply could not understand. "They
have totally fucked up on Jack, Bill & myself," he wrote in his
journal. He condemned the commercialism of the New York
publishing world. "They gamble on inconsequential kicks think-
ing they'll latch on," he observed. "But they have very little taste
or insight into what's good." In the wake of the commercial and
literary failure of his first novel, Kerouac began to doubt himself
and to grow angry and embittered. "I have had the worst shitluck
possible with that book and it is the same thing all the time with
whatever I do," he told Neal Cassady in 1950, at the age of
twenty-eight. In a characteristic moment of grandiosity, he in-
sisted that he had inherited the "curse of [Herman] Melville."

Part of the problem, Ginsberg, Kerouac, and Burroughs

agreed, was that America was in decline. American values had been corrupted, literary standards had fallen, and in publishing no one recognized talent or genius anymore. "It is a decade starting off inauspiciously in mediocrity and war," Kerouac fumed in 1950, shortly after the start of the Korean War. At times, he maintained his idealism and sense of hope. He wanted humanity to "gather in one immense church of the world," but he also lashed out at human beings, including Ginsberg, and he railed at all the "cruds of New York." Now and then his anti-Semitism flared up and he denounced the "millionaire jews" [sic] and Jewish editors. No one would publish *On the Road*, his picaresque novel about himself and his friends, and someone had to be the scapegoat. As Ginsberg reminded him, it wasn't Jewish editors who were to blame. And Kerouac's failure to find a publisher for *On the Road* was only part of the problem. In 1951, he went to jail, albeit briefly, for failing to pay child support to his ex-wife, Joan Haverty, who had given birth to a daughter that Jack refused to accept as his own. He wandered tirelessly across the country, and to Mexico in 1952, where, he confessed in his journal, he was "unbearably lonely" and filled with "long, dark depression" and "thoughts of suicide." He was certain that he was on the cusp of insanity. "I've been in the madhouse once and will be in the madhouse again," he wrote. Here was one of the best minds of his generation nearly destroyed by madness.

Burroughs—the "Wandering WASP"—was for years addicted to heroin, which he had begun to use at the end of World War II with the help of Herbert Huncke. Yet Burroughs was a hardy survivor. He was less vulnerable than Kerouac, and in the manner of James Joyce he knew when to be cunning, when to go into exile, and when to be silent. He knew, too, when it was time to come home. In 1953, he returned to New York and lived briefly with Ginsberg on the Lower East Side, which looked to him like a phantasmagoric landscape, a modern hell with "blocks of ruined buildings . . . muggers and policemen and junkies and the CIA stealing out of hallways and blackmailing each other." It was a vision of the megalopolis that would influence Ginsberg two years later when he began to write *Howl* in San Francisco. Burroughs also knew when it was time to abandon silence and to speak his mind. In 1965, he would explain to his *Paris Review* interviewers, "All of my work is directed against those who are bent, through stupidity or design, on blowing up the planet or rendering it uninhabitable. Like the advertising people . . . I'm concerned with the precise manipulation of word and image to create an action, not to go out and buy a Coca-Cola, but to create an alteration in the reader's consciousness."

Burroughs's own consciousness had been battered by drugs, madhouses, and jails—in New York, Texas, and in Louisiana—on a variety of drug charges. His life looked like a downward spiral, and yet the further down he descended the more inspired he became to tell his own story. In 1950 in Mexico Burroughs hit bottom—the inner circle of his own hell—when he shot and killed his wife, Joan. Locked up in Lecumbere Prison, he hired an able Mexican lawyer, whom he paid handsomely. Joan's death was an accident, he claimed, and he was soon released on bail. Before long he made his way to Tangiers for the drugs, the young boys, and the chance to write his novel, *Naked Lunch*. Allen Ginsberg was traumatized by Joan's death. He had lived in her apartment on the Upper West Side and later at her house in Texas. She had been a mother to him. During his stay at the New York State Psychiatric Institute, she'd written to say that he shouldn't feel ashamed of himself. She had been in Bellevue and she knew that "anyone who doesn't blow his top once is no damn good." Now he added Joan's name to the list of dead friends and acquaintances—David Kammerer, Phil White, and William Cannastra—and he sat down and wrote an elegy entitled "To Joan Adams (Burroughs) on her Death."

## Should I Go to California?

For Ginsberg, New York in the 1950s felt like an inferno and a madhouse all in one. He knew that he had to escape before his own sanity crumbled, before he himself went up in flames. He hated his lowly job in market research and advertising and felt guilty about the commodities—especially the toothpaste—he helped to promote. Then, too, he was envious of his friends and acquaintances: Louis Simpson, whom he knew from Columbia and who was teaching at the New School; Anatole Broyard, who was writing for the *New York Times;* and Milton Klonsky, who was making a name for himself as an art critic. New York City and ordinary New Yorkers unnerved him. In 1952, at a rally in Madison Square Garden for Adlai Stevenson, the Democratic Party candidate for president, he sat "in the bleachers with the lower classes the vulgar I detest," he wrote, as though he was a refined character in a Henry James novel. On another occasion, while watching Charlie Chaplin's *Limelight* in a Manhattan theater, he was afraid that the "ruffians" in the balcony would physically assault him simply for being an intellectual.

He had no hope of finding a scrap of heaven anywhere, he told himself, but purgatory might be possible, and purgatory seemed to lie in the West. "Should I go to California?" he asked in his journal in the spring of 1953. California held out the promise of a new life. Kerouac had lived in San Francisco and had written his first book of poetry there. At first Kerouac didn't approve—"it's a shallow place. It's all show," he wrote—but he gradually fell in love with the city. "San Francisco, I finally admit, is 'my city, my Parisian city across the desert,'" he wrote. In the mid-1950s, San Francisco seemed like America's most romantic city. Joe DiMaggio and Marilyn Monroe were married there in 1954. Ginsberg's heartthrob, Neal Cassady, was living just south of San Francisco in San Jose with his wife, Carolyn—who had attended Bennington College and who had studied dance with Martha Graham—and their children. But the marriage, the family, and the children didn't prevent Allen from pursuing him or from entertaining erotic fantasies about Neal and writing romantically about him in poems like "The Green Automobile," in which he allowed himself to imagine, "We will go riding / over the Rockies, / we'll go riding / all night long until dawn."

Before leaving New York, he visited his fifty-nine-year-old mother at Pilgrim State Hospital on Long Island and now, for the first time, Naomi looked like she was going to die. He was certain that she didn't have much longer to live, and he broke down and wept. Later, at home, he wrote the draft of a poem about her entitled "In Hospital Visiting Naomi," an early forerunner of *Kaddish*, in which he borrowed the words "The horror! The horror!" from Conrad's *Heart of Darkness* to describe her situation. His feelings about Naomi were emotionally knotted, too knotted to untie. He loved his mother; she exhibited "natural exuberance & innocent perception," he explained—and he identified with her and he was prepared to do battle with the world on her behalf. "I feel that I could half start a conspiracy of the insane with her," he wrote in his journal. But he also conspired against her. He—not Louis, Eugene, or anyone else in the family—committed her to Pilgrim State Hospital. Then, too, he signed the official documents that allowed the doctors to perform a lobotomy. Soon after that decisive act, he began to realize that he felt resentment and hostility toward Naomi. "I am beginning to hate my mother," he wrote to Kerouac, who made sure to let Allen know that he loved his mother, Gabrielle.

From his brother, Eugene, Allen learned that at his mother's funeral there were not enough Jewish men to form a minyan and so she was denied kaddish, the traditional prayer for the dead. Gradually, he realized that he would have to write a poetic prayer for Naomi, and that he would have to call his poem *Kaddish*. It was the most Jewish of all his work and *the* work in which he was clearly a Jew. In the original draft of *Kaddish*, Ginsberg describes—in more detail than in the final published version of the poem—his final encounter with Naomi at her apartment, just before she entered the madhouse. In a great rage, he slaps her across the face, hits her in the stomach, and bangs her head against the wall. Great "howls" emerge from deep inside him. "Don't be mad anymore!" he screams. "I want you to love me! Mama! Mama! Help me, don't go mad." Now, he felt as though he had betrayed his mother, and he saw himself as Judas. As he prepared to leave New York for California, he was filled with a sense of guilt and shame. He regarded Naomi as a victim of the American system of injustice—an Ethel Rosenberg of sorts. This was not an entirely strange association, since both Ethel and Naomi were Russian Jews, members of the American Communist Party, and mothers of two sons. Moreover, both of them, in their own way, had been persecuted. In the summer of 1953,

Allen sent a telegram, packed with all the metaphors he could muster, to the White House to protest the electrocution at Sing Sing of Ethel and Julius Rosenberg—who had been convicted as spies for the Russians. "Rosenbergs are pathetic," Allen's telegram read. "Government Will sordid. Execution Obscene. America caught in crucifixion machine. Only barbarians want them burned. I say stop it before we fill our souls with deathhouse horror." Allen felt deeply about electrocutions—public "burnings," he called them—and he had a series of nightmares about Naomi, including one in which she was burned alive. "Burning," he noted in his journal, was "a beautiful horrible slang for official electrocution."

In 1953, he left New York and traveled to Washington, D.C., hoping to visit Ezra Pound at St. Elizabeth's Hospital, but Pound refused to see him. (In the 1960s, he would finally catch up with Pound in Italy, and would write admiringly about his work.) Then, it was on to Miami—a "dream of rich sick Jews," he called it—and then to Havana, where he played the part of the hipster tourist, visiting cafes and bars, listening to Cubans "drumming / . . . whistling, howling." The words "howl" and "howling" had already appeared in his journal. Now they began to show up with increasingly regularity in his journal entries and in his poems, too. In Mexico, where he again played the part of the tourist, the dogs all seemed to "howl" and he began to howl, too, and to think of howling as a way to express his deepest concerns.

In letters and poems to friends at home, he also augmented his own personal mythology. He was the "intrepid American adventurer" and the "great explorer." He was the anthropologist, archeologist, and romantic poet in the mold of Shelley, wandering through jungles, discovering ancient artifacts, and befriending strange tribes. In Chiapas he met an American woman named Karen Shields whom he described as the embodiment of Robert Graves's "the White Goddess" and who initiated him, he claimed, into all the "Mayan secrets." There seemed to be romance with Shields, but he also felt lonely and he longed for a "sweet brown man's body."

Death had been a recurring theme in the poems collected in *Empty Mirror*. Now, he returned to the theme of death in *Siesta in Xbalba*, the one major poem that emerged from his experience in Mexico. Here he describes his visit to the ancient mummies in the city of Guanajuato and his obsession with an ancient "deathshead." He also relates his experiences in the Yucatán, where he has come with his "own mad mind to study / alien hieroglyphs of Eternity." The crucial words in the poem are "mad," "madness," "mystical," "mythical," "naked," "nakedness," "nudity," "obscure," "wild"—many of which would become key words in *Howl*. In *Siesta in Xbalba* he utters them as though they were a kind of incantation or mantra. The self-portrait that emerges is of a strange young man searching for the key to the mysteries of the universe. At the end of *Siesta in Xbalba* he seems to have found it, as well as the key to himself. In the journal he kept in Mexico, he recorded a prose snapshot of himself crossing the border to the United States: "alone naked with knapsack, watch, camera, poem, beard." He took some of those images and incorporated them into the next-to-the-last stanza in *Siesta in Xbalba*, where he is "tanned and bearded / satisfying Whitman, concerned / with a few Traditions, / metrical, mystical, manly." If he saw himself clearly, as in a photograph, he also saw the United States clearly, too, as the "nation over the border" with its "infernal bombs," "industries / of night," and "dreams / of war."

Mexico made it possible for him to look at America with fresh eyes and to see himself in the tradition of Whitman. Mexico played a pivotal part in his liberation from himself and from America. Ginsberg had of course read and admired Whitman in high school. At Columbia in the 1940s, he lost track of his work and embraced Eliot, Auden, Yeats, and Rimbaud. In Mexico, he apparently read *Ode to Walt Whitman* by the Spanish poet Federico García Lorca, and García Lorca rekindled his appreciation for *Leaves of Grass*. Many of García Lorca's images and phrases reverberate in *Siesta in Xbalba* — García Lorca's image of "America . . . inundated with 'machines and tears,'" for example, as well as the image of the bearded Whitman. That Ginsberg reconnected with Whitman through García Lorca is also suggested by "A Supermarket in California," the 1955 poem that describes Ginsberg "shopping for images" while he shops for groceries. In his surreal supermarket, Ginsberg sees Whitman "poking / among the meats in the refrigerator / and eyeing the grocery boys." He sees García Lorca "down by the watermelons."

When he arrived in California in 1954, he had a new sense of pride about his own manhood, and for the first time he identified himself as an American poet in the tradition of Whitman. Accordingly, he began to write poems about America, including one poem entitled "America" in which he called upon God to inspire him to "salvage some remnant of the truth / of all society" from his own "solitary craze." Now, madness was a condition to be cultivated. Now, he was convinced that out of his own individual insanity he might discover larger truths about the insanity of

America. His voyage from New York to California via Mexico had yielded yet another vision, and this time the vision seemed to be grounded in reality. In California in the summer of 1954, he devised a bold new literary strategy. He would "reveal in short-hand and symbolic images / the paradigm of fortune for United States; / witness the downfall and roar of daily life, / in riches and despair amid great machinery."

# CHAPTER SEVEN

# Another Coast's Apple for the Eye

## Dread Frisco

In the 1950s, *Howl* shocked the middle-class Pollyannas and the pundits of positive thinking. Ginsberg aimed to wake Americans from what seemed like a narcotized slumber. "God damn the false optimists of my generation," he raved in his journal in the winter of 1955, as he was readying himself to write what he hoped would be a big new poem about America. The state of the nation troubled him, and he wanted to say something to the country at large about how much America had promised and then disappointed the world. "America is new," he wrote in his journal shortly before he began to write *Howl*. He added, "Here in America we are gathered independently of one soil's history and begin anew with the dream-like arrival of strangers gathering and propagating on a continent newly created and historically empty at their arrival." In San Francisco in 1955, he was at the end of the continent, and it felt to him like the end of the world and the end of history. There was no good reason to be optimistic. It wasn't the "American Century" at all, as Henry Luce of *Life* had promised the nation. From Allen Ginsberg's point of view, the American nightmare had set in.

For the most part, readers didn't hear negative political news about America in the mid-1950s; they certainly didn't read it in *Life* or *Look*. For the most part, readers didn't read poetry, either. But that was Allen Ginsberg's project: he wanted to tell the truth in poetry in his own way—to scream it in a uniquely American way. "I occasionally scream with exasperation," he wrote. "This is usually an attempt to communicate with a blockhead." The form of his poem itself would have to be shocking, he was convinced, especially to those poets and readers of poetry who believed, as the poet Richard Wilbur did, that "limitation makes for power," and that the "strength of the genie comes of his being confined in a bottle." In his college poems Ginsberg had confined the genie; after all, he had been a formalist. Now he wanted to release all the force from the bottle, and let it carry him away. San Francisco was the place where he was finally able to let it happen and let himself go. As William Everson—the California Catholic poet and Beat fellow traveler—noted, San Francisco's relaxed atmosphere "opened his mind." San Francisco in the 1950s liberated him so that he could write about New York in the 1940s—the city that he loved and that he had lost. The opening of his mind enabled him to look back and write with a certain ironic and comic detachment about minds destroyed by madness, including his own mind.

In August 1954, just before he arrived in San Francisco, he described the city as "dread Frisco." Without a job, money, family, or friends—Kerouac was on the road, Burroughs back in Tangiers, Cassady at home with his wife and children in San Jose—he didn't expect to enjoy life there. But he was pleasantly surprised. Eight months later, in April 1955, he called San Francisco "Athens-like"—a place that inspired him to write some of his best poems. San Francisco plays a significant role in several Ginsberg poems from this period. "In the Baggage Room at Greyhound" portrays a sad city of faceless, nameless travelers— "millions of the poor rushing around." San Francisco also appears in the 1955 poem "Sunflower Sutra," a pastoral poem for the industrial age that contrasts the world of men and machines with the world of nature. Here San Francisco is a city of "box house hills" and smog, smoke, and grime. It's T. S. Eliot's wasteland a quarter of a century later, relocated on the West Coast of the United States. In "Sunflower Sutra," Ginsberg describes a late afternoon in the company of Jack Kerouac. The two men walk along a stream with "oily water" and "no fish." There's a garbage dump and a junkyard littered with rusty cars, empty tin cans, broken machinery, and an old Southern Pacific locomotive—"a once / powerful mad American locomotive." In the poem, Ginsberg remembers the wastelands of New York and New Jersey—the "Hells of the Eastern rivers, bridges clanking Joes Greasy Sandwiches, / dead baby carriages, black treadless tires forgotten and unretreaded." He's surprised to see a sunflower growing in the midst of San Francisco's urban, industrial wasteland—"A perfect beauty of a sunflower!" He remembers his own vision of Blake in 1948, and Blake's poems, especially "Ah! Sun-Flower." At the end of "Sunflower Sutra," he offers a "sermon" to Kerouac and to his readers in which he states that human beings are "not our skin of grime," but "golden sunflowers inside." Allen hadn't felt this optimistic since he left Paterson at the age of seventeen to live in New York.

From the time he arrived on the West Coast in 1954 until he departed in 1957, Ginsberg traveled all across California. After a trip to Yosemite in the summer of 1955—just before he wrote *Howl*—he waxed poetical about the "valley floor being primeval, Eden, Shangri-la, but primeval with giant ferns and tropical valley life surrounded by secret giant cliffs." And yet for all his enthusiasm about the natural world, he didn't write a poem about Yosemite or Eden or California's virgin land. It was the corrupt, fallen world of men, machines, and robotic monsters that inspired him. Weekend sojourns in Yosemite were pleasant enough, and occasional backpacking adventures were delightful too, but Ginsberg wanted most of all to make a home in the city and to write city poems in the tradition of Baudelaire, Eliot, and Blake.

### Islands of Freedom

The surrealist poet Philip Lamantia knew the city that Ginsberg encountered as well as anyone else. Born in San Francisco, Lamantia was expelled from high school in the 1940s as a troublemaker—as a teenager he identified with Edgar Allan Poe and H. P. Lovecraft, the quirky author of *The Outsider and Others*. As soon as he could, Lamantia fled to New York and joined the company of André Breton, the French surrealist. He described San Francisco just before the Beat Revolution of the mid-1950s as "terribly straight-laced and provincial," though he also noted that there were "islands of freedom" and a "whole underground culture that went unnoticed by the city at large." When Ginsberg arrived in San Francisco in 1954, he couldn't help but be invigorated by the underground cast of characters—the hipsters, bohemians, pacifists, artists, anarchists, mystics, homosexuals, and lesbians. Some were natives, and some—like the Chicago-born writer Kenneth Rexroth—were in self-proclaimed exile from cities all across America. San Francisco had lured poets for decades by the time Ginsberg arrived, and they had become San Franciscans. In 1947, *Harper's* magazine ridiculed the whole nonconformist crew—the followers of Rexroth and the followers of the novelist Henry Miller—in a sensational article by Berkeley author Mildred Edie Brady entitled "The New Culture of Sex and Anarchy." Brady was condescending and dismissive. She mocked the California bohemians because they read poetry that was "all but incomprehensible to the uninitiated," and because they "offered sex as the source of individual salvation in a collective world that's going to hell." Brady ridiculed them because they didn't own houses or cars—they hitchhiked—and because they wore beards and sandals, lived in "uncarpeted rooms: abstract paintings against rude board walls, canned milk and pumpernickel on a rough table, ceramic ashtrays and opened books on a packing box." It seemed ludicrous to her that these young, penniless poets—"the mustachioed papas and the bosomed mamas"—lived in an "approximation to a primitive tribal group" and that they embraced religion, art, and anarchism.

To Ginsberg and to many of his peers, Brady's piece sounded like an invitation to a party, not a warning to keep out, and as soon as he arrived in San Francisco, he began to explore the city's cultural underground and its islands of freedom. He learned about San Francisco's radical history from living radicals like Rexroth and from the murals—in Coit Tower, for example—that had been painted in the 1930s by Works Progress Administration (WPA) artists. He browsed at City Lights Bookstore, the nation's first all-paperback bookstore, which was just a year old, and he admired the books that City Lights was publishing in the Pocket Poets Series, including Lawrence Ferlinghetti's *Pictures of the Gone World*. He read the local avant-garde magazines *Ark* and *Circle*, and he tuned in to listener-sponsored radio station KPFA—only five years old and still finding its voice and its listenership.

He saw groundbreaking blockbuster movies: *Rebel without a Cause* and *East of Eden*, with James Dean as the rebel and the wayward son; and *The Wild One*, with Marlon Brando as the leather-clad leader of a motorcycle gang ready to rebel against anything and anybody. Watching Dean and Brando on screen in San Francisco with Neal Cassady and Natalie Jackson added to the intensity of the experience and gave Allen a sense of participating in the start of something new and exciting in America. American youth was breaking out, breaking loose, and the irreverent behavior was contagious. Perhaps the most memorable photo he took in San Francisco was of Neal and Natalie standing together on Market Street under the marquee of a theater that read "Marlon Brando: *The Wild One*." In *Howl*, he would acknowledge the film in the phrase "saintly motorcyclists." So, too, listening to rock'n'roll on the radio in Neal's car gave him a sense that something new was happening to popular music in America. In *Howl* he celebrates the rock'n'roll revolution that was sweeping America in phrases like "all night rocking and rolling." Elvis Presley wasn't his heartthrob—Elvis was too white and too Southern for Allen—but he was a big fan of Little Richard, Fats Domino, and Johnny Ray. The mid-1950s teen idols, and the teens themselves—"the vast lamb of the middleclass," as he called them—persuaded him that America was breaking from conformity, and he was eager to help the breakout. So, *Howl* mirrored the cultural changes that were taking place; as it turned out, the poem would accelerate the pace of change, too.

In San Francisco, he tried all the food—Mexican, Chinese, Italian—the city had to offer. He ate in exclusive French restaurants, all-night diners, and "sukiyaki joints." In Foster's Cafeteria on Montgomery Street—which reminded him of the Pokerino, his main Times Square haunt in the 1940s—he spent hours drinking coffee, smoking cigarettes, eating French fries and chili, talking with friends, and writing poetry. He read ravenously in the public library, and with his library card he took home armfuls of books by native poets like Robert Duncan, Philip Lamantia, and Josephine Miles, and newcomers like Michael McClure, who had just arrived from Kansas, eager to join the poetry scene. With his new friends, he rode the cable cars and the ferries, climbed the hills, and gazed at the bridges. At San Francisco State's newly founded poetry center, he heard famous international poets like his college hero W. H. Auden, as well as unknown local poets, and he did his best to ingratiate himself with the center's creator, Ruth Witt-Diamant, the city's grand lady of letters. He frequented the bohemian nooks and cafés—Jackson's Nook, the Black Cat Café, Vesuvio's, Miss Smith's Tea Room, 12 Adler Place, and Mike's Place, which Ferlinghetti memorializes in his poem "Autobiography" as *the* place to be.

"Art is a community effort—a small but select community," Ginsberg noted in his journal in 1954. Energetically, he went about the business of assembling his own small, select community of artists, writers, and hipsters, many of them homosexuals. His new friends in San Francisco reminded him of old friends from New York. He noted how much he was haunted by the New

York past and how the "dear shadows" preoccupied him more than the real people he was meeting. But he soon made new friends and quickly conquered San Francisco, putting his stamp on the city, which distressed some of the local poets, who resented a New Yorker stealing their poetic thunder.

Robert Duncan paid a call on Ginsberg at the Marconi Hotel on Broadway—his first home in San Francisco—and though they exchanged ideas about writing and the power of the imagination, there was never genuine mutual respect. In public, Ginsberg was cordial to Duncan, as one would expect; Duncan was a fellow poet and a homosexual, born in Oakland, educated at the University of California—a cultural pioneer who belonged to a small, select literary circle of his own. Duncan was one of the Bay Area's literary luminaries, and Ginsberg saw him on stage in a wild performance of his own play, *Faust Foutu*. He was duly impressed—even envious—when Duncan boldly yet casually took off his clothes, faced the audience and said, "This is my body." Here was another poet preoccupied with the body, and that spoke well of him. But Allen didn't think much of Duncan's work; he found it too stiff and formal. He didn't think much of Rexroth's work, either, though many readers, like Ann Charters—a UC Berkeley English major in the 1950s—felt that Allen was influenced by Rexroth's antiwar poem "Thou Shalt Not Kill."

Like *Howl*, "Thou Shalt Not Kill"—which was written in 1953—was about the war between the generations. Like *Howl*, it offers images of "madhouses," and like *Howl* it depicts a ravenous beast—a "behemoth" rather than a "Moloch," but still a robot-like killer of youth. If Rexroth was an influence, Ginsberg wouldn't or couldn't say. "Rexroth is [a] poor poet with big ego," he confided to Kerouac, though he also befriended Rexroth and attended literary gatherings at his home on Scott Street. He even wrote a tender poem about him. "Rexroth's face reflecting human / tired bliss / White haired, wing browed / gas mustache, / flowers jet out of / his sad head," he observed in "Scribble." In 1955, Rexroth was only fifty, still writing poetry and literary criticism, but to Ginsberg he seemed old and worn out, a survivor from another era.

"Scribble" was penned in accord with Kerouac's technique of "sketching," which, he assured Ginsberg, would help him write better poems. If he could only train himself to make sketches of what was right in front of him, he would surely develop his talent. Kerouac had other compelling ideas about writing. He drew up a "List of Essentials"—thirty of them—which Ginsberg tacked to the wall of his room at the Marconi Hotel. The local poets were impressed, especially Duncan, who "dug it," Ginsberg reported, especially the "conception of spontaneity," which sounded like something new and innovative. "Scribbled secret notebooks, and wild typewritten pages, for y[ou]r own joy," Kerouac put at the top of his List of Essentials. "The unspeakable visions of the individual" was another suggestion, and so was "composing wild, undisciplined, pure, coming in from under, crazier the better."

In San Francisco in 1954 and 1955, Ginsberg took Kerouac's essentials to heart, aiming for craziness, ecstasy, wildness, and more. "Bookmovie is the movie in words, the visual American form," Kerouac wrote in his List of Essentials. In *Howl*, Ginsberg would make a bookmovie—a poem with moving images—and in *Howl* at last he found an American literary form he could call his own. "Writer-Director of Earthly movies Sponsored & Angeled in Heaven," Kerouac urged. In *Howl*, Ginsberg took on the role of writer/director and leading actor, too, creating a language that bridged the world of angels with the world of devils.

For all his liberation and sense of spontaneity in San Francisco, he still kept one foot in the world of respectability, order, and discipline. He went to work in the field of market research, as he had done in New York, though he felt it was killing him. Once again he divided his time, once again he went back and forth from the bohemian underground to the world of corporate sales, statistics, and advertising. He remained deeply ambivalent. He worked hard trying to be straight. His hair was short; he wore a tweed jacket, white shirt, and tie. And, after the debacle with Neal in San Jose, he began a relationship with a young woman named Sheila Williams Boucher—a hip chick, in the vernacular of the day, who flipped over jazz and dug Negroes. She was cool, Ginsberg told Kerouac proudly; he and Sheila made a handsome couple, and in the unpublished poem "In Vesuvio's Waiting for Sheila," he describes himself as he straddles respectability on the one hand and the underground on the other. Here he wears a "Dark suit," and has "money in my wallet— / Checkbook abreast." At Vesuvio's bar he waits for Sheila and imagines "an evening / of fucking and jazz."

## Moloch

In San Francisco in 1954, Ginsberg's seminal experiences didn't take place on the town and in the midst of crowds. The pivotal moments were intensely personal and remarkably solitary. They often happened while he was on drugs—Dexedrine, marijuana, and peyote—and the drugs opened an interior world that led to *Howl*. Peyote provided the seeds for Part I and Part II of the poem—the most depressing sections, though even here there are glimpses of ecstasy and joy. In his essay "Notes Written on Finally Recording *Howl*," Ginsberg explained that he "got high on peyote" in his Nob Hill apartment in the city and "saw an image of the robot skullface of Moloch in the upper stories of a big hotel." The big hotel was the Sir Francis Drake, a San Francisco landmark, but as his journals and letters indicate, he didn't see Moloch immediately, as he would later claim. Moloch came to him slowly, not in a sudden revelation; he shaped and selected his images gradually, not in a flash.

The first time he looked at San Francisco under the influence of peyote, he saw New York City as though it was right outside his window—so close and so real that he could almost touch it. "Another coast's apple for the eye," he wrote in his journal. He gazed at the scene, took it in, and described it in his "scribbled secret notebooks," as Kerouac called them—without bothering to organize, analyze, or explain. The images welled up, pilled up. "Fixed eye & noticed the vegetable horror of the Sir Francis Drake Hotel," he noted. "A N.Y. Gotham midtown Murray Hill unreal Wall Street miniature panorama." That was only one of a series of images. There was another: "Found suddenly the gothic eyes of the skull tower glaring out . . . with horrible cross check Dollar sign skull protrusion of lipless jailbarred inhuman longtooth spectral deathhead . . . This phantom building robot was smoking in inaction as if it had been stuck there in eternity." The associations were surreal and phantasmagoric, and they electrified his imagination.

Looking at San Francisco from his window, he was reminded of Rembrandt's dark, ominous paintings, Fritz Lang's science fiction films, especially *Metropolis*, and T. S. Eliot's poetry. The first-person narrator of *Howl*—the unnamed "I" who sees and who is also a seer—is akin to Eliot's J. Alfred Prufrock and also akin to Tiresias, the blind Greek prophet who appears in Part III of *The Waste Land*. Like Tiresias, the narrator of *Howl* sees the secrets of the human heart and the human soul. In Part V of *The Waste Land*—"What the Thunder Said"—Eliot offers images of the collapse of the cities of the world. In Part III, "The Fire Sermon," he emphasizes the surreal quality of modern urban life, describing London as a city that's unreal. Ginsberg borrowed Eliot's images. In his journal he wrote, "I came to the window and glanced out into the night space at the unreal city below in which I inhabit a building." He envisioned the Sir Francis Drake as a "Golem waiting for the Rabbi of electricity to pull the switch for it to topple forward into the city destroying." Curiously, when he came to write *Howl*, he didn't define his robot-monster with Jewish or Hebrew images. The rabbi and the Golem both vanished; Buddha and Christ took their place, and the poem became increasingly Christian and Buddhist, in large part under the influence of Kerouac, who was studying Buddhism and sharing his studies with Allen.

For years, Ginsberg had been writing poems about the destruction of the cities of the world. In "Two Sonnets" (1948), he depicts New York as a "City of horrors . . . so much like Hell" and a "tomb of souls." As in *The Waste Land*, the cities of the world are falling down: London is burning, San Francisco is collapsing, and Moscow is dying. Those apocalyptic images came bubbling to the surface again in San Francisco, and in *Howl* they found near-perfect expression. That expression took months to develop, though he didn't like to admit it. Slowly but surely his notebook images of the "Unreal City" evolved into the surreal

New York of *Howl*, and gradually the notebook descriptions of the archetypal Towers of Hell turned into the real tenements that appear in the poem. In Ginsberg's peyote-induced vision of the "Unreal City," there wasn't a single living soul. When he came to write *Howl*, he populated his city with a cast of dead souls and underground men. His real friends, the hipsters who lived in poverty in cold-water flats and quested for holy visions, provided the inspiration. Some of his acquaintances also served as models for the poem's cast of squares: the book editors, the men in their gray flannel suits, and the effeminate fellows who work in the fashion industry.

## Megalopolis

Ginsberg knew New York of the 1940s better than he knew any place in the world, better even than Paterson in the 1930s—which he would describe in detail in *Kaddish*. By turning to New York, he turned to a rich body of personal lore. New York was his library and his museum, his archeological site and his archive. By the time he moved to California, he said, he had "given up on New York 'cause it was too restrictive and too much in the closet and too academic." All that was true. But New York never gave up on him, never let go of his imagination. The city haunted him, stalked him, and seduced him. Nearly a dozen American cities appear in the pages of *Howl*: Atlantic City, Baltimore, Birmingham, Denver, Houston, Laredo, Los Alamos, Newark, and Paterson. In *Howl*, America is a nation of cities and New York is the city of cities, the megalopolis. With the exception of a few brief interludes, Ginsberg had lived in New York for nearly a decade—on the Upper West Side and the Lower East Side, as well as in Harlem and Lenox Hill. New York was embedded in his consciousness. He prided himself on his firsthand knowledge of Times Square, Greenwich Village, Rockefeller Center, where he worked briefly for United Press International, and of the legendary streets of Manhattan—Fifth Avenue, Wall Street, Madison Avenue, and Forty-Second Street.

There wasn't a borough that he didn't know firsthand, and, with the exception of Queens, all five boroughs and many of their landmarks appear in *Howl*. The New York City subway system appears in *Howl*, and so does the Bronx Zoo, the Empire State Building, Chinatown, the Staten Island Ferry, the East River, the Hudson River, and City College of New York. Ginsberg's old haunts also appear—from Bickford's Cafeteria to Fugazzi Bar & Grill. Other New York landmarks appeared in early drafts of *Howl*—Birdland, the jazz club where Charlie Parker performed, as well as Longchamps, the legendary restaurant, but they were cut. Long Island appeared in an early version, but it too was cut. There are dozens of precise images of life in New York: fire escapes, tenement roofs, storefronts, neon signs, steam heat, blinking traffic lights, and the pushcarts of the street peddlers. Ginsberg captured the ambiance and the atmosphere of New York—its real and surreal weather. He filled his canvas with the colors of New York: the "drear light of Zoo"; "submarine light of Bickford's"; and the "darkness under the bridge." He recorded the sounds of New York—the "noise of wheels," the "ashcan rantings," and the wailing of the Staten Island Ferry.

There are almost no dates in the poem, and there are very few references to specific historical events. There are references to "wars," "wartime," and to the "scholars of war," but what wars and what wartime, Ginsberg doesn't say. It's an Orwellian world of constant and continuous war—"eternal / war" is the phrase Ginsberg uses in Part III of *Howl*. Still, if he refuses to place his poem in a specific year or even a decade, he is very particular about the time of day. It's usually nighttime, often midnight and even "winter midnight" in *Howl*. The same dreadful experiences transpire one night after another, as though day never dawns, as though the season of darkness never ends. Occasionally, night seems friendly and protective, but mostly nighttime is terrifying and lonely. The characters have "waking nightmares." They write compulsively all night, talk uncontrollably all night, listen to jazz habitually all night. On those rare occasions when the sun rises and morning arrives, it's rarely a bright, new day. The characters drag "themselves through the negro streets at dawn looking for an angry / fix." When afternoons arrive they're as flat as "stale beer."

### Great Suicidal Dramas

By 1955, Ginsberg knew at least half a dozen individuals who had either attempted or committed suicide. He had listened to Kerouac talk about suicide for years, and he'd watched Burroughs's self-destructiveness, too. There were his own ongoing suicidal impulses and there was suicidal American society at large— American military and material self-destructiveness. But by the time he wrote *Howl*, he could look at suicide with a sense of ironical detachment and even with a sense of humor. Like his friends and acquaintances—and like Ginsberg himself—the characters in *Howl* create "great suicidal dramas." They leap "off fire / escapes off windowsills off Empire State," and, like Tuli Kupferberg, who lived to tell the tale of his attempt at suicide, off the

Brooklyn Bridge. Ginsberg's hipsters throw "themselves under meat trucks" and "cut their wrists three times successively unsuccessfully." Even when they aren't actively trying to kill themselves, they're barely surviving. They stagger, cower, sink, fall to their knees, drag their feet, and fade out. No one stands tall or walks with a sense of dignity, head held high. Still, Ginsberg extends compassion toward his cast of drug addicts, suicides, outlaws, criminals, and depressives. As he noted, Part I of *Howl* is a "lament for the Lamb in America with instances of remarkable lamb-like youths." The youths of Part I are "burned alive in their innocent flannel suits on Madison Avenue." In Ginsberg's eyes, the advertising industry, the fashion industry, and the book industry are at the very heart of the inferno. They dominate the ninth circle of his urban hell.

The New York of *Howl* is bleak and depressed, but the language is exhilarating, especially in alliterative phrases like "battered bleak of brain / all drained of brilliance" and in playful, surrealistic images like the "drunken taxicabs of Absolute Reality." How right he was to make the ubiquitous New York taxicab into an emblem of the tangible world, and how playful and delightful an allusion to Rimbaud's image of the "drunken boat." Ginsberg describes a deadly, destructive world, but his poem is alive from beginning to end. There's a tremendous sense of velocity. Things and people are in constant motion, and constantly clashing. In the midst of death, destruction, sadness, and suicide, there's gallows humor and madhouse humor. The characters throw "their watches off the roof to cast their ballot for Eternity," and they appear "on the West Coast investigating the FBI in beards and shorts." It's an absurdly comic world—topsy-turvy—and sometimes it seems like it's right out of a Marx Brothers' movie. As

Ginsberg himself pointed out, his poem was a "tragic custard-pie comedy of wild phrasing."

In *Howl*, Ginsberg's hipsters are on never-ending joyless rides in the inferno of New York. They wander "around and around" and chain "themselves to subways for the endless ride." They also escape from New York and travel across America. *Howl* follows the journeys—in search of sex, drugs, and spirituality—of his friends Kerouac and Burroughs, who are vividly described in the passage, "who retired to Mexico to cultivate a habit, or Rocky Mount to tender Buddha / or Tangiers to boys." Ginsberg biographers Barry Miles and Michael Schumacher have argued that *Howl* isn't about Kerouac or Burroughs; yet they are deeply embedded in the poem from beginning to end. Cassady's travels are depicted here, too, as he goes "out whoring through Colorado in myriad stolen night-cars" and seduces women in gas stations, alleys, and on mountaintops. In the 1940s, Ginsberg had traveled to Colorado, Texas, Mexico, and Dakar, and *Howl* traces his odyssey. It's not a linear journey; there is no straight line here and no strict chronological order. The poem zigzags across the continent, painting a collage of the whole country. By the end of the poem, America becomes the main character, and the poem itself turns into a paean to the nation. Not to the nation depicted in *Life* and *Look*, but to America's outcasts and downtrodden.

### The Suffering of America's Naked Mind

At the end of Part I, Ginsberg describes his literary journey— the process of writing *Howl;* thus *Howl* is also a poem about itself, a poem that refers to itself and communicates with itself: an autotelic poem. Ginsberg depicts himself as he runs "through the icy streets obsessed with a sudden flash / of the alchemy of the use of the ellipse the catalogue the meter." At the end of Part I, he sees himself "confessing out the soul to conform to the rhythm of thought in his / naked and endless head." Now, he isn't only a poet of New York, Denver, or Texas, but of the entire country, and he identifies himself as an inspired jazz musician—a saxophonist—who blows the "suffering of America's naked mind." Part I ends with a sense of triumph and personal satisfaction.

It made sense to end his poem with an account of the act of writing the poem. But *Howl* wasn't done with Ginsberg; the poem wasn't completed yet. The peyote-induced image of the Sir Francis Drake Hotel—the "Drake Monster," as he called it—came back to haunt him. In August of 1955, nine months after his first hallucination in San Francisco, he took peyote again—this time with Peter Orlovsky, the new love of his life. "We wandered on peyote all downtown," he wrote Kerouac. "Saw Moloch Moloch smoking building in red glare downtown . . . with robot upstairs eyes and skullface, in smoke, again." Now for the first time he gave the monster a specific name, a name from the Old Testament, which he had read as a boy and on his voyage to Dakar and was now rereading. He began to write about Moloch—not on his typewriter, but by hand at the bottom of the page of the "who" section that he'd already written. His first description of Moloch was short—it added up to less than a full page. Here again Ginsberg borrowed from his memories of gloomy New York, and once again he wrote about subways, garbage cans, and ugliness. He also offered two powerful images of children— "children screaming under the stairs," and "children breaking their / backs under the subway. Breaking their backs trying to lift the / Whole City on their backs." The "Whole City" is icy, heavy

New York City; Ginsberg's children carry the weight of "Rocke-feller Center tons." They also carry the immense political weight of the twentieth century on their own backs, and that seems to be how Ginsberg felt as a child growing up in the 1930s in a left-wing household. "Hitler! Stalin!" he wrote in the first manuscript draft of Part II, echoing the names he'd heard so often at home in Paterson. The Moloch section of *Howl* was as dark and de-pressing as anything he had written, but a new note of joy could also be heard. The children raise the city to "Heaven which ex-ists and is everywhere about us." Even in the inferno, paradise might be found.

### Cottage in the Western Night

Soon after he wrote the initial draft of the "Moloch" section of *Howl*, Ginsberg moved from San Francisco to Berkeley, and in Berkeley—"the campustown," as he called it—he became even more optimistic. *Howl* became more hopeful, too. The last image in the poem—it's almost picture-postcard perfect—is of a "cot-tage in the Western / night," an idyllic sanctuary from the inferno of the American megalopolis. The image of the cottage was in-spired by the real cottage at 1624 Milvia Street in Berkeley, where Ginsberg lived from the summer of 1955 to the summer of 1956. Sixteen twenty-four was a commune of sorts—the perfect place to envision a more perfect world and more perfect human beings. Philip Whalen lived there and so did Jack Kerouac, briefly—af-ter returning from Mexico and before leaving for North Carolina to visit his sister. The full-time residents were joined by friends like Neal Cassady and lovers like the twenty-year-old woman who appears in Kerouac's *The Dharma Bums* as "sex mad and man mad." It was on Milvia Street, his mini-paradise, that Ginsberg wrote Part III of *Howl*—the most playful and the most joyful section of the poem—and where he also rewrote and revised Parts I and II. At 1624 Milvia, he also wrote several signature poems about Berkeley, including "Sather Gate Illumination," which describes the campus at the University of California at Berkeley, and "America," in which the Berkeley Public Library makes a brief appearance. His most significant Berkeley poem is "A Strange New Cottage in Berkeley," which he wrote in 1955 but that wasn't published until the mid-1960s, in *Reality Sandwiches.*

In "A Strange New Cottage in Berkeley," Ginsberg describes a glorious afternoon as he putters lazily about his house and in his garden. It's another poem written in accord with Kerouac's idea of sketching. It's also worlds away from the eschatological emphasis on last things—the "last fantastic book," the "last door," and the "last telephone"—that appear in *Howl.* The man, not the cottage, is at the center of this poem about genesis, and the self-portrait is of an American Adam who smokes marijuana and works without an Eve, without a snake, and where eating the fruit of the tree doesn't bring calamity or disaster. Under the hot sun, Ginsberg prunes the blackberries, waters his vegetables and his flowers, giving "godly extra drops" to the string beans and the daisies. (He's an Adam who plays God.) When he's hungry, he picks and eats the plums from a small tree that he describes as "an angel thoughtful of my stomach." Life seems perfect in "A Strange New Cottage in Berkeley." By all appearances, Ginsberg's life at 1624 Milvia was idyllic, too. In a seductive letter he wrote to Jack in August 1955, Allen describes the thirty-five-dollar-a-month rental as a "Shakespearean Arden cottage with brown shingles and flowers all about, big sweet garden, private."

Kerouac was so impressed by the glowing description that he joined Ginsberg in the "little rose-covered cottage," and that was exactly what Allen wanted—Jack's companionship while he revised *Howl*, and when he performed *Howl*, too, at the Six Gallery. Kerouac loved the "perfect little kitchen," the "perfect little bathroom," the little library "with hundreds of books from Catullus to Pound," the long-playing records of Bach, Beethoven, and Ella Fitzgerald, and Ginsberg's "three-speed Webcor phonograph that played loud enough to blast the roof off." With Bach and Fitzgerald in the background while he was rewriting *Howl*, it's no wonder that he called the poem a "jazz mass" and a "Bach fugue." The poem took on the complexity and the spontaneity of Bach and the exhilaration and the soulfulness of jazz.

At his rose-covered cottage in Berkeley, Ginsberg made his poem less topical and less specific to New York—he expunged the phrase "Rockefeller Centers Tons" and dispensed with "Hitler! Stalin!" At the same time, he added a wealth of specific details about his monster. With revision, Moloch became the "vast stone of war!" and Moloch was linked to "Robot apartments!" and "demonic industries!" Ginsberg also drew increasingly on his own life, especially his memories of childhood, which sprang up as he wrote *Howl*. In Part I, he describes his vulnerability as a boy at school "who broke down crying in white gymnasiums naked and trembling before / the machinery of other skeletons." He also added passages that describe his self-abandonment and the ways that the culture of repression was embedded in his own consciousness from an early age. "Moloch who entered my soul early!" he wrote with a sense of sadness. "Moloch who frightened me out of my natural ec- / stasy!"

In 1975, twenty years after he wrote *Howl*, he insisted that the "key phrase" of the whole poem was "Moloch whose name is the / mind!"—a phrase that derives from Blake's image of "mind-forg'd manacles." What Ginsberg seemed to be saying was that the human mind was its own worst enemy—a notion that was reinforced by his readings in Buddhism in 1955. *Howl* sounds a note of ambivalence about the causes of human suffering. Ginsberg offers two contrary, though not necessarily irreconcilable, ideas—one Marxist and political, the other Buddhist and spiritual. In *Howl*, human beings are the victims of war, injustice, and poverty—capitalist society inflicts suffering. But human beings are also the authors of their own suffering. While the author rages against Moloch and identifies with the Blakean "lamb-like youths," he also suggests that the lamb-like youths aren't simply innocent victims. They have led themselves to slaughter, much as they have "chained themselves to subways for the endless ride from Battery to holy / Bronx." *Howl* derives its power from Ginsberg's ability to entertain what Keats called "negative capability"—the strength of mind to hold "opposite, contradictory thoughts . . . without an irritable reaching after fact and reason." Ambivalence, irony, and paradox are at the heart of *Howl*, and in that sense it's a poem of the 1940s and the era of Eliot and the New Criticism. But it's also a poem of the 1950s and the era when Buddhism began to influence poets and writers from Salinger to Kerouac. Ginsberg would say he wanted a world without war and without the Bomb, and yet he would also say that he loved the Bomb. Hating it and wanting to ban it would only add to its power over humanity, he felt. The point was to negate it through acceptance. By the end of *Howl*, he'd come to that realization. The Bomb was holy too.

# CHAPTER EIGHT

# Mythological
# References

*Howl* was shaped by a host of writers, many of whom belonged to antithetical literary traditions: John Donne and William Blake; T. S. Eliot and Walt Whitman; Arthur Rimbaud and William Carlos Williams; the prophets of the Old Testament and Herman Melville. It was a complex heritage to which Ginsberg belonged and it was constantly shifting. Probably no two writers influenced him more profoundly than William Burroughs and Jack Kerouac. Of what use was the literary past, he wondered when he settled in San Francisco, if the present moment was so exhilarating? At times, Burroughs and Kerouac seemed to offer all the literary influence he needed.

When he wrote *Howl*, he saw America through his own eyes as a land of the lost and the lonely—a land of terror and beauty. He also saw the country through the eyes of Burroughs and Kerouac, and he told his story with Kerouac's epic lyricism and with Burroughs's paranoid and conspiratorial vision of the atomic age.

Shortly before he began to compose *Howl*, he wrote "On Burroughs' Work," which serves as homage to Burroughs and as a concise statement of his own aesthetic. "A naked lunch is natural to us," he wrote. "But allegories are so much lettuce. / Don't hide the madness." It was a useful reminder to himself not to conceal the naked truth and to avoid allegory. Joan Burroughs was also on his mind in the months before he began to write *Howl*. In "Dream Record: June 8, 1955," he froze, as in a photograph, the last moment of her tragic life: "her / face restored to a fine beauty / tequila and salt had made strange / before the bullet in her brow." "Dream Record" was a rehearsal for *Howl*, a poem that enabled him to salvage the past and to resurrect memories of old friends. Joan's beautiful face of death and the faces of his friends from the 1940s—William Cannastra, Phil White, Herbert Huncke, and Walter Adams—haunted him when he sat down to write *Howl*.

No ghost haunted him more than the ghost of Jack Kerouac. Even as he wrote his poem he envisioned Kerouac reading and responding to it. He remembered their quarrels about art and autobiography, language and literature, and now he took Kerouac's side in their ongoing quarrel. In June of 1952, after reading the latest draft of *On the Road*, he fired off an angry letter to Kerouac. "It's crazy (not merely inspired crazy) but unrelated crazy," he exclaimed. And he fumed, "It's so personal, it's so full of sex language, so full of our local mythological references, I don't know if it would make sense to any publisher." Identical charges could be leveled against *Howl*. It too sounds like the "confessions of an insane person." It too seems unrelated, disjointed, and nonsensical. Moreover, like *On the Road*, *Howl* is personal, local, and mythological. It mythologizes Ginsberg's own life as well as the lives of a small group of friends "destroyed by madness." It also offers candid "sex talk." In *Howl* Ginsberg wrote the kind of literature he had warned Kerouac against. Kerouac himself had doubts about his and Ginsberg's habit of creating their own contemporary myths. "Who are Allen and I to invent private poetic myths in a real, serious world?" he asked. Like Kerouac, Ginsberg took ordinary, unknown men—Cassady and Solomon—and turned them into archetypal Americans caught up in the madness of the society. He made Solomon into a mythic lunatic ranting and raving behind the bars of the asylum, and he turned Cassady into an icon of the relentless searcher in quest of ultimate freedom. He took their language—the language of drug addicts, homosexuals, and sexual outlaws—and brought it where it had rarely if ever been before: into the pages of American poetry.

### Sex Language

In *Howl*, Ginsberg describes anal sex, oral sex, and what middle-class Americans in 1955 would surely have called promiscuous sex, in a language that expands the vocabulary of poetry. If no reputable New York publishing house would touch *Howl* in the mid-1950s, it was precisely because the "sex talk" was pornographic and subject to criminal prosecution. *Lady's Chatterley's Lover* was still banned, and so were Henry Miller's *The Tropic of Cancer* and the *Tropic of Capricorn*. At a time when "fuck" was unprotected speech, Allen Ginsberg used that and other obscenities. Occasionally, he used polite words—"copulated," for example—but mostly slang: "cunt," "snatch," and "cock." *Howl* celebrates the "cocksman"—men and their penises, not women and their vaginas. Ginsberg's cocksmen have sex indiscriminately and scatter their seed "freely to whom / ever come who may."

There's no sex between married couples in *Howl* and no sex between longtime lovers, though there's occasional tenderness; one anonymous "sweetheart" appears in the poem. Sometimes sex is depicted romantically; the homosexual sailors are "human seraphim" who provide "caresses of / Atlantic and Caribbean love." Mostly there's a sense of despair and desperation about sex. The characters enjoy casual sex in "empty lots & diner / back-yards" and in "hometown alleys." Ginsberg's heroes hunger for sex much as they hunger for everything else in life, from food and wine to jazz and spirituality. Americans were insatiably hungry, he felt, and always trying to feed the emptiness inside with things, images, and their own inflated ideas of themselves.

The sexual hero of *Howl* is Neal Cassady, who appears as the "Adonis of Denver" and who is a "joy to / the memory of his innumerable lays of girls." Ginsberg describes Cassady "flashing buttocks under barns and naked in the lake," alluding, if obliquely, to his own sexual attraction to Cassady. But Ginsberg had to be careful to conceal the homosexual relationship that began in 1947, and that they resumed in 1954, when Ginsberg arrived at Cassady's house in San Jose—"Nowheresville"—Carolyn Cassady called it. Writing about romantic love between men was still a taboo topic in the 1940s. Men who had male muses had a "morbid pathology," Robert Graves wrote. "The main theme of poetry is, properly, the relations of man and woman, rather than those of man and man." In writing about Neal, Jack, Bill, and others, Allen went against the grain, and he felt defensive about it. As late as 1981, he felt that he had to justify writing love poems about men and young boys; the poem

"Old Love Story," in which he recounts and celebrates the theme of homosexual love through the ages, is an example.

In 1954, Kerouac had already given up on Neal as a friend and pal, though in the guise of Dean Moriarty, he would appear in 1957 as the hero of *On the Road*. Kerouac came to see Neal as an imposter; he had taken on "that familiar American pseudo-virility of workingman & basketball players, 'tough guy,'" he complained to John Clellon Holmes. Allen still revered him, still romanticized him as a working-class hero, and sexualized everything about him. "I dream beautiful sexual dreams and wake up burning with ardor and tenderness," he wrote of Cassady soon after he arrived in "legendary Calif[ornia]." What he wanted in the summer of 1954 was much the same as what he had wanted in the winter of 1947: a union of bodies and souls. There was intense sex in San Jose in the summer of 1954, but it wasn't beautiful, tender, or soulful. Neal abused Allen—though Allen seems to have encouraged the abuse. "I want to be your slave, suck your ass, suck your cock, you fuck me, you master me, you humiliate me," he wrote in his journal. "I want to be tied and whipped, spanked on the behind over knees, want to be made to cry and beg and weep for love." Neal provided pain without pleasure and torture without tenderness, and Allen was understandably distressed. "Neal has been cruel to me," he complained. "He makes me suck his cock. He orders me around. He makes me subservient."

In *Howl*, there isn't a peep about their intense, sadomasochistic relationship. Rather, Ginsberg chose to present Cassady as the Don Juan of the American West—a sexually liberated playboy—even as Hugh Hefner made it his mission in *Playboy* magazine (which began publication in 1954) to celebrate the sexual prowess of the heterosexual American male. While Hefner's playboy was suave and sophisticated, Ginsberg's playboy was a car thief who patronized whorehouses. Neal Cassady is the "secret hero" of *Howl* because his bisexuality remains under wraps. *Howl* conceals even as it reveals, covers up even as it appears to undress and go naked. Surely the public would have been shocked by Cassady's homosexuality—he was a married man with three children—as shocked as Carolyn Cassady was when she caught Allen and Neal in bed together, with Allen performing fellatio, as usual. The highly charged confrontation with Carolyn reminded Allen of his relationship with his mother, Naomi, and the "unbearable horror" of the childhood journey by bus he had taken with her to Lakewood, New Jersey, when he was a boy. On that trip his mother also outed him. These two women seemed larger than life; they seemed to have the power to make him feel both painfully insignificant and deeply ashamed. Carolyn was "nagging" and "violent"—a *"charnel"* who would "stain Neal," he insisted.

It's not surprising that the women in *Howl* are almost all shrews. In the mid-1950s Ginsberg embraced misogyny; he knew it and admitted it. "How I hate women," he wrote Kerouac in December 1954. In Part I of the poem, he borrows from Greek mythology and describes "three old shrews of fate." All of them are grotesquely "one eyed" and they're the sworn enemies of men. They're greedy and acquisitive—whore-like sisters to the mythical succubus. One shrew is associated with the "heterosexual dollar," another with seductiveness—she "winks out of the / womb"—and the last is a kind of evil fairy-tale witch who "does nothing but sit on her ass / and snip the intellectual golden threads of the craftsman's loom." He did, however, offer a fantasy of blissful sex with Carolyn and with Neal in "Love Poem on Theme by Whitman"—which he wrote at the Cassady home in San Jose and which was inspired by the erotic poems in Whitman's *Children of Adam*. Here he imagines himself in bed with Neal and Carolyn. He lies down between the "bridegroom" and the "bride" in a ménage à trois without jealousy, suspicion, or guilt. Their bodies are "fallen from heaven . . . / shuddering naked, hot hips and buttocks screwed into each / other." Even in this poem, which is meant to celebrate both the male and the female, it's the male who is less objectified. The bridegroom has a "cock." The bride only has a "hole." Ginsberg may have imitated Whitman, but he never wrote lines like those in which Whitman described the beauty of the "female form" and the "divine nimbus" of woman.

The fantasy of sex with Neal and Carolyn was never to be realized, but after Ginsberg moved to San Francisco from San Jose, other sexual fantasies began to come true. He had female lovers and male lovers and bedroom orgies with men and women. At last he felt that he was the great lover he had wanted to be. Robert LaVigne's sketches depict the pansexuality he enjoyed in San Francisco. In one sketch, Ginsberg is naked and in bed with a naked Peter Orlovsky and a naked Natalie Jackson. Now he felt that he could finally take pride in his own sexuality. "I'm changed in Calif[ornia], like a dream," he wrote Kerouac at the end of December 1954. A few weeks later, at the beginning of 1955, he told Jack, "Something great happens to me in Frisco. After girl now for first time in life boy." And there were boys and girls together in his own bed. The girl was Sheila Boucher Williams, who allowed almost everything sexual, including anal sex, and for a few weeks Ginsberg boasted that he was "living in splendor" with

Sheila. California was dream-like not because he was writing great poetry, but because he was enjoying great sex, and in his poems he added to the mythology of California as a land of sexual liberation, a vast erogenous zone.

The boy in his life was Peter Orlovsky, an ex–New Yorker with a mother who was crazy and with two older brothers, Nicholas and Julius, at Central Islip State Hospital. Peter's younger brother, Lafcadio, seemed likely to end up in a mental hospital, too. The whole family seemed insane. With Orlovsky as with Cassady, Ginsberg wanted a sexual relationship in which he would be the slave—the passive lover and the masochist. "I want to be tied to bed & screwed, whipped," he wrote when his mind turned to thoughts of sex with Orlovsky. Allen wanted to turn his "erotic imagination" into flesh and blood reality; he wanted "sexual ecstasy." If that wasn't enough, he also wanted a "mystical Sanctity union with God." Peter Orlovsky seemed like a highly qualified candidate for his immense enterprise. Orlovsky was young and impressionable, just twenty-three, and he was handsome. Further, he was attracted to women, which made him attractive to Allen, who found himself attracted to men—like Neal Cassady and Jack Kerouac—with wives and girlfriends. In Allen's fantasy, Peter would be the "master in bed" while he would be Peter's "master in book."

The advent of uninhibited homosexuality, which he was enjoying for the first time in his life, made him ecstatic. "I'm happy, Kerouac, your madman Allen's / finally made it: discovered a new young cat," he gushed in "Malest Cornifici Tuo Catullo," which was inspired by the work of Catullus, the Roman poet of lust and love whom he was reading and translating from Latin into English in 1955. (In an early draft of the poem that he wrote in his journal, he described Orlovsky not as a "new young cat," but as his "lost sex kid.") The heavenly sex didn't last long. Allen and Peter quarreled, slept in separate beds, and then separated—though they were soon back together again. Like almost all lovers, they had spats, and after their first spat, Ginsberg thought it was all over between them. In January 1955, looking back at what seemed like a brief affair, he felt guilty about his seduction of Peter; he'd stolen him from the painter Robert LaVigne and he was ashamed. He'd first seen Peter—or rather Peter's image—in LaVigne's portrait of him sitting naked. How romantic that was—to fall in love with a picture, not the real person! Now, after their breakup, he noted, "I hardly do know him, just my idea of him from a few pictures of Rob[er]t."

Ginsberg felt that he'd lost his innocence and gained a sense of evil. "The two of us doomed . . . as in [ Joseph] Conrad, [Henry] James," he moaned. Without Peter, he felt "alone in San Fran-[cisco]" and living through "empty days." He was either up or down, exhilarated or in despair, and he began to dream complex, wild dreams about madness and women. In one especially vivid dream that winter, he saw Natalie Jackson, along with his mother, Naomi, and the poet Ezra Pound. All three of them were in a mad-house that seemed to be a combination of St. Elizabeth's Hospital in Washington, D.C., and Greystone in New Jersey. It was a dream that went to the heart of his identity as a poet, and to his creativity, too: once again poetry and madness were indivisible.

### Inspired Crazy, Unrelated Crazy

For years, Ginsberg had been thinking and writing about mad-houses, madmen, and madness. Now, for the first time, he was conscious of those thoughts, and that consciousness moved him closer to *Howl*. "Madness! Madness!" he wrote in his journal in 1954. "Oh how often I hear that word in my brain." In 1955, he would go on hearing the word "madness," and as always he would feel ambivalent about it. There was the good kind of madness and the bad kind of madness, creative madness and self-destructive madness—"inspired crazy" and "unrelated crazy." In San Francisco, he once again found himself surrounded by madmen and madwomen; Natalie Jackson lived on the edge, and as Ginsberg knew, she was capable of doing something really crazy, which made her lovable and yet alarming. Natalie did finally do something crazy—leapt to her death from the roof of a building in San Francisco. So her name was added to the list of lost souls. Soon after she committed suicide, Ginsberg started an elegy about her in which he wondered if he should have given her "money? or more love? / or a rest home in my crazy lovely garden?" He might have finished his elegy about Natalie, but then his mother died and he had no choice but to write about Naomi, not Natalie. And yet perhaps there was some of Natalie's spirit in *Kaddish* after all.

Of all the men in his life in San Francisco, Neal seemed the craziest. He wandered through "North Beach talking about cunt," and he was obsessed about chess and Edgar Cayce. "Neal's madness," Ginsberg wrote in his journal, "makes me think I'm mad." He was ambivalent about his own madness, much as he was ambivalent about almost everything else, including his own sexuality. "There's something good about my kind of madness," he noted. What seems to have driven him madder than anything else was his own unresolved sexuality. "My mind is crazed by homosexuality," he wrote in his journal.

But he wasn't so crazed that he couldn't take care of himself. To make a living, he went to work for thirteen dollars a day at the Greyhound Bus Terminal in San Francisco, an experience mythologized by "In the Baggage Room at Greyhound," a neo-proletarian poem in which he calls himself "a communist"—with a small "c"—and in which he also describes himself provocatively and humorously as a worker with "pectoral muscles big as / vagina." To address his psychological and emotional issues he went into therapy—at one dollar a session at Langley Porter in San Francisco. For the first time in his life he found a psychiatrist whom he could trust, a therapist who loved poetry, especially Blake's poetry, and who had a sense of humor.

The son of a midwestern minister, Dr. Philip Hicks was born in 1928—which made him two years younger than Allen. "I was a naive twenty-six-year-old," Hicks would say years later. "I'd never met anyone like Allen before." After his boyhood in North Dakota, Philip Hicks attended medical school at Boston University, then moved to San Francisco to begin his career. "For the first few weeks of treatment Allen Ginsberg was prickly and snotty," Dr. Hicks remembered. "He was clean shaven and he wore a Brooks Brothers suit. Over the next year or so I saw his transformation to the wild poet of North Beach." Dr. Hicks played a pivotal role in Ginsberg's own metamorphosis and also in the evolution and development of *Howl*. In his psychiatric report at Langley Porter on October 11, 1955, Dr. Hicks noted that Allen Ginsberg had entered therapy a year earlier—on October 25, 1954—"to overcome a block in his writing." Over the course of therapy, Dr. Hicks noted that Ginsberg developed "greater acceptance of himself and began writing more profusely and being able to perform with less anxiety." The Langley Porter records show that Ginsberg ended his therapy just four days after he read *Howl* at the Six Gallery. The therapy had certainly helped him perform with less anxiety. The reading at the Six Gallery on October 7, 1955, seemed to be all the proof he needed that his therapy was an unmitigated success. Dr. Hicks gave his patient the permission he seems to have needed to feel proud of himself as a poet, and to explore, without shame, his own homosexuality. "He actually liked me and wanted to see me pleased and happy and free to develop in my *own* way," Ginsberg told Jane Kramer. Dr. Hicks liked his patient and his poetry, and he refused to take a traditional Freudian approach and scold Allen for his homosexuality as the doctors at the New York State Psychiatric Institute had done in 1949. He also helped Ginsberg come to terms with the trauma of his childhood and to alleviate his fear of going mad—like his mother, Naomi, and like Carl Solomon, who was an inmate again, this time at Pilgrim State Hospital on Long Island. "He loved his mother—her spirit, her moxie and her communism—and he kept part of her close, but he also rejected part of her," Dr. Hicks explained. "He was afraid that he might be schizophrenic, too. He had this deep-seated fear of losing it, of becoming mentally ill. Carl Solomon was a close friend, and his institutionalization was alarming to Allen, too, which is part of the reason he came to Langley Porter for therapy. I told him that I didn't think that he'd end up in a mental hospital like Carl or like Naomi."

The therapeutic sessions with Dr. Hicks helped Ginsberg write *Howl*, and the process of writing *Howl* proved to be therapeutic, too. His art had healing powers. Ginsberg resolved his fears of going mad by writing about the madness of Carl Solomon, who appears briefly in Part I of *Howl* and then again in Part III as the major character. The first line of the last section of *Howl* begins "Carl Solomon! I'm with you in Rockland." His name was perfect for a poem about madness and wisdom; like the Solomon of the Old Testament, Ginsberg's Solomon was a wise man. All the "Solomons" of the modern world were in madhouses, and that's what was wrong with the modern world, Ginsberg felt. Neal Cassady didn't seem to mind the fact that Allen mythologized his sex life, but Solomon was disturbed that Allen altered the facts about his mental condition. He complained vociferously and Allen apologized profusely for his "unlicensed poetic version of his adventures." Solomon had a long list of complaints about Allen and about *Howl*. "I was never in Rockland," he wrote. Indeed, he wasn't at Rockland but at Pilgrim State Hospital. "Rockland" sounded far more menacing than "Pilgrim State"— it was a cold, hard place, not a place for pilgrims. Solomon also objected to the way that Ginsberg described him as a mental patient at the New York State Psychiatric Institute in 1949, where the two men first met, and about his days as a college student, too. "This section of the poem garbles history completely," Solomon wrote of the stanza that begins "who threw potato salad at CCNY lecturers on Dadaism."

Solomon insisted that Ginsberg had it all wrong: the potato salad incident took place off campus, not on campus; the college where he studied was Brooklyn College, not CCNY; and the incident itself was an expression *of* Dadaism, not a protest *against* Dadaism. In *Howl*, Ginsberg writes that in the "madhouse," the doctors gave Solomon "insulin Metrazol electricity / hydrotherapy psychotherapy." Solomon clarified the record. "No Metrazol or electricity for me," he explained. In fact, it was Naomi, not Carl Solomon, who received Metrazol and electric shock therapy. Allen appropriated Solomon's name and felt guilty about it. "Although I do believe in candor," he explained, "it becomes embarrassing when the writing gets circulated widely enough so that my candor involves other people. So it's like an invasion of other people's privacy."

In *Howl* he invaded Solomon's privacy at the same time that he concealed his own secrets; for example, he never overtly describes himself as a patient in a mental hospital. In his own defense, Ginsberg insisted that *Howl* was a "gesture of wild solidarity, a message into the asylum, a sort of heart's trumpet call." His compassion and empathy are apparent in the refrain, "I'm with you in Rockland." From the beginning to the end of the poem, the "I" who tells the story of madness moves from an observer to a participant. The narrator becomes less detached, more involved, more implicated in the tale he tells. The *he* evolves into a *we*. And yet Ginsberg also held himself back. He turned himself into a diagnosing doctor and Carl into a patient under his observation, especially in the phrase, "you're madder than I am."

Thirty years after he finished *Howl*, Ginsberg admitted that he was "mistaken in my diagnosis of his 'case.'" Carl Solomon was not madder than he was. His "lifelong virtues," Allen wrote, included "endurance, familial fidelity and ultimate balance." Then, too, he realized that while he sacrificed Solomon, he simultaneously protected Naomi. Granted, when he addresses Solomon in Part III, he observes that "you imitate the shade of my mother." But the passage does not explain what he meant. It wasn't until he wrote, "Footnote to Howl" in 1955 that he clearly made the link between Carl Solomon and Naomi Ginsberg. "Holy my mother in the insane asylum!" he wrote. It wasn't until 1986 that he explained, "I'd used Mr. Solomon's return to the asylum as occasion for a masque on my feelings toward my mother, in itself an ambiguous situation since I had signed the papers giving permission for her lobotomy." He added, "Thereby hangs another tale." It was a tale that he would never tell—how and why he gave permission for Naomi's lobotomy. He didn't tell it in *Kaddish* and not in "White Shroud" or "Black Shroud," the last two poems he wrote about his mother. His relationship with Naomi would remain shrouded, and so would his own real experience with Carl Solomon at the New York State Psychiatric Institute.

# CHAPTER NINE

# Famous Authorhood

## Ripeness Is All

In San Francisco in the summer of 1955, Ginsberg was surrounded by friends and lovers—Peter Orlovsky, Sheila Williams, Peter Du Peru, Robert LaVigne, Natalie Jackson, Neal Cassady, and Al Sublette. He loved them dearly and needed them for support, but they came between him and his work. A literary circle was essential, but so was solitude. More and more, he began to turn his back on the group, withdraw into his own private world, and type at his desk, even while Neal, Natalie, and Peter drank, talked, smoked, and made love. Finally, by the height of summer, he had all the solitude he required. Peter went to New York to rescue his youngest brother from a mental hospital, Neal and Natalie turned to one another, and Sheila took a new husband. There was no one to distract him, and he set to work in earnest. For several months, he had been experimenting—in his journal and in drafts of poems he never published—

with what T. S. Eliot called the "telescoping of images." He was linking seemingly unrelated images and ideas in a brief phrase. Then, too, he'd been exploring Eliot's idea that the poet's mission was "to find the verbal equivalent for states of mind and feeling" so that the poem captured the rapid, often random, movements of the mind itself. There were other influences in addition to Eliot—including Japanese haiku and William Carlos Williams. Ginsberg would acknowledge them, but didn't acknowledge Eliot, though his journals provide a trail that leads directly back to Eliot. In San Francisco in April and May 1955, he was reading Eliot aloud with Peter Orlovsky, and he recorded in his journal one of the key lines from *The Waste Land:* "These fragments I have shored against my ruins." His own poem would be made up of bits and pieces and it would be written to keep himself from falling apart and going mad, as Eliot had done at the time he was writing *The Waste Land*. Ginsberg was also studying Eliot's work, including "Sweeney among the Nightingales," one of his favorite poems, and consciously imitating Eliot even as he drew closer to Whitman.

In a journal entry that he entitled "A Few Notes on Composition," he wrote this advice to himself: "Join images as they are joined in the mind: only thus can two images connect like wires and spark." And he told himself, as William Carlos Williams had told him years earlier, "Do away with symbols and present the facts of the experience. They will speak for themselves." In the winter and spring of 1955, he could feel the wires connecting in his own head. He could see the sparks fly and his whole body seemed electrified. In *Howl*, the image of the "hydrogen jukebox" is the clearest example of what he had in mind when he wrote, in

*Howl* itself, about making "incarnate gaps in Time & Space through images / juxtaposed." "Hydrogen jukebox" links the hydrogen bomb and the jukebox to make an infernal machine that seems perfect for an age of mechanization and mass destruction. How he arrived at the image of the "hydrogen jukebox" he never explained, though the image appears in his journal in 1955 as an example of what he called the "apt relation of dissimilars"—and an example, too, of Western Haiku. Ginsberg's journals show that he had been preoccupied for nearly two decades with bombs and bombing—ever since the Nazi bombings of Spain in 1937, and increasingly after the dropping of atomic bombs on Hiroshima and Nagasaki in 1945. The explosion of the first hydrogen bomb in 1952, followed by the testing of bigger H-bombs in the mid-1950s, rekindled his fascination with bombs, bombing, and nuclear destruction. In the winter of 1955 he wrote in his journal about the "evil brilliance of [the] H Bomb," concluding that the "apocalypse is here." In *Howl* he would write one of the great poems of apocalypse of the twentieth century, a poem in which global disaster seemed imminent, and terror was lurking in the next room. Perhaps he was a paranoid alarmist—or maybe it was prescience—but in any case he thought that his own balding, as well as some of Cassady's medical problems, might be the result of nuclear fallout.

"Ripeness is all." That line from *King Lear* had been reverberating in his head ever since he was an undergraduate at Columbia. Now he understood it more profoundly than ever before. Near the start of his therapy at Langley Porter—feeling that he was on the verge of a personal breakthrough—he wrote, "The time seems to be ripe. 'I am ready.'" Now, the time was ripe for poetry and he was ripe, too, riper than he had ever been before.

In the short poem "Blessed be the Muses," which he wrote just before he began to write *Howl*, he thanked the muses for "dancing around my desk, / crowning my balding head / with Laurel." He was ready to be inspired and at the same time prepared for the worldly fame that he felt was forthcoming. "I suppose I'll wake up to find myself famous," he wrote in the summer of 1955.

When he celebrated his twenty-ninth birthday on June 3, 1955, he marked the occasion in his journal, recording a favorite line—"I fill'd with woes the passing Wind"—from Blake's poem "The Crystal Cabinet." In a year he would be thirty. Time was running out; soon enough he would be like Eliot's J. Alfred Prufrock, who worries about growing older and showing his age. At twenty-nine, Ginsberg was already conscious of growing old, losing his hair, and not having any immortal poetry to show for his efforts. Time was running out, too, on the 1940s—the decade he was eager to explore, map, and define for all America. It had to be now, or he'd forget it forever—lose the sense of it and the feel of it, the sense of how different the 1940s were from the dreary, depressing 1950s. Everything in President Eisenhower's America seemed "to run on a routine of unspiritualized mediocrity," he complained in his journal. "Standardization and mechanization and control of the individual psyche" seemed "a fait accompli." The arrival of television was especially alarming. In San Francisco at night, he gazed at apartments and saw "futuristic television light windows" and terrifying television antennae on rooftops. Television seemed to be taking over, and in the first draft of *Howl*, he offered an image of "television treetop," which suggested television towering above trees, the machine triumphing over nature. When he revised the manuscript, he took out the word "television," substituting the lines "Moloch whose smokestacks and / antennae crown the cities," conveying how television dominated the landscape. He had learned that a part could express a more vivid sense of the whole, making it seem more ominous.

Ginsberg and Kerouac often took opposing sides on electoral politics and the political issues of the day. In 1952 Kerouac supported Republican senator Robert Taft while Ginsberg supported Democratic senator Adlai Stevenson. And, while Kerouac defended Senator Joseph McCarthy, Ginsberg reviled him. Still, Ginsberg saw eye to eye with Kerouac about many of the alarming cultural shifts in America in the 1950s. In his essay "About the Beat Generation," Kerouac observed that in the early 1950s, and especially during the Korean War, "a sinister new kind of efficiency appeared in America." It was the era of "silent conformity" resulting from the war and from the "universalization of Television," he wrote. Even *Dragnet* and Sergeant Friday seemed sinister to Kerouac; the hit program was symbolic of the "Polite Total Police Control" that had become a way of life in America. Allen couldn't have agreed more. The 1940s were a dark time and yet when compared to the 1950s, they seemed more spiritual and less conformist. Now, he was afraid, as Kerouac was afraid, that teenagers—the "new Rock n' Roll youth," in Kerouac's phrase—would never know what it had been like to be a hipster in the 1940s. When Kerouac looked back at the 1940s, he remembered "a generation of crazy, illuminated hipsters" who were "characters of a special spirituality." To his way of thinking, they were "subterranean heroes" because they "turned from the 'freedom' machine of the West and were taking drugs, digging bop, having flashes of insight, experiencing the 'derangement of the senses,' talking strange, being poor and glad." Kerouac might have been thinking of Ginsberg when he wrote that passage. Ginsberg had done everything that Kerouac described—he took drugs, talked a strange argot, listened to bop, experienced what Rimbaud called "the derangement of the senses," and experienced profound visions. He had turned from the machine of the West to find his own individual freedom. Now, in 1955, Ginsberg felt that it was time to sing about those subterranean heroes of the 1940s, and to sing about himself, too—to use himself as a model for his own art.

Ever since he arrived in San Francisco in 1954, he had experimented with drugs, but when he wrote *Howl*, he didn't resort to marijuana, peyote, or amphetamines. There were no last-minute visions or hallucinations. He was as clear-headed as he'd ever been. It seems likely that he wrote all night long—he was a nocturnal poet—and it seems likely, too, that nighttime in San Francisco reminded him of nighttime in New York, the city that fills the pages of *Howl*. Ginsberg enjoyed the company of fellow poets, but he also insisted on isolation—never more so than when he was writing *Howl*. "I was alone," he wrote, describing the experience of writing *Howl*. By his own account, he "sat idly" at his desk one afternoon looking out a window that faced Montgomery Street in San Francisco's financial district—which reminded him of Wall Street in New York—waiting to be inspired. The typewriter in front of him was secondhand, and on his desk was a stack of "cheap scratch paper." He could hear the sounds of the city as well as the sound of his own voice reverberating in his head; it was the sound of his voice that helped him begin to put words down on paper.

Ever since 1949, he had been recording himself reading his own poems. When he arrived at Cassady's house in San Jose in the summer of 1954, he began to record himself again, and now, a year later, he was familiar with the sound of his own voice and confident of where he might take it. From the start, he envisioned *Howl* as a poem to be performed in public, not simply read silently in private. He saw himself reading *Howl* aloud to a small, select audience that would include Cassady and Kerouac. He was alone at his desk at 1010 Montgomery Street, but he imagined that Kerouac "would hear [the] sound" of his "long saxophone-like chorus lines." And, like an inspired saxophonist about to perform for an audience, he was conscious of his own breathing and the breath he would need to compose and perform a long poem with long lines. *Howl* was a kind of exercise in breathing, as well as an experiment in language and form. "Each line of *Howl* is a single breath unit," he explained. It was a hot breath, too, "not cooler average-daily-talk short breath," and his long breath, he felt, enabled him "to mouth more madly."

But he didn't mouth madly at the start of *Howl*. As Berkeley professor and ex–poet laureate Robert Hass observed, when Ginsberg wrote the opening lines of the poem, he wasn't instantly on fire but "just getting warmed up." As you read the manuscript revisions and listen to his recordings of the poem, it's clear that he became more self-confident and excited as he went along. Gradually, the work took on a rhythm of its own, and the rhythm kept him going. When he reached the fourth stanza he changed direction dramatically and wrote one of the poem's pivotal lines, "Who poverty and tatters and hollow-eyed and high sat up smoking in the / supernatural darkness of cold-water flats floating across the tops of / cities contemplating jazz." He would repeat the word "who" another fifty-nine times before reaching the end of Part 1. Now, he had the fixed point he needed and to which he could return. He also had a license for flux and flexibility. With the fourth stanza he was, as Hass noted, finally "on a roll" from which there was no stopping. As Ginsberg himself explained, he knew from the fourth stanza on that he could depend "on the word 'who' to keep the beat . . . to keep measure, return to and take off from again onto another streak of invention." Page after page, he came back to the word "who," coining one dazzling image after another. He was in the midst of what Carl Solomon called a "verbal orgy"—one image triggered another. Moreover, he was doing what he had long wanted to do—steer away from abstract symbols and stick to the facts, as he knew them. When he wrote, "I saw the best minds of my generation destroyed by madness," he meant to be literal, not metaphorical. He was a reporter and his obligation, as he saw it, was to the "truth of the reporting." From his point of view, he had in fact stood witness as many of the brightest men and women from his own generation—Kerouac, Solomon, William and Joan Burroughs—had gone crazy; now he mythologized the madness of his friends. To some Californians, like Robert Hass, the opening—"I saw the best minds of my generation"—sounded like "East Coast chauvinism," the words of a New Yorker who assumed that the "best minds" were all from New York. And yet the first line wasn't a fatal flaw. The poem carried readers along and won them over.

### Revising It

How long he sat at his typewriter—how many hours or days— isn't clear. He certainly never said. At some point, he removed the last page of the manuscript from the typewriter and began to read what he'd written and to make changes in pencil. Though he knew that he wasn't finished with the poem, he sent the manuscript to several of his closest friends, usually with an explanatory note or letter. "Started a poem, came to me like inspiration, reads like Kerouac style," he wrote laconically to Burroughs, who was in Morocco. At the top of page one of the typescript that he sent Burroughs, he also wrote in his own hand, "SF 1955" and in capital letters "STROPHES." He didn't call it "Howl" and there was no mention of Carl Solomon in the version he sent Burroughs. There was no epigram from Whitman, either, and he didn't type or sign his own name. A year or so later, when he wrote the dedication, he was so confused about the origin of the title that he mistakenly gave Kerouac the credit, not himself.

Ginsberg insisted that *Howl* was a work of inspiration, but he didn't explain what he meant by inspiration, perhaps because it seemed obvious. Of course, inspiration has meant many different things to many different poets. For Stephen Spender there were several distinct kinds of inspiration. In one kind, the poet hallucinated and heard voices that dictated the poem to the poet. The poet had only to write down the words he or she was given. In another kind of inspiration, Spender explained that the poet felt that he was given just the opening line and then proceeded to extract the entire work from it. Robert Graves wrote in *The White Goddess* that the inspired poet went into a trance and foretold the future. It was essential, Graves argued, that inspiration be followed by a kind of critical detachment in which the poet shaped and regulated his visions and hallucinations. When Ginsberg wrote the first draft of *Howl*, he seems to have gone into the kind of trance that Graves describes—he let his imagination take him where it would. And when he emerged from his trance, he used his critical faculties to rearrange and revise the poem. He detached himself from the work and looked at it critically with an eye to improving it. Then, too, one might say that the whole poem was inspired by the apocalyptic first line, with its storehouse of powerful images and ideas—of the poet's generation, along with destructiveness, madness, nakedness, hysteria, and hunger. Years after he wrote *Howl*, Ginsberg told Burroughs that inspiration often came as he sat alone at a typewriter, confronted by a blank sheet of paper. "The typewriter imagination tells the writer what to write," he explained. Indeed, it is an experience that many poets have shared. You don't know what you'll write until you sit down at the keyboard and begin to write, and the words in front of you inspire you to continue to write.

Gary Snyder remembered that the first time he saw the poem it was called "Strophes." The word "strophes"—from the Greek—meant a great deal to Ginsberg ever since he'd read Whitman in high school. "These long lines or Strophes as I call them came spontaneously as a result of the kind of feelings I was trying to put down, and came as a complete surprise to a metrical problem that preoccupied me for a decade," he explained in 1956. The phrase "complete surprise" seems to be an exaggeration, but he was a poet who liked to be taken by surprise, especially since he often felt repressed and shut down.

From Ginsberg's point of view, spontaneity wasn't appreciated for what it was: "A CRAFT." He had arrived at the gates of spontaneity, he explained, only after long "experience writing and practicing." Like a pianist who sat at a piano and practiced hour after hour, day after day, he too practiced his craft, rehearsed his art, and undertook exercises to perfect his work. How far apart he was from Kerouac on the subject of spontaneity—in theory, if not always in practice—is indicated by their correspondence in August 1955. Ginsberg sent Kerouac a six-page typescript of *Howl*, with all sorts of revisions. In the very first line, for example, he used a pencil to cross out the word "mystical" and to add the word "hysterical," and in the middle of the page he crossed out "anarchy" and substituted "Arkansas." In his cover letter to Kerouac, Ginsberg wrote, "I typed it up as I went along . . . [it] was the first time I sat down to blow, it came out in your method, sounding like you, an imitation practically." Perhaps he *thought* he was imitating Kerouac, much as he thought he was imitating Whitman, but in fact he was finding himself, his voice, his method. Kerouac admitted that *Howl* was "very powerful." He enjoyed the poem's sex language, especially phrases like "with a vision of ultimate cunt and come" and "waving genitals and manuscripts." What Kerouac did not like was that his old friend had tampered with the first draft. He noted that Ginsberg had edited and revised his work. The manuscript he received in the mail was seriously flawed, he felt, because it had "secondary emendations made in time's reconsidered backstep." What Kerouac wanted was Allen's "lingual SPONTANEITY or nothing." That's not what he would get.

For the next year or so, Ginsberg continued to "backstep," as Kerouac called it—to reconsider and emend, to do everything in his power to make the poem as perfect as he could make it. No "spontaneous" poem was more thoroughly rewritten. The ongoing debate about spontaneity continued when Kerouac moved to 1624 Milvia Street in Berkeley in September 1955 and became Allen's writing coach and critic, a kind of mentor and muse at the same time. Week after week, month after month, he watched Allen rework the whole poem, trying to stop him from revising. Philip Whalen listened to the dialogue between Ginsberg and

Kerouac as it unfolded. "On visits to Ginsberg's cottage in Berkeley I watched as he reframed various passages and sections of the poem while Kerouac encouraged him to cut out as little as possible," Whalen wrote. Ginsberg had never been more self-confident—and never less dependent on Kerouac.

He not only reframed whole passages and sections, he also changed individual words and phrases. There were hundreds of emendations, and in 1986, on the thirtieth anniversary of the poem, he explained some of them, as well as providing information about the biographical and autobiographical roots of *Howl*. The "crucial revision," he explained, was the substitution in line one of "hysterical" for "mystical." That single change helped set the "tone of the poem," he argued. It initiated the sense of "comic realism" and "humorous hyperbole" that runs through *Howl*.

Ginsberg offered a modicum of helpful hints but declined to explain most of the emendations. He did not explain why—when he revised the first draft—he added the crucial line "angelheaded hipsters, looking for the shuddering connection between the wheels & wires of the machinery of the night." The image of those angelheaded hipsters is essential to the poem and yet it wasn't there from the start. Nor did Ginsberg explain why he changed "negro fix" to "angry fix," and "angry streets" to "negro streets." Perhaps the changes reflect his own ambivalence and even confusion about blacks. Were they to be feared, or admired? He was of several minds: they were romantic savages, downtrodden workers, and the coolest of Americans. In his journal in 1954 and 1955, he used the word "nigger" in phrases like "nigger radio" and "nigger whore," to describe black music and black women. At the same time, he denounced segregation and racism. Perhaps the civil rights movement in the South, which was emerging even as he was writing *Howl*, persuaded him to use the word "negro" instead of "nigger."

Like Kerouac, Ginsberg had a penchant for black culture—he loved folk, jazz, and the blues. He traveled all the way to Dakar to be among Africans, and he moved to Harlem, too, to be among sophisticated urban black folk—but unlike Kerouac he never boasted about wanting to be a Negro. Being a Jew, a homosexual, and a communist felt like more than enough of a burden to bear. In *On the Road*, Kerouac wrote, "I walked with every muscle aching among the lights of 27th and Welton in the colored section of Denver, wishing I were a Negro." Kerouac felt that whiteness was bland and empty; he wanted to belong to any ethnic group but white. Ginsberg never described himself or regarded himself as white. He was in exile from himself, and his burden was to come home to himself—to his homosexuality, his Jewish identity, and his own idiosyncratic version of communism.

The hard work of revision improved *Howl*. The poem became tighter, richer; more expressive and more compact. It also became more personal. Ginsberg added his own experiences to the poem, making it increasingly autobiographical. Most of all, perhaps, the language of the poem became more vivid, more alive and acrobatic. In the first draft, he used the verb "looking" to describe the spiritual quests of the angelheaded hipsters. "Looking" became "exploring" and "exploring" became "burning," a subtle but significant change that fit perfectly with the poem's underlying image of New York as a city on fire and its citizens in flames. Every detail—even the exclamation marks in the Moloch section (all eighty-three of them)—contributed to the intensity of the whole. Though he boasted of his spontaneity, he in fact searched for what Flaubert called "le mot juste"—the precise word to fit the specific context.

With revision, the verbs helped to shape the poem as a conscious vocal exercise. There's a whole lexicon of words to describe the varieties of human expression, from the eloquent to the loquacious, the reverential to the irreverent. There's whispering, screaming, saying, singing, shrieking, crying, moaning, groaning, howling, talking, yacketayakking, conversing, praying, and confessing, along with vomiting and disgorging. In *Howl*, Ginsberg was no longer blocked. At long last, he broke down his own internal inhibitions—literally disgorged what was trapped inside—and released a torrent of words, images, emotions, and experiences.

The original typescript version of *Howl* ends with a suggestion of homosexuality: "I am with you in Rockland / where we hug and kiss the United States under our bedsheets." With revision, he moved that stanza from the end, moving the "cottage in the Western night"—which had been embedded in the text—to the conclusion. The revised version of Part I ends on a note of serenity; at last the vagabond poet—the wandering Jew and the exiled American—is at home in his own California cottage.

### Reading It

If he initially wrote the poem with the idea of performing it for a small group of friends, performing Part I of the poem in public in 1955 at the Six Gallery convinced him to write new sections to be read to audiences. The more he performed the poem, the more it turned into a performance piece. Accordingly, he wrote

Parts II and III with verbal pyrotechnics, rhetorical flourishes, and dramatic phrases. Lines like "Moloch! Moloch! Nightmare of Moloch!" and "Carl Solomon! I'm with you in Rockland" were meant to be performed aloud before a live audience.

In the fall of 1955, he read *Howl* all over San Francisco, first at the Six Gallery, of course, and then in a hall on Telegraph Hill, where the audience was drunk and disorderly and he was distressed by their antics. He also read at the San Francisco Poetry Center, where in deference to Ruth Witt-Diamant, he censored the obscenities, substituting the word "censored." When he read the poem's most infamous line, it came out, "who let themselves be censored in the censored." On March 18, 1956, shortly before his thirtieth birthday, he read the whole of *Howl* in public for the first time at a multimedia event. This time the performance was at Berkeley's Town Hall Theater, where Robert LaVigne's nude sketches were on exhibit, including a shocking sketch (at least to some undergraduates at Berkeley) that depicted Orlovsky making love to Ginsberg.

At Town Hall Theater, Ginsberg read for the first time the cycle of Berkeley poems that emerged in the wake of *Howl* and that provide a kind of gloss on *Howl:* "America," "Sunflower Sutra," and "A Strange New Cottage in Berkeley." This time the reading was recorded, albeit by amateur engineers, and this time the reading was much more challenging. *Howl* was much longer now—it took more time and energy to read—and the audience was wilder than the audience at the Six Gallery. Listeners were too quick to laugh, Ginsberg complained, and he had trouble composing himself on stage. "The beginning of the reading is quite muted," he explained after listening to the recording. "I'm not stable on my feet, and I'm worried I'm going to be interrupted if they laugh too much." And, though he'd been reading the poem for months, he began to worry that he had lost his own reading voice and was now merely imitating Dylan Thomas, who had toured America in the early fifties and had set a new standard for poetry readings in public. Still, if the reading at Berkeley's Town Hall Theater disappointed him, it was moving and memorable to many who attended. It was a polished, professional performance. Ginsberg knew when to go slowly, when to build up speed, when to pause, when to rant, when to be solemn, when to emphasize the ironical and which words—"mad" and "Moloch," for example—to make emphatic.

A year after the Six Gallery reading, he was still energetically reading *Howl*, sometimes with Gary Snyder or Gregory Corso as an opening act. On October 30, 1956, he read the poem at a private house in Hollywood. This time, he took off his clothes in front of the audience, writing proudly to Ferlinghetti, "I disrobed finally. Been wanting to onstage for years." Earlier that year, he had disrobed before friends in Berkeley; this was the first time in front of a crowd of strangers. Indeed, the desire to disrobe in public seems to go back all the way to his childhood. In Hollywood, he finally broke an old taboo. He did what he wanted to do and yet was terrified of doing. For years afterward he would undress in public, take photographs of himself without any clothes, and allow other photographers to take pictures of him in the nude. "Why am I interested in seeing myself naked?" he asked in an essay for an art exhibit in New York in the mid-1960s that included nude photos of himself. He replied, in characteristic fashion, that he was both attracted to and repelled by his own body. "For years I thought I was ugly, I still do," he wrote. But he went on to explain that he was a gnostic and felt that it was essential to live in his own body, ugly though it might be, while it still existed. It was the only body he had.

Ginsberg was excited about the Hollywood reading. Marlon Brando, to whom he had sent an invitation, didn't attend; but there were other Hollywood luminaries in attendance—certainly a different crowd from that at the poetry center. The most distinguished member of the audience at the Hollywood reading was Anaïs Nin, who had been alerted to the event by Ruth Witt-Diamant—herself a member of the audience at the Six Gallery in October 1955. Ginsberg was a "messiah of a sort," Witt-Diamant wrote to Nin, although he didn't have much to offer "outside the particular agonies of his own experience." Nin wasn't at all put off by Witt-Diamant's dismissive comments: she relished Ginsberg's zany performance. Having lived in Paris and having read widely in French literature, she understood immediately what many of Ginsberg's American contemporaries ignored or didn't see—his connection to French surrealism and to the art of the collage. In her view, *Howl* was a "great long, desperate wail, a struggle to make poetry out of all the objects, surroundings and people he had known." She added that "at times, it reached a kind of American surrealism, a bitter irony; it had a savage power, . . . It reminded me of Artaud." Nin had known Artaud—had been his lover in Paris. Madness didn't frighten her—either in real life or in poetry.

Other members of the audience in Hollywood and in Venice—where Ginsberg also read and recorded his work— were less generous. Mel Weisburd, a southern California critic and poet, dismissed Ginsberg, Corso, and company. They "*cannot* be associated with any true underground literature," Weisburd proclaimed. He argued that Ginsberg was a vulgar salesman for himself and his own crude brand of poetry.

And it's true that Ginsberg was doing everything in his power to promote himself and his work, which he knew faced an uphill battle for attention in a highly competitive literary marketplace. Reading at small venues in San Francisco, Berkeley, Seattle, and Hollywood attracted a modicum of attention, but it certainly didn't bring as much attention as reading, say, at the Frick Museum in New York, or at the Library of Congress in Washington, D.C. Circulating his work was a challenge. As Kenneth Rexroth noted, San Francisco's distance from New York made it "harder to get things, if not published, at least nationally distributed." Lawrence Ferlinghetti had just founded City Lights and the fledgling publishing house didn't have the means to promote *Howl* in a big way. To get the attention he wanted and needed, Ginsberg had to resort to shocking tactics like disrobing in public, courting the very mass media he scorned. Yet publicity wasn't his only motivation. His performances were also sheer fun. "I do nothing but write and drink and carouse & take off my clothes at parties," he wrote in the fall of 1955. "So life is fine."

The British-born poet Denise Levertov, who had recently met Allen, genuinely admired *Howl*. "*There's* something I can accept unconditionally," she wrote to William Carlos Williams enthusiastically. But she didn't accept unconditionally Ginsberg's advertisements for himself. By promoting himself as a poet, Allen went against the unwritten but powerful injunction of the day: poets should shun the commercial world. In the eyes of a great many poets, teachers, and critics of poetry, he was behaving unpoetically by promoting his poetry. "It seems Allen Ginsberg is conducting a regular propaganda campaign," Levertov complained to William Carlos Williams after a visit from Allen, and after seeing his picture in *Mademoiselle*. "He will damage his work surely if he puts so much energy into advertising." Perhaps so. Or perhaps Ginsberg set the pace in this as he did in so many other ways; a great many American poets today seem to assume that they must promote themselves and their work. For better or worse, they have followed in Ginsberg's footsteps.

Williams wanted to lend Allen the support he needed, but he, too, worried that Allen's antics might damage his art. "He is a Jew during an age which makes a god of advertising," Williams wrote of Ginsberg. "He can walk into any business office and demand recognition . . . if he can make the man he faces believe that it means MONEY! to him." Louis Ginsberg had long suspected Williams of anti-Semitism, and he and Allen discussed the matter. "I don't think he's anti-Semitic since he has Jewish friends & attacks Pound's anti-Semitism," Allen told Louis. But Williams's letter to Levertov would probably have affirmed Louis's deeply held suspicions. Advertising was indeed a god in America in the 1950s; but Americans of Jewish descent were hardly the only ethnic group to worship in the temple of advertising, as Williams seemed to believe. Ginsberg himself had specifically lashed out at the advertising industry in *Howl*. Moreover, he felt that there was a world of difference between his own efforts to advertise himself and the Madison Avenue advertising industry. (Years later, he defended himself after he appeared in an ad for the Gap that was published in the *New Yorker:* the money he made went to good causes, he insisted.) In spite of Louis's concerns about Williams's alleged anti-Semitism, Allen continued to remain friends with the older poet. Along with Kerouac and Corso, he visited Williams at his home in New Jersey, and when Williams died, Ginsberg wrote "Death News," an elegy that celebrated the poet's gentle, noncompetitive personality. "The poet / of the streets is a skeleton under the pavement now," he explained. "There's no other old soul so kind and meek."

Ferlinghetti had promised to publish *Howl*, but publication would take time. Meanwhile, Allen sent friends, family members, and former teachers typewritten copies and then mimeographed copies of the poem. Briefly, he joined the mimeograph revolution that in the 1950s made it possible for nearly every poet to publish and to reach an audience almost instantly. The people who read the mimeographed version of *Howl*—and later the City Lights book, *Howl and Other Poems*—saw it through their own individual perspectives. The poem provided a kind of Rorschach test. Lucien Carr, who was working as a reporter for United Press International, noted that it was a "considerable departure and improvement over earlier stuff" and, in his characteristic sarcasm, he encouraged Allen to "keep it up, as we of the petit Bourgeoisie say." Lionel Trilling, who was still teaching at Columbia and who published a collection of essays entitled *A Gathering of Fugitives* in 1956, couldn't yet bring himself to aid and abet a literary fugitive like Ginsberg or his fugitive poem, *Howl*. When Allen read *Howl* at Columbia in 1959, Trilling didn't show up, though his wife Diana did. Lionel stayed at home with W. H. Auden as though boycotting the event. But Louis Ginsberg was on hand, and Allen was so happy he wept tears of joy. Louis was still writing poetry, though he had not published a book of poems for twenty years. He was delighted that his son was finally receiving the attention he wanted—and at Columbia no less. Louis allowed that *Howl* was not his "type of poetry." But there "were many mansions in poetry," he said—borrowing Whitman's image to describe Edgar Allan Poe—and *Howl* was one of them.

Naomi Ginsberg's 1956 observations about *Howl* might have provided Allen with a sense of comic relief except that he received her letter at nearly the same time he received a telegram from his brother, Eugene, informing him of their mother's death in June of that year, at Pilgrim State Hospital. Mother Ginsberg found her son's syntax "a little too hard." Yet Naomi understood well enough to say, "I hope you are not taking any drugs as suggested by your poetry." To the end, she lived up to the stereotype of the Jewish mother. "I hope you behave well," she told Allen. She wanted him to get a job, marry a "beautiful" woman like Eugene's wife, and, like Mr. and Mrs. Brooks, who lived on Long Island, raise a family of his own. Whatever Allen's feelings about his mother's observations, he was grief-stricken. "My mother Naomi is dead," he wrote in his journal. "My heart is empty . . . I must continue writing. My youth is ending all my youth."

He did continue to write even as he felt his youth slipping away, and not surprisingly what he wrote sprang from his grief and sense of loss. Years later he would insist that he gave birth to *Kaddish* in Paris in 1957. In fact *Kaddish* began to gestate in 1956, when he worked as a yeoman in the Military Sea Transportation Service aboard the *Sgt. Jack J. Pendleton*—even as he was in the midst of proofreading *Howl*. Since he was at sea, he entitled the poem to his mother *Kaddish or the Sea Power*, and it was in part the awesome power of the sea that enabled him to rise above his grief and loss. "We all die, life's a short flash," he noted one night on the prow of the ship. But he also felt a sense of "universal joy at creation," and it was that sense of death and creation going on

simultaneously that informs *Kaddish* and gives it much of its re-
demptive power.

Of course, in 1956 *Howl* took precedence over *Kaddish*. Just as
soon as City Lights published the book he sent copies to almost
all the major American poets—from W. H. Auden to Louis
Zukofsky—and to his closest friends, too, many of whom replied
enthusiastically. Perhaps Gary Snyder's comments pleased Allen
more than those of anyone else in his extended literary family.
Snyder read *Howl* as soon as the City Lights edition arrived on
his doorstep. Reading it to himself, he was reminded of the Six
Gallery reading, and he heard Allen's "voice ringing" in his ears.
Snyder wasn't simply an enthusiastic reader. He also wanted to
help distribute the complimentary copies of *Howl* he had re-
ceived from City Lights. An anarchist and an admirer of the In-
dustrial Workers of the World, Snyder described the books he
received in the mail as "bombs." The only question was where to
place them so that they might most effectively foment the com-
ing cultural revolution.

Make no mistake about it, Ginsberg wanted fundamental cul-
tural and social ferment. At the same time, "famous authorhood"
was addicting and he couldn't get enough of it, he confessed.
Money was good, too; soon after *Howl* was published he began to
receive checks from Ferlinghetti, and that made him very happy.
The sales provided a delightful "new source of loot," he was
proud to report. Yes, fame and fortune were very good. But they
were even better when combined with the political transforma-
tion he had longed for and dreamt about. In 1949, at the New
York State Psychiatric Institute and in the company of Carl Sol-
omon, he had begun to plan "incredible logical revolutions." In
several of the stanzas near the end of Part I of *Howl*, he described

his imaginary revolutionary scenarios, albeit in a comic vein: "I'm with you in Rockland / where there are twentyfive thousand mad comrades all together sing- / ing the final stanzas of the Internationale." In fact he wasn't prepared to plot a socialist revolution, sing the "Communist Internationale," or even begin to call anyone "comrade." What he had in mind was something more irreverent, more like the Marx brothers than Karl Marx and more in the spirit of the comic genius Charlie Chaplin than the humorless American Communist Party. "You have no idea what a storm of lunatic-fringe activity I have stirred up," he wrote to his father with a sense of sheer delight.

Before the reading at the Six Gallery in San Francisco, he was briefly a graduate student at the University of California at Berkeley, where he planned to conduct research about problems of prosody in poetry. He was especially interested in T. S. Eliot's prosody, and he was reading a study of the subject by Sister Mary Cleophas entitled *Between Fixity and Flux*. But graduate school both stifled and intimidated him. There were assigned books to read, information to memorize, lectures to attend, and papers to write. At Berkeley there was too much structure, and not nearly as much fun, as reading his own poetry before drunken audiences, getting drunk himself—in the tradition of drunken poets like Dylan Thomas—and undressing at parties with Peter Orlovsky and Gregory Corso. In the spring of 1956, instead of taking classes at Berkeley, he gave a class at San Francisco State.

Kerouac had always said that Allen was an academic at heart— a budding Lionel Trilling—and that he belonged in the classroom. He did belong there—he was theatrical and engaging and he had a sense of humor. When asked about his academic title, he would explain that he occupied the "chair of guest gorilla." In that persona, he did everything he could to persuade his students not to write according to preconceived ideas of what literature was supposed to be, but instead to do what he liked to think he himself had done—"actually express secret life in whatever form it comes out." To achieve that aim, he told his father, "I practically take off my clothes in class." In the classroom he was nearly as outrageous and provocative as he was on stage and at private parties. No doubt about it, Louis was shocked and dismayed by his son's unconventional academic career on the West Coast. Louis had taught poetry for at least thirty years to high school and college students, and he had never had to lambaste them or "precipitate great emotional outbreaks and howls of protest." In his own defense, however, Allen claimed that there was a method to his pedagogical madness, and that it did "actually succeed in communicating some of the electricity & fire of poetry and cuts through the miasmic quibbling about form vs. content etc." Little by little he did indeed become an effective classroom teacher.

From 1986—befitting on the thirtieth anniversary of the publication of *Howl and Other Poems*—to his death in 1997, he was a professor at Brooklyn College and an inspiring poetry teacher. Ellen Belton, the dean of undergraduate studies and a professor of English at Brooklyn College, remembers vividly Ginsberg's contributions to the campus, his curiosity about the way things ran, and his friendships with students. She also remembers his first arrival on campus. "When we interviewed him for the job we weren't quite sure what we were getting into," Belton says. "We thought that he might show up as a wild and crazy Beat poet. He actually came dressed in a tweed jacket with elbow patches, looking very professorial." Belton had read *Howl* when she was a graduate student, and she was delighted to hear him read *Howl* at Brooklyn College, and delighted, too, that he taught a class on the Beats that was attended not only by students but by members of the community. "He was a wonderful teacher with a wide range of teaching styles," she says. "He assumed that the audience was on his level and he invited all of us to be part of a global conversation about literature and life." There was also something endearing—something charming—about him. "I remember that he was working on his *Collected Poems* and that he said, 'It's sort of like getting to do a dissertation on yourself,'" Belton says.

Three decades earlier, in the mid-1950s, Ginsberg wanted a revolution in the classroom, a radical change in the way that poetry was taught. He was prepared to chase the New Critics from the halls of academia. Interpreting a poem without placing it in a social and historical context, and without discussing the life of the poet—which many of the New Critics insisted on—made no sense at all to him, and he used his own poem to make his point. In order to understand *Howl*, he explained, it was important to understand the Cold War and the warring impulses in his own character and personality.

Teaching method aside, it was really his poetry that stirred up students and helped to foment the revolution he wanted to make. The poem "America," which he described to his father as a "sort of surrealist anarchist tract," was probably the most effective of the overtly political poems that he wrote in the wake of *Howl*. It's probably also *the* poem that best answers the question that Burroughs asked after reading *Howl* in March 1956—"I am wondering where you will go from here."

In "America"—which may sound as though it was written

spontaneously, but which he revised again and again for more than a year—he was finally self-confident enough to write with all the comedic force he could muster, "It occurs to me that I am America," and "Go fuck yourself with your atom bomb." Neither line appears in the first draft, and some of the lines in the first draft—including, "I Allen Ginsberg Bard out of New Jersey take up the laurel tree / cudgel from Whitman"—do not appear in the final draft. Ginsberg had wanted to make himself into Mr. America and become the voice for the silenced nation for nearly as long as he had wanted to disrobe in public. Now it was time for America to disclose itself, and he asked, "America when will you be angelic? / When will you take off your clothes?" In the manuscript draft he had also asked, "America when will you give me back my mother?" but he cut that line, probably because he realized that his mother deserved a poem all to herself. "America" was an instant hit with audiences, a bit of stand-up comedy in which he broke almost all of the taboos of the 1950s: he admitted that he was a "queer," that he smoked marijuana, that he had read Karl Marx, and had been a communist. Moreover, he was "not sorry." He wasn't apologizing for anything he had done, or would do, and he wasn't asking for forgiveness. Perhaps Senator Joseph McCarthy would have issued him a subpoena, and would have interrogated him, but at the end of 1954, just as Allen was making his home in San Francisco, McCarthy had been censored by the U.S. Senate and now he was out of the business of investigating citizens. "America" both reflected and furthered the initial crumbling of the anti-communist crusade.

For most of his adult life, Ginsberg had been terrified of the bomb and anxious about nuclear war between the United States and the Soviet Union. For at least a decade he'd listened with anxiety to the "hydrogen jukebox." Now, he was able to make fun of his fears and to invite Americans to laugh at their own paranoia and preoccupation with the Russians and the bomb. "America it's them bad Russians," he wrote, tongue in cheek. Yet he wasn't anti-American. He wanted his fellow citizens to know that he had the best interests of the nation at heart. So he ended the poem with an image of himself doing his part. "America I'm putting my queer shoulder to the wheel," he wrote. At the same time that he was taking on America, he was ready to take on Russia, too. The time was ripe. The Soviet Union was in the midst of "Destalinization," and Allen followed the news with the feeling that a miracle had taken place. He wanted to go to the USSR, write poetry on the walls of the Kremlin, meet Russian poets, and make them his brothers despite the Cold War.

At the same time that he was entertaining such grandiose global political ideas, he was also attending to the last-minute practical details of publishing his book. He selected an epigram from Whitman's *Song of Myself* to set the tone for *Howl* as a poem of liberation: "Unscrew the locks from the doors! Unscrew the doors themselves from their jambs!" At the last minute, he also wrote a dedication; this originally included Lucien Carr, along with Kerouac, Burroughs, and Cassady, but Carr objected—he wanted anonymity—and Ginsberg removed his name. The poem's long, detailed dedication was a way for him to publicly acknowledge the influence of Kerouac, Burroughs, and Cassady on his life and his work. It was also an advertisement for his three friends and their unpublished work. Ginsberg mentioned that Burroughs was the author of *Naked Lunch*, a novel that would make everyone insane, that Kerouac had written eleven books, all of them unpublished, including *On the Road*, and that Cassady had written an autobiography entitled *The First Third*. In spite of his attention to all sorts of publication details, he didn't think about copyrighting the book. Only after it was printed did he realize that needed to be done.

As Ginsberg told Ferlinghetti, *Howl* was his first book and he wanted to get it right. At first, the printers set the poem incorrectly; the long lines he had typed so carefully to give the look and feel of prose paragraphs were all chopped up. His beloved work of art had turned into a typographical nightmare. It would cost him money to have it reset—"[I] hate to put out gold like that," he told Eugene—still he was willing to spend the money.

News of the innovative West Coast poetry readings began to reach New York in the spring of 1956, and the *New York Times* promptly dispatched Richard Eberhart, a fifty-year-old poet and critic, to report on the scene. Eberhart attended the reading in Berkeley in March, and immediately afterward he told Ginsberg that *Howl* sounded like "a negative howl of protest." Allen did not reply then and there. He was stunned into silence. Two months after the reading, in a letter to Eberhart, he begged to disagree. *Howl* wasn't negative at all. In fact, it was an "'affirmation.'" It was meant to remind human beings of their own dignity. People weren't "smelly shits," he argued. They were "angels." The message of the poem—he made it sound positively Christian—was to "forgive and love yourself" and then to "forgive another and love another." Not surprisingly, he also turned to the subject of madness, trying to clarify it. Allen explained to Eberhart that "what seems 'mad' in America is our expression of natural ecstasy." If that expression of ecstasy is suppressed—if there is no "validation" from society for that feeling—the slightly confused individual will begin to think that he is "mad" and really "go off

[his] rocker." It was society that was to blame for madness, Allen argued. Innocent angels were driven mad by an insensitive system. Near the end of his letter to Eberhart, he reiterated his main point: *Howl* was not a work of "nihilistic rebellion." It was a religious work and if it advocated anything at all, it was the "enlightenment of mystical experience—without which no society can long exist."

Eberhart's review appeared in the *New York Times* on September 2, 1956. Under the headline "West Coast Rhythms," the author noted that San Francisco was at the epicenter of a movement of young, radical poets, and that the "most remarkable poem" that had emerged from the movement was *Howl*. The poem itself had not yet been published, Eberhart noted. It was odd and unheard of, indeed, to review an "unpublished" poet, but the poet and the poem were so unusual that the *New York Times* was willing to break with its own tradition. Eberhart did not expose Ginsberg as a homosexual in his review, but he did disclose a great deal else about him, some of which tended to undermine Ginsberg's self-mythologizing. Far from being a mad poet who had appeared out of nowhere to write a raw, original masterpiece, he was in fact the son of Louis Ginsberg, a well-known poet, Eberhart explained. The secret was out. The orphaned poet was no orphan at all. Moreover, he was no unschooled genius. Eberhart noted that he had studied poetry at Columbia and had harnessed himself to traditional forms. Only after "years of apprenticeship," Eberhart wrote, did he develop his "brave new medium." Behind the image of the spontaneous poet was a disciplined artist and craftsman.

Though Eberhart did not mention that he knew Ginsberg personally—or that he had corresponded with him—his positive review was obviously shaped by his personal connection to the poet himself. Indeed, he admitted to his readers that he had changed his mind about *Howl*. "My first reaction was that it is based on destructive violence," he wrote in the *Times*. He had come around to thinking that it was imbued with a "positive force" and that it expressed "a redemptive quality of love." Allen could hardly have written a more favorable review, and soon after it appeared in the *Times*, he showed up in New York to promote *Howl* in person. Only a short time had passed since he had left New York for California, but he was very much changed. He was a famous poet, albeit in a small circle. He had benefited greatly from therapy at Langley Porter; he had more fully come to terms with his homosexuality; and he had new friends—Snyder, McClure, Whalen. He felt a sense of confidence that had often eluded him.

When he arrived in New York in the fall of 1956, Ginsberg was afraid that *Howl* would sit on shelves in bookstores growing dustier by the day. Perhaps the thousand copies that had been published wouldn't even sell out. But Eberhart's review had helped spread the word about *Howl*, and so had word-of-mouth praise. City Lights didn't have an advertising budget or a marketing campaign, so Ginsberg became a one-man walking-talking advertisement, and a marketing director, too. He walked all over Manhattan, from bookstore to bookstore, checking to see if *Howl* was available and urging booksellers to stock the latest volume in the City Lights Pocket Poets Series. "Nobody I know in the Village has seen or bought it," he complained to Ferlinghetti soon after his book was published.

At the Eighth Street Bookstore he found a few copies, but they were buried under a stack of Rexroth's new book; he made sure that *Howl* was displayed more prominently. He went to the *New York Times* and tried to persuade Harvey Breit to run another article about *Howl*, and he pestered Louise Bogan at the *New Yorker*, too. "One review . . . could break the ice," he observed. His own dogged efforts paid off, and by the start of 1957 he could report to Ferlinghetti that the Eighth Street Bookstore had sold all its copies, and that all over the city sales of *Howl* were brisk. Bigger sales and greater success were just beginning.

# CHAPTER TEN

# This Fiction Named Allen Ginsberg

## Square Poet, Avant-garde Poet

For decades, Louis Ginsberg had been far more famous than Allen. The elder Ginsberg taught poetry at Rutgers and played a leading role in the prestigious, though stodgy, Poetry Society of America. He had two books of poems to his name, dozens of poems in anthologies, and publications in most of the leading literary magazines. Then, in 1956 and 1957, with the advent of *Howl*, attention suddenly shifted from father to son. Allen was the bright new star in the literary firmament. Never again would Louis outshine his son, though for a brief time in the late 1960s and early 1970s, father and son shared the stage and gave poetry readings together from California to New Jersey. "I'm a square poet," Louis would say provocatively. "Allen's avant-garde." Frequently he was Allen's most enthusiastic fan. He wrote effusively about his son and boasted that the "high school and college kids love him. He is the audible voice, unabashed and uninhibited, of their secret hidden dreams and desires." Louis used Allen's name and reputation to promote himself, much as Allen used Louis's name when and where it suited him. (When he begged the *Saturday Review of Literature* to hire him as its poetry editor, for example.)

Other fathers might have bridled at a son who was more famous than they were, and other sons might have used their fame to berate their fathers and settle old scores. Allen's fame brought him closer to his father; now that he was famous he could pay homage to Louis and his work. In "To My Father in Poetry," which he wrote in 1959, he acknowledged, at long last, his father's influence on his own work—something he had long ignored and long denied. He heard his father's voice in his own voice. Louis was delighted that his famous son respected him. "While our methods in writing poetry may differ, we both aim at the central ideal of greater awareness, deeper insight, and richer delight in the astonishing phenomenon of life," he wrote. The father-son love feast notwithstanding, they disagreed as strongly as ever about politics, poetry, sex, and the self. In "To Allen Ginsberg"—one of his best poems—Louis compared his son to Theseus, the legendary Greek hero who slew the Minotaur, and expressed the hope that Allen would find his way through the labyrinth of his own self until he found his own genuine identity. Allen was well aware of his various selves, but unlike Louis, he felt that no single self was truer than another. They were all parts of himself and equally valid. What was essential, he argued, was to be detached, to remain in flux and never become fixed to any one identity. "I'm not really a Jew any more than I am a Poet," he told Louis. "Sure I'm both. But there is a nameless wildness—life itself—which is deeper." And he added, "All conceptions of the self which limit the self to a fixed identity are obviously arbitrary." When he wrote those lines to Louis he was living in Europe, an experience that intensified his awareness of his identity. "So finally it even begins dawning on me to stop thinking of myself as an American. And often in the dead of night I wonder who this fiction named Allen Ginsberg is—it certainly isn't me."

Surely, fame would have taken a far greater toll had he not understood that "Allen Ginsberg" was a fiction. His ability to remain detached from any one fixed identity had helped to make *Howl* an extraordinary poem. In *Howl*, he was the paragon of the protean poet. In the moment of creation, he was everyone and he was everywhere, from Alcatraz to Madison Avenue. He was himself, and he was also almost everyone else in the poem. He could become one with the angelheaded hipsters and with the Adonis of Denver. He was Moloch and he was Carl Solomon, too. His ability to remain detached from "Allen Ginsberg" enabled him, in large part, to go on writing extraordinary poems in the wake of *Howl*—overtly political poems as well as deeply personal poems—including "Death to Van Gogh's Ear!" "At Apollinaire's Grave," and, of course, *Kaddish*, which he started in 1956 and continued to work on in Paris and in New York in 1957 and 1958. Living in Europe deepened his vision of both Europe and America and helped him understand the experience of a generation of European immigrants like his mother who were born in the Old World and came to the New World. Now he could imagine what it must have been like for Naomi Levy to leave Russia, travel across the Atlantic, and arrive in New York, the strangest of cities. He could transcend his own resentment and anger and see his mother as a beautiful woman in her own right. And he could put himself on the sidelines and put his mother at the center of his poem.

### The Future Is Not Ours

The late 1950s was a perfect time for him to peer out at the world and to watch the Cold War as it went on unfolding. He had been concerned with Russian-American conflicts since the start of the Cold War in the 1940s, and he'd tried to capture in poetry the ways in which the two superpowers mirrored one another. Now, in 1957 and 1958, he continued to monitor East-West tensions, and he continued to think about the Cold War. In October 1957, after the Russians launched Sputnik, the first satellite to orbit in space, he followed the news intently and noted that it was the "greatest story since [the] discovery of fire." Like the Roman Empire, America was in a state of decline and fall, he concluded, while the USSR was rapidly rising. "The future is not ours," he observed. He tried hard to remain detached and not identify himself with either the USSR or America, East or West. "Neither side is right," he observed. "Sides are an illusion." The Russians were brutal and cruel in Hungary, he admitted, but they were no worse than the French in Algeria or the British in Kenya.

And, while he believed that he was personally better off as an American living in America than he would be as a Russian living in the USSR, he roundly condemned America's political role in the world and the American political system at home. The success of *Howl* gave him the courage to speak his mind and to express views he had long held but had not been eager to publicize. Now, he announced that he detested the anti-communist crusade, the American arms industry, and capitalism itself. Readers who read between the lines of *Howl* might have guessed that he held these views. Now they didn't have to guess. He spelled it out. In Allen's view, the White House and the Pentagon tolerated "mad dictatorial developments" everywhere on the face of the earth. Of course, he disapproved of Soviet-style mind control and brainwashing, and he rejected official Communist Party ideas about literature and the arts, and about the obligation of the artist to serve the needs of the people. He would never write for the Communist Party or for the people, he proclaimed. No matter what country he lived in, he would always write for himself or he would write for no one. The Soviet Communist Party had driven Mayakovsky into madness and suicide. It surely would drive him mad, too.

Meanwhile, America was driving him mad. The American mass media was engaged in brainwashing and "mass hypnosis," he argued. The function of television, he insisted, was to control people, and he denounced it at every opportunity. By 1961 he would write about the deadliness of TV in "Television Was a Baby Crawling toward That Deathchamber," a long angry poem in which he proclaimed that he could never tell his own secrets on TV and that television kept vital information a secret from Americans. In the late 1950s he argued that the USSR wasn't as evil as the talking heads on American television made it out to be. He was convinced that the USSR was a "great nation," that Russian writers were as original and creative as writers anywhere, and that "communism had tried & succeeded in improving material living conditions." He didn't want a communist society in the United States, but he wasn't opposed to communism in the Third World. What would work best in the West, he believed, was a "shift to cooperative socialism [and] an abandonment (perhaps) of money itself."

At times he was in despair about the future, and in frustration he retreated to the elitist point of view he had long held. "The masses are wrong," he wrote to Ferlinghetti. "The world is going to hell, there's no more hope of improvement . . . Things will get worse not better . . . there's nothing left to do but keep the light burning for whoever can understand now or later." At other times, he was far more optimistic about the future, and he reiterated his faith in the land of Jefferson, Lincoln, and the "old line socialists"—Eugene Victor Debs, Scott Nearing, and Ella Reeve Bloor—whom he had admired when he was a boy in Paterson and whom he memorializes in "America" and *Kaddish*. In his most hopeful moods, he would say, "American democracy is a beautiful thing," but in the late 1950s that sentiment was increasingly rare. American democracy itself seemed to him to be increasingly rare.

### Like Going to College

He thought a great deal about America during his sojourn in Europe. He became increasingly anti-American, and yet there was something uniquely American about his anti-Americanism. In many ways he was the archetypal innocent abroad, the idealistic young man making the grand tour, the wide-eyed tourist who fell in love with almost everything about the Old World, and came to detest almost everything about the New World. Europe was a "great experience," he wrote effusively to Louis in September 1957. It was "like going to college."

Like hundreds if not thousands of Americans before him, he found Paris "beautiful" and he was tempted to "expatriate & settle down." And, like so many other Americans, he loved the Latin Quarter and the little cafés where the existentialists smoked, drank, and talked, and where you might catch a glimpse of Jean-Paul Sartre, if you were lucky. Europeans were genuine intellectuals, he decided. They cared about ideas, he insisted, whereas making money was the American thing, and there were no moral standards. Even New York, the most European of American cities, paled by comparison with Paris, Rome, Florence. From the vantage point of Europe, New York looked "hard, closed, commercial, ingrown." Europeans were less materialistic than Americans, he thought, and less racist, too. "Europeans have more better personal relations with Negroes than Americans have," he concluded. In Holland, "big black nigger looking spades" dated "nice white girls," he noted, and no one paid any attention. Yes, he was still using racist language, still trying to shock his father, and he would go on using racist language for some time to come. Even as late as 1966, in the midst of the civil rights movement, he would use racial epithets in *Wichita Vortex Sutra*. No one challenged him, or scolded him.

By the mid-1960s he was largely beyond reproach. In 1967, for example, when he read in London, the British poet Ted Hughes described him as the prophet of a spiritual revolution, and one of the most important men of the twentieth century. From Hughes's point of view, *Howl* was the single work that began a global revolution in poetical form and content. It had, indeed, broken all sorts of verbal barriers, and Ginsberg went on breaking them when he described himself as "queer" or wrote about his own body and his bodily functions, or used words like "niggers" and "spades." In the late 1950s, the Europeans he met seemed less repressed than Americans about sex and race and about language, too. They were far more verbally liberated. About the only thing he didn't like in Europe was the Roman Catholic Church. At first he imagined that European Catholics belonged to a mystical secret society that provided a wonderful sense of community. Gradually, however, he changed his mind and came to feel that the Roman Catholic Church operated like the secret police in a totalitarian society, and that Rome was in the business of mind control and censorship. All those medieval cathedrals depressed him, while the Renaissance inspired him, especially the art of Michelangelo, which depicted "naked idealized realistic human bodies."

Europeans seemed more artistic and far more poetic than Americans—Americans hated poetry and poets, he insisted—and he pursued poets and the legacy of poetry, too. In Italy, he visited "mad Shelley's grave," plucking a few tender leaves of clover and mailing them to Louis, who was delighted to receive them. There were visits to living poets, too, especially W. H. Auden, whom he had adored when he was an undergraduate at Columbia, and whom he had been trying to meet for years. He loved to be in the company of famous people, especially famous writers and musicians, and for years he would seek out celebrities, from Ezra Pound to Bob Dylan and the Beatles, though celebrities also sought him out. Now, with the fame that *Howl* had furnished, and with all the notoriety that the media provided, he could knock on doors and find himself ushered into tea or served a glass or two of wine. What he wanted was adulation and acceptance. At the same time, he wanted to be the enfant terrible, the anti-poet, and poetic iconoclast. For years, he'd hoped for, and even dreamt about, a meeting with Auden; in one dream, he was Auden's disciple and the envy of every other student in the class. In person, Auden was slow to accept him, hesitant to warm to him. In Italy, he told Allen he didn't like Shelley and didn't like *Howl*, either. It had "no vitality or beauty," and it was "full of the author feeling sorry for himself," Auden complained. Meeting Auden and debating with him about literature persuaded Ginsberg that "the republic of poetry needs a full-scale revolution." Meeting Auden also made him feel that he belonged to the literary and cultural tradition of Emerson, Thoreau, Whitman, and Williams. In the spirit of his forefathers, his rally cry became "spiritual democracy" and "indestructible individuality."

All over Europe he promoted himself, distributing and talking about *Howl*. During his stay in England, he recorded *Howl* for the BBC. He visited British poets, and though he didn't knock on T. S. Eliot's door—that would have been too audacious, even for him—he reread *The Waste Land* and was once again inspired by Eliot. On a walking tour of London, he remembered Eliot's lines about London, and soon enough he had a marvelous dream—a kind of letter from his unconscious—that he recorded in his journal. "Last nite I dreamed of T. S. Eliot," he wrote. In the dream, Eliot serves him tea at his flat in London, treats him as his literary equal, and listens to his opinions about poetry and poets, from Mayakovsky to Creeley. Like a good father, Eliot tucks Allen into bed and says, "ah Ginsberg I am glad / to have met a fine young man like you." When he woke, he felt "ashamed" of himself. He wasn't supposed to like Eliot and he wasn't supposed to want Eliot's approval. Supposedly, he had broken away from Eliot's poetry and idea of tradition. The dream was a reminder to him of Eliot's power over his imagination, and a reminder, too, that as always he couldn't control his unconscious and his dreams. "Am I that great?" he wondered in the wake of his dream. "What English Department / would that impress?" He concluded that his had been an "overambitious dream of [an] eccentric boy."

Ginsberg wrote only once again at length about Eliot. In 1977, in the essay "T. S. Eliot Entered My Dreams," he describes an imaginary conversation with Eliot in which he argues that poets ought to be revolutionaries. He denounces "robotic modernity" and praises Eliot for having criticized "homogenized commercial Tawdriness" in *The Waste Land*. Briefly there's a meeting of the minds. Ginsberg and Eliot seem to be kindred spirits, but that isn't meant to be. Ginsberg denounces the CIA and Eliot defends the CIA. Moreover, Ginsberg has Eliot confess that he once worked for the CIA and Ginsberg says he suspected as much all along.

### Attacking the Beats

In 1957 and 1958, he was in a conspiratorial frame of mind, though he didn't accuse the CIA then and there of playing a role in the subversion of culture. As far as he was concerned, it was only the Columbia College English department that was responsible for the onslaught on the Beat Generation, the San Francisco Poetry Renaissance, and the attacks on *Howl*. Lionel Trilling had condemned his poem, and now two former students of Trilling's— as well as his own former classmates—condemned it in print, also attacking Kerouac and the Beat Generation. Allen felt betrayed. Maybe Trilling himself was behind the assault on *Howl*, he thought, if not directly then indirectly. Perhaps some of Trilling's former students wanted to show that they were still loyal, and that they hadn't turned, as Allen seemed to have turned, on his former professor and on the values and traditions of the Columbia English department.

John Hollander's review of *Howl and Other Poems*—and half a dozen other books of poetry, including Rexroth's *In Defense of the Earth*—appeared in *Partisan Review* in the spring of 1957, when Allen was abroad. Hollander had met Ginsberg for the first time a decade earlier when Allen was an undergraduate. Like almost everyone else on campus, Hollander knew that Allen had been suspended for writing obscenities in the dust of his dorm window and that he'd been to Dakar and back—which meant that he'd traveled much farther afield than anyone else at Columbia and farther even than Kerouac. Hollander had read Ginsberg's poems and essays, which were published in the *Columbia Review*, and he watched in amazement as Ginsberg took on different personae, from the poet maudit—the poet accursed by bourgeois society and perhaps by God as well—to the poet scholar. Soon after they met, Ginsberg became Hollander's "poetic mentor as well as friend." "I showed him everything I wrote, and I can still remember his cheerful and serious tone of voice as he would read aloud," Hollander wrote years later. Hollander listened to Allen's poems in imitation of Andrew Marvell and listened attentively as he talked about Rimbaud, Wordsworth, and his own mother, Naomi. There had been real intimacy between the two young poets, and there had been a sense of trust, too. Naturally, Ginsberg was surprised to read Hollander's comment that *Howl and Other Poems* was a "dreadful little volume." Hollander did acknowledge Ginsberg's "real talent"—his "marvelous ear," and his grotesque sense of humor. In his review, he also hinted at their college friendship. "Even without knowing his profound and carefully organized earlier writing (unpublished in book form), one might suspect a good poet lurking behind the modish façade of a frantic and *talentlos* avant-garde," he wrote. As far as Ginsberg was concerned, there was nothing redemptive about the review; it was just "nasty." And the literary nastiness kept coming hard and fast—from all directions. In the summer of 1957, the *Sewanee Review* published a largely negative review of *Howl and Other Poems* by the Georgia-born poet and critic James Dickey. Like Hollander, Dickey allowed that beneath Ginsberg's "exhibitionist welter of unrelated associations," there was "comic talent" and a "passion for values." But from Dickey's perspective, Ginsberg was a poseur. He was all "Attitude"—and it was "really not worth examining," he concluded.

The biggest assault on Ginsberg, *Howl*, and the Beats was still to come. In September 1957, the *New Republic* published Norman Podhoretz's essay "A Howl of Protest in San Francisco," which dismissed almost all of the poets and the poetry to emerge from northern California—though Podhoretz did acknowledge that Ginsberg's "hysteria is tempered with humor." He admired *Howl* because it did not idealize or romanticize "dope-addicts, perverts, and maniacs." Podhoretz's big battle was against the Beat Generation itself, which seemed to him to be in rebellion against America simply for the sake of rebellion. The Beats embraced "homosexuality, jazz, dope-addiction, and vagrancy as outstanding examples of such rebellion," but no genuine political or social rebellion, he complained. Podhoretz's essay in the *New Republic* was a warm-up for a longer, heftier article, "The Know-Nothing Bohemians," which appeared in *Partisan Review* in the spring of 1958 and which attracted national attention.

In case anyone in academia and in publishing had not noticed,

Podhoretz's second article made it clear that there was a raging intellectual battle, if not in the streets of America, than at least in the pages of its major literary magazines. Indeed, *Howl* had triggered a culture war between academia and bohemia, New York and San Francisco—a culture war about tradition and the individual talent, politics and the arts, manners and morals. Kerouac's *On the Road* intensified the war when it was published in 1957—and appeared albeit briefly on the *New York Times* bestseller list. When Burroughs's novel *Naked Lunch* appeared in print, literary battles broke out all over again. Once again there was an obscenity trial, this time in Boston, and this time Ginsberg went to court and testified for Burroughs. As Norman Mailer noted, the Beats generated "enormous antipathy" in the "vested centers of literary power." The war started as a skirmish among members of the Columbia family. Ginsberg, Kerouac, and Ferlinghetti—all of them Columbia men—were on one side. Hollander, Podhoretz, and Trilling—Columbia men, too—were on the other side. The family feud quickly spread from coast to coast, campus to campus, magazine to magazine, until it took in nearly the whole of American literati in the late 1950s and early 1960s. African American writers like Le Roi Jones and James Baldwin took sides—Jones was pro-Beat; the Beats were his brothers. Baldwin was anti-Beat; Kerouac and his companions were nothing more than "Suzuki rhythm boys," Baldwin wrote. *Life*—the all-purpose American magazine—reported on the pop culture phenomenon as it spread from "Beatsville" to "Squaresville," informing the general public of what was cool and hip and what wasn't. Lawrence Lipton, the southern California poet and critic, penned his defense of the Beats, *The Holy Barbarians* (1959). Gene Feldman and Max

Gartenberg added fuel to the fire with their anthology, *The Beat Generation & the Angry Young Men* (1958), which included writers on both sides of the Atlantic—Kingsley Amis, Jack Kerouac, Allen Ginsberg, and Colin Wilson. Eventually FBI Director J. Edgar Hoover weighed in and announced to the nation that the Beats were a bigger threat than the communists themselves. Ginsberg agreed. He and Kerouac and Burroughs, and all the rock'n'rollers of the 1950s, did more than any left-wing activists to undermine American hegemony, he argued.

For the most part, Hollander discussed poetry and aesthetics in his *Partisan Review* piece—two topics unlikely to generate heated debate in the culture at large. Norman Podhoretz, on the other hand, was an ideologue and a polemicist with a flair for sweeping ethical statements and melodramatic innuendo. He was also a protégé of Lionel Trilling, which added to his stature as a critic. By the time Podhoretz concluded his *Partisan Review* article, he had touched on the nature of bohemianism, the American middle class, race and racial conflict, and even the "history of modern times." The Beats provided Podhoretz with a convenient springboard for his all-embracing assault. Then, too, his assault on the Beats helped to catapult him into the front ranks of American intellectuals. As Norman Mailer noted, "There were people who made a career out of attacking the Beats." Podhoretz was one of them. A year after his blistering article appeared in *Partisan Review*, he became the editor of *Commentary*. It certainly didn't hurt his career that he'd condemned Kerouac and the Beats. In "The Know-Nothing Bohemians," he had little to say about *Howl*—though he did describe it, patronizingly, as a "little volume of poems." Nor did he have much to say about Ginsberg, though he did "out" him for the first time in print. In 1958, before Allen was fully prepared to step out of the closet, Podhoretz noted that "homosexuality" was Allen's "preserve." (Allen would out himself at a reading when a listener in the audience asked why there were references to homosexuality in *Howl*. That was because *he* was a homosexual, he said. If doubts remained in the minds of his readers, and in the nation at large, he put them to rest little by little. He posed in the nude with his lover, Peter Orlovsky, and became a poster boy and advocate for the gay liberation movement.) Perhaps Podhoretz pushed him to out himself. In 1958, Podhoretz also noted that Allen's poetry expressed the "darker side" of the Beat Generation and that it spoke for "violence and criminality, main-line drug addiction and madness." Kerouac was less violent, less crazy, but in Podhoretz's estimation both writers were anti-intellectual. Podhoretz had not yet read *Naked Lunch*, but that novel would no doubt have confirmed his view of the Beats as dark, sinister, and violent. After all, Burroughs had shot and killed his wife, albeit by accident. He had been a heroin addict for most of his life and thought that addiction offered a paradigm for understanding nearly everything, from war and money to sex and drugs.

Podhoretz's review verged on hysteria, and it whipped up hysteria too, especially when it compared the Beats to the kind of violent teenagers depicted in the 1955 movie *The Blackboard Jungle*. Still, Podhoretz offered some insightful comments. He focused attention on the controversial passage in *On the Road* in which Kerouac wrote about the Negroes of Denver, Colorado, and how he wanted to be a Negro. Podhoretz observed that few apologists for slavery or segregation had depicted a "more idyllic picture of Negro life" than Jack Kerouac. Moreover, he astutely noted that though Kerouac admired Negroes, he didn't support the civil rights movement for integration that was gathering steam in the American South. Podhoretz observed that Kerouac was no liberal supporter of civil rights; he proceeded to paint him with a broad brush as a kind of crypto-fascist who "worships primitivism, instinct, energy, 'blood.'" From there, Podhoretz took an ideological leap, linking the Beat Generation to gangs and gang violence. "The spirit of hipsterism and the Beat Generation strikes me as the same spirit which animates the young savages in leather jackets who have been running amuck in the last few years with their switch-blades and zip guns," he wrote. At Columbia in the 1940s, Ginsberg had indeed called for young savages to assault genteel civilization, but his savages were far more metaphorical than real. Knives and guns never were his style, or Kerouac's, either.

### We're Not Martians

Kerouac rose to his defense and wrote several incisive articles— "About the Beat Generation," "Lamb, No Lion," and "Beatific: The Origins of the Beat Generation"—in which he depicted himself and his Beat brothers as spiritually minded, not violence prone. "The Beat Generation is no hoodlumism," he proclaimed. He was proud of the fact that there was "a Beat Generation all over the world, even behind the Iron Curtain," and he predicted that the Beat Generation would be the "most sensitive generation in the history of America." Kerouac appeared on television and brought his message to millions, but he was unsuited for polemic debate with the likes of Norman Podhoretz. He took it all too personally.

Ginsberg was angered, annoyed, and saddened by Podhoretz's

"The Know-Nothing Bohemians." As soon as he collected his thoughts—and, at the same time, worked himself into a frenzy—he mounted a spirited literary defense of himself, Kerouac, and the Beat Generation. In print and in face-to-face meetings that often turned confrontational, Ginsberg blasted his former college friends—both Hollander and Podhoretz—and almost everyone else in the New York literary and academic world. But he was also capable of maintaining a sense of humor about it all. His open letter to Hollander began "Dear John," and ended playfully, "Yours in the kingdom of music"—and he spelled his own name backward, "Nella Grebsnig." Ginsberg's letter wasn't simply a personal note to an old friend, as it might have seemed at first glance. He circulated copies among friends. Later, the letter was printed in its entirety in Jane Kramer's *Allen Ginsberg in America*, where it served as a literary manifesto and a cultural call to arms.

Sitting at his typewriter, Ginsberg poured out much of the bile that had been building up for at least a decade. Halfway through the letter to Hollander, he paused and asked a rhetorical question, "Well what's all this leading up to?" And he answered, "I don't know yet I'm just obviously blowing off steam." But the steam was carefully aimed at what he called the "whole horror of Columbia," at Lionel Trilling ("who is absolutely lost in poetry"), the New Criticism, *Time* magazine, and *Partisan Review*. He raved and ranted about America's ignorant intelligentsia, the "American Egghead," "Podhoretz & the rest of the whores," as well as the plain ordinary "jerks who have no interest but their ridiculous devilish social careers and MONEY MONEY MONEY." More than anyone else, he detested Podhoretz. His article was just "*wrong* (unscientific)," he wrote, and the expression of "ridiculous provincial schoolboy ambitions." All the hurtful names he'd been called—ambitious, schoolboy, and provincial—he now hurled back.

Ginsberg was not exclusively negative in his long letter to Hollander. He made it clear that he loved the Black Mountain School of poets. He revered Robert Creeley, Paul Blackburn, and Joel Oppenheimer, all of whom would be included in Donald M. Allen's popular anthology *The New American Poetry* (1960)—along with the Beat poets, which helped enormously to bring the poetry revolution to campuses all across America.

Despite his screams of frustration and anger—"THEY CAN TAKE THEIR FUCKING literary tradition AND SHOVE IT UP THEIR ASS"—Ginsberg's letter to Hollander offers insightful ideas about the theory and practice of poetry, most of which derived from the actual experience of writing *Howl.* "Poetry is what poets write, and not what other people think they should write," he exclaimed. On a more personal note, he said, "I am sick of preconceived literature and only interested in *writing* the actual process and technique, wherever it leads." About *Howl,* he insisted that it was an experiment with form itself. "FORM FORM FORM," he insisted. It was indeed a brave attempt to reinvent worn-out poetical forms, and traditionalists distrusted its unconventionality.

Throughout his letter to Hollander, Ginsberg practically begged to be read and understood as a poet with integrity and sincerity. "John," he cried out at one point, have the "heart and the decency" to "take me seriously." Despite his seemingly all-powerful ego and his protective personae, Ginsberg was exceedingly vulnerable. He had a profound need to be treated with respect and with kindness—as shown by the entries in the journal—and not treated as a cultural clown. The critics and the reviewers didn't take the Beat writers seriously, he complained. In the same breath, he argued that he and Kerouac were taken too seriously. He had to have it both ways; that was his nature. For years, he explained, he had been reading "outright vicious blather" about the Beats, and he was astounded, surprised, weary, and hurt. "They should treat us more kindly," he wrote, and with a sense of playfulness he added, "after all, we're poets and novelists; we're not Martians in disguise trying to poison the minds with anti-earth propaganda." Moreover, he predicted that his poetry and Kerouac's novels would be taught at Columbia "in 20 years, or sooner." The pendulum would swing in the opposite direction: the Beats would be as loved and as revered as they were now hated and reviled. That thought disturbed him greatly. He was afraid that Beat books, values, and ideas would find their way into the mainstream in some sort of watered-down form. Nothing alarmed him more than that. His very worst fear, he noted, was that the Beats would be read "too familiarly" and "accepted in some dopey platitudinous form."

Perhaps nothing that Ginsberg wrote was more prophetic. It didn't take long for the adversary culture of the Beats to become absorbed into the culture at large, much as it didn't take long for Beat spirituality to be brokered, packaged, and marketed. His worst fears were realized before he knew it. As William Burroughs noted, "Kerouac opened a million coffee bars and sold a million pairs of Levis to both sexes," though of course he didn't directly profit from the commercialization of the counterculture.

After he wrote *Howl*, Ginsberg set an impossible task for himself: to write original poetry time after time. "The only pattern of value or interest in poetry," he wrote in his Paris diary, was the pattern that was "discovered in the moment . . . at the time of composition." In his open letter to Hollander, he made much the same comment. "Any poem I write that I have written before, in which I don't discover something new (psychically) and maybe formally, is a waste of time, it's not living," he exclaimed. After *Howl*, he wrote original poems and extraordinary poems, but he couldn't and didn't discover something new psychically and formally each time. He couldn't and didn't duplicate the breakthrough he had made with *Howl*. Moreover, he couldn't continue to remain detached from the "fiction named Allen Ginsberg." The older he became, the more attached he became to a fixed identity. It became increasingly difficult to embrace the "nameless wildness." By the early 1980s, he recognized the attachment to his persona as the famous Beat poet and author of *Howl*. Even *Kaddish* follows much the same basic form he created in *Howl*, and at his worst he fell back on literary formulas. Not surprisingly, many of his best late poems were about his own "fixed identity" and about the "fiction named Allen Ginsberg." He expressed that concern in the 1983 poem "I'm a Prisoner of Allen Ginsberg," in which he wondered—bitterly, ironically, and humorously—"Who is this Slave Master makes / me answer letters in his name / Write poetry year after year, keep up / appearances." He returned to the theme again and again. In "After Lalon," a brilliant 1992 poem, he warns against the dangers of fame and the attachments to the things of this world. And yet he couldn't detach himself. Shortly before his death in 1997 he called the White House to ask if President Bill Clinton might grant him a literary award—some final recognition by the nation of his lifetime achievement.

# CHAPTER ELEVEN

# Best
# Minds

In the winter and spring of 1957—as the media discovered the
Beats—Ginsberg, Kerouac, and company made a series of pil-
grimages to honor the writers and artists they admired. Oddly
enough, though they celebrated their own generation, they
reached out to men from an earlier generation, as though they
consciously wanted to belong to a tradition of nonconformists.
Their first stop was Manhattan, where they met the Spanish sur-
realist Salvador Dalí. Then it was on to Rutherford, New Jersey,
to visit William Carlos Williams, then seventy-three years old
and an enthusiastic supporter of the Beat Generation's literary
revolution. Williams was impressed that Ginsberg's "gang" had
been reading to audiences of "up to 400 people FOR Free." After
New Jersey, they were off to more exotic locations, especially
Tangier, Morocco, where they explored the Casbah, experi-
mented with drugs, and visited Burroughs, who had been an ex-
patriate for years. Ginsberg helped transform the disorganized

papers in his apartment into *Naked Lunch*, and before long the phantasmagoric novel would be published in Paris and then in the United States.

In the summer of 1957, while Ginsberg continued his travels, Kerouac returned to America. With his mother, Gabrielle, whom he had tended for much of his adult life, he moved to a small house in Berkeley and complained to friends that he was "bored"—and that Berkeley itself was a "real horror." *On the Road* was on the way to the printer and he was anxious for his long-delayed novel to arrive in his hands—and the hands of reviewers and readers. At the last minute, he thought he might link his work to the latest popular music bandwagon by changing the title of *On the Road* to ROCK AND ROLL ROAD as a way to "double the sales." Then again, there might not be any sales at all. He was terrified that Viking, his publisher, might get "chickenshit" and "put off the publication" of his novel. He wasn't entirely paranoid. For years, *On the Road* had been read and rejected by editors. Now, it seemed likely that the book would encounter more adversity and hostility. In San Francisco in 1957 Kerouac was unnerved by the controversy surrounding *Howl*, which he thought might endanger his own as yet unborn book. In his darkest moods, he thought that he might be doomed to live in the shadow of Ginsberg, and he didn't like it. "I'm introduced as 'that guy that HOWL is dedicated to!' (you rat!)—Cant be famous on my own," he complained.

In the summer of 1957, Ginsberg was awfully famous and getting more and more famous by the month, if not the week, thanks in large part to the puritanically minded folk in San Francisco who were troubled by the obscenities in *Howl*. From the start Louis Ginsberg had complained about the "dirty, ugly words." They would only "entangle" his son in trouble, and Louis urged his son to "cut them out." Of course, Allen wasn't in a frame of mind to heed his father. But in the fall of 1956, and at the proverbial last minute, Villers, the rather prudish British firm, refused to print *Howl* word for word. There were too many dirty words; Allen was forced to make revisions. It was self-censor, or no poem, and so there were the inevitable delays as he made changes and expunged the four-letter words. Finally, the book went to press and arrived safely at the port of San Francisco. Where the words "fucked" and "ass" had once been there were now a series of dots—"who let themselves be . . . in the . . . by saintly motor- / cyclists, and screamed with joy"—leaving readers to guess just what had been omitted. At first, the edition of *Howl* that Villers printed passed through customs, and before long it was "selling like hotcakes," as Ginsberg proudly reported to his brother, Eugene. Then, on March 25, 1957, 520 copies of the second edition of *Howl* were seized by Chester MacPhee, the collector of customs, on the grounds that the poem was obscene, and because, as he told the *San Francisco Chronicle,* "you wouldn't want your children to come across it." *Howl* was, of course, only a poem, but it had raised a ruckus in San Francisco far beyond the local poetry circles, and the local philistines felt impelled to cleanse their community of the offending text. Throughout the mid-1950s the San Francisco Police Department waged a relentless—and inevitably futile—war against the city's burgeoning homosexual subculture, raiding bars, arresting suspects, and dispersing homosexuals when they gathered in public parks, on the beach, and on street corners. Now, despite all that intense police repression, homosexuality reared its head in *Howl,* and that was intolerable. Poets like Robert Duncan and Jack Spicer had been outrageous from time to time, but they were local lads who seemed to know their place when push came to shove. Ginsberg was another story—a loud, pushy New Yorker. In the eyes of conservative San Francisco, he was an outside agitator who was disrespectful of the city and its culture. City Lights—which had been founded by two New Yorkers—wasn't far behind on their list of enemies.

Lawrence Ferlinghetti was no innocent bystander in the literary storm that broke across the city. Ginsberg exaggerated when he noted that Ferlinghetti was the "most advanced publisher in America in that he publishes 'suspect' literature." There were other publishers who fit that description in the 1950s, including Barney Rosset at Grove Press and James Laughlin at New Directions, but Ferlinghetti was certainly one of the most advanced publishers, and he knew what he was getting into when he offered to publish *Howl* in October 1955. A longtime student of controversial literature and the history of publishing in America in the nineteenth and twentieth centuries, Ferlinghetti anticipated trouble from the start. As he knew, Whitman had had more than his share of troubles with *Leaves of Grass*. It was likely that censorship would rear its ugly head once again. Accordingly, Ferlinghetti submitted a copy of the manuscript of *Howl* to lawyers for the American Civil Liberties Union (ACLU).

Months before it was published, the ACLU lawyers, including the legendary Jake Ehrlich, agreed to defend it for free, if and when trouble arose. "I almost hope it does," Ginsberg confessed. "I am almost ready to tackle the U.S. Gov[ernmen]t out of sheer self delight." Henry Miller's books, including *Tropic of Cancer*—which he was reading for the first time in San Francisco and which he called a "great classic"—had been banned and he was ready and willing to be banned, too. Fomenting a literary and a cultural revolution was at the top of his agenda. Now, he was delighted that customs had confiscated his book since it would mean increased sales. "I guess the seizure works out fine as publicity," he observed. From Europe, he followed the situation as it unfolded and kept in regular contact with Ferlinghetti about the legal situation. Jack Kerouac followed the situation from Berkeley and kept Allen informed, too.

On April 3, 1957, about a week after MacPhee seized the second printing of *Howl*, the ACLU served notice that it would contest the legality of his action. At the same time, Ferlinghetti authorized the printing of a new edition within the United States, a shrewd move that put *Howl* out of the reach of customs. Before long, books were back on the shelves at City Lights, sales were brisk, and a real literary controversy erupted. *Howl* proved to be irrepressible and uncontainable. *Evergreen Review*, which was edited by Barney Rosset and Donald Allen, published an entire issue devoted to the "San Francisco scene." *Howl* was the highlight of the volume, though there was also excellent work by McClure, Kerouac, Snyder, Whalen, Ferlinghetti, and William Everson, a lay brother in the Catholic Church known as Brother Antonius. The Austrian-born photographer Harry Redl, who was the same age as Ginsberg, provided stunning black-and-white portraits of eight of the contributors to the volume. Michael McClure looked like he was trying to look like James Dean. Allen Ginsberg looked—with his dark glasses and intense eyes—like a bohemian intellectual.

*Evergreen Review* boasted an essay entitled "San Francisco Letter" by Kenneth Rexroth in which he noted that William Everson/Brother Antonius was the "finest Catholic poet" in

America and that Robert Duncan was the local representative of the "international avant-garde." In Rexroth's view Ginsberg was "one of the most remarkable versifiers in America," and *Howl* was "the most sensational book of poetry of 1957." That description was apt, though there were other powerful—though less sensational—books of poetry published in 1957, including Denise Levertov's *Here and Now* and James Wright's *The Green Wall*. Rexroth added that *Howl* was neither violent nor obscene. "It is Hollywood or the censors who are obscene," he argued. If Ginsberg continued to write, Rexroth predicted, he would become the "first genuinely popular, genuine poet in over a generation—and he is already considerably the superior of predecessors like Lindsay and Sandburg."

Everyone seemed to have a definitive opinion about *Howl* and the case against it. On April 7, 1957, William Hogan, the book review editor of the *San Francisco Chronicle*, noted in his weekly column that MacPhee's seizure was unfortunate to say the least. As Hogan pointed out, the U.S. Supreme Court had recently ruled that reducing adults "to reading only what is fit for children" was a violation of the First Amendment. He added that MacPhee might "face some real problems if a shipment of some editions of the Bible, among other of the world's literature, ever enters this port." On May 19, 1957, the *Chronicle* published a feisty article by Ferlinghetti that intensified the debate. *Howl* was, in Ferlinghetti's opinion, the "most significant single long poem to be published in this country since World War II, perhaps since T. S. Eliot's *Four Quartets*." Echoing Rexroth, Ferlinghetti added that *Howl* wasn't obscene. The real obscenity was the "sad wastes of the mechanized world, lost among atom bombs and insane nationalism." Curiously, it was the Catholic poet William Everson who argued not only that *Howl* was indeed obscene but also that its obscenity was the mark of its genius. "It was Ginsberg's insight into the operative power of the obscene that gave him the leverage to effect a revolution in American poetry [and] precipitate a new concept of the poem," he wrote. From Everson's point of view, Allen had broken down barriers. He made the private public—put the naked mind and body in the open—and that was obscene to the Babbitts and the Puritans of the 1950s.

Given the prevailing cultural climate in San Francisco, as well as the U.S. Supreme Court's recent rulings on obscenity, the U.S. attorney in San Francisco declined to prosecute City Lights, Ginsberg, or Ferlinghetti, and on May 29, 1957, MacPhee released the 520 copies he had seized two months earlier. But that wasn't the end of the story. The San Francisco police leapt into the fray—even before MacPhee let his confiscated copies of *Howl* go. Captain William Hanrahan of the juvenile department concluded that *Howl* was unfit for children and therefore unfit to appear anywhere in the city of San Francisco. On May 21, 1957, two police officers, Russell Woods and Thomas Pagee, entered City Lights, bought a copy of *Howl* from Shigeyoshi Murao—the store's clerk and mainstay—for seventy-five cents, and obtained a warrant for his and Ferlinghetti's arrest. Kerouac followed the story closely—he even visited City Lights to size up the situation for himself—and described everything he heard and saw to Ginsberg, who was in Europe, thousands of miles away. "Let me report on HOWL," he wrote. "The local dumb Irish cops . . . bought HOWL in the store and arrested the nice Jap[anese] cat who was instantly bailed out by [the American] Civil Liberties Union but I went there & there were no more HOWLS on the shelf." Ferlinghetti was out of town,

Kerouac explained, but he would return soon and surrender to the authorities.

Kerouac was genuinely worried. He confessed to Allen that he was afraid that America would become "like Germany, a police state." Still, he noted that there were a few brave souls, like Rexroth, who would rise to the occasion and fight fascism to the end. "So Allen do not worry," he wrote. "Write a big poem called WAIL beginning 'Wail for the cripples of Morocco crawling on their bellies.'" In Morocco, surrounded by both poverty and Old World culture, the legal assault on *Howl* seemed surreal to Allen, and he never took it seriously—not as seriously as the reviews and articles by his college classmates John Hollander and Norman Podhoretz. In large part, he regarded the legal matter as Ferlinghetti's problem, not his own. Granted, he told his brother, Eugene, he was "sorry to miss" the "excitement in San Francisco," and he was thinking of giving a "big reading" of *Howl* at San Francisco State. He would send invitations to the police, deliberately provoke the authorities, "get arrested and end up in jail," he wrote. He would become a literary cause célèbre. But that never came to pass. Ginsberg never seriously considered appearing at the trial of *Howl*, which took place in the summer of 1957, and indeed, his own personal cause, as well as the cause of his poem and of City Lights, may well have been helped, not hindered, by his conspicuous absence.

The outcome of the trial was, to a certain degree, known even before it began. There was tremendous local opposition to the prosecution from the *San Francisco Chronicle* and from the academic world. Indeed, there was a solid liberal community in San Francisco. Moreover, just months before *Howl* went on trial, the U.S. Supreme Court ruled in *Roth v. the United States* that literature was not obscene if it had "redeeming social importance." It seemed likely, from the start, that *Howl* would be found to have some redeeming social value. The case was heard before a single judge, and though Judge Clayton Horn seemed conservative— he taught Bible class in Sunday school at his local church—he also believed unequivocally in the First Amendment. He had, of course, read the *Roth* decision, and he understood obscenity law as redefined by the U.S. Supreme Court. Before and during the trial, Judge Horn thought long and hard about Justice Brennan's benchmark opinion that the Constitution guaranteed citizens the right to discuss publicly, openly, and without fear of punishment matters of public concern, including sexual matters. He also thought about Justice William O. Douglas's stunning opinion. Indeed, he turned out to be far closer to Justice Douglas— who believed that American citizens on their own were fully capable of judging what was obscene—than to anyone else on the U.S. Supreme Court.

### The Classroom Comes to the Courtroom

Even before the trial began, Ferlinghetti and his able ACLU attorneys—Jake Ehrlich, Lawrence Speiser, and Albert Bendich— provided Judge Horn with a wealth of opinion from experts about the merits of *Howl*. Ruth Witt-Diamant, director of the San Francisco Poetry Center, and her assistant, Robert Duncan, noted that *Howl* was not "salacious" and that it was indeed "noble." U. C. Berkeley English professor Thomas Parkinson—who would become a friend of Allen's—testified that *Howl* was "one of the most important books of poetry published in the last ten years." Barney Rosset and Donald Allen said that they had published *Howl* in

*Evergreen Review* because it was "a significant modern poem." The Northern California Booksellers Association (NCBA) was a bit timid. "It may or may not be literature," the association's statement read, but it had "literary merit." Moreover, the NCBA felt that the "proposition that adult literature must meet the standards of suitability for children is manifestly absurd."

The pretrial publicity promised a dramatic courtroom drama, and in fact the city of San Francisco followed the trial closely throughout the summer of 1957. In many ways, however, it wasn't so much a trial as a seminar in which many of the best minds of the Bay Area had the opportunity to hold forth, on the witness stand, about literature and society, art and morality, poetry and poets. It was as though the classroom came to the courtroom, and the language of college English departments entered the domain of the law. The First Amendment seemed to offer protection to the defendants, and so did the California Constitution, which, as Judge Horn pointed out, guaranteed that "every citizen may freely speak, write, and publish his sentiments on all subjects." Ferlinghetti and Murao were charged with violating Section 311.3 of the penal code of the State of California, which made it a felony for any citizen to write, compose, print, publish, sell, distribute, keep for sale, or exhibit any obscene or indecent writing, paper, or book. Obscenity had never received First Amendment protection, and as always the issue before the court was the nature of obscenity. Just what was it? In *Roth v. the United States*, the U.S. Supreme Court offered a series of tests that made Judge Horn's task easier than it might have been otherwise.

Judge Horn knew that he had to make his ruling on the basis of contemporary community standards in San Francisco—not the standards of the Victorian past or of Peoria—and that he had to be guided by the viewpoint of the average citizen. He knew, too, that *Howl* had to be judged as a whole, not on the basis of isolated four-letter words. So, for example, the word "bullshit"— which appears at the end of the Moloch section in the phrase the "whole boatload of sensitive / bullshit!"—could not justify censorship of the entire volume. It was clear to Judge Horn that Ferlinghetti had read Ginsberg's manuscript and had decided to turn it into a book and distribute it, four-letter words and all. However, it wasn't clear that Shig Murao was aware of the poem's language when he sold a copy of *Howl* to the police. At the opening of the trial, Murao was all dressed up in a light blue summer suit, prepared to testify, but the charges were promptly dropped against him, and Ferlinghetti emerged as the lone defendant. The prosecution offered a pathetic case. Ralph McIntosh, the deputy district attorney, argued that the average person would not and could not understand *Howl*. He added that he himself did not "understand it very well." Still, he remembered parts of it well enough to quote them, and to note, "I think it is a lot of sensitive bullshit." But there wasn't much bite to his bark.

The prosecution called only two witnesses, neither of whom was versed in the field of obscenity and neither of whom had a national reputation. Gail Potter, an English instructor who had taught at Dominican College and Golden Gate College, testified that reading *Howl* made her feel dirty. "It has no literary merit," she concluded. David Kirk, an assistant professor of English at the University of San Francisco, said that after reading *Howl* for only a few minutes he realized that it was worthless—a "weak imitation" of Walt Whitman and a hopeless monument "to a long-dead movement—'Dadaism.'"

Jake ("Never Plead Guilty") Ehrlich, the lead attorney for the

ACLU, was brilliant. He had done his homework, and in the courtroom he demonstrated his ability to wax poetic. He also discussed the nature of censorship and quoted from the landmark obscenity cases of the twentieth century, including Judge John M. Woolsey's groundbreaking opinion in the 1933 trial against James Joyce's *Ulysses*. "The desire to censor," Ehrlich noted, was "not limited to crackpots and bigots," but could be found in all walks of life. Language itself was not "a crystal, transparent," but rather the "skin of a living thought," he said, sounding like an erudite professor of literature. Ehrlich specifically defended the use of the word "fuck." To make his point he read from Christopher Marlowe's sixteenth-century poem "Ignato," which begins, "I love thee not for Sacred Chastity" and which ends with the author insisting that he loves the woman about whom he writes because, "zounds I can fuck thee soundly." Surely no defense attorney in an obscenity trial—except in the trial against *Naked Lunch*—ever had a more impressive group of creative writers and veteran teachers in his corner. They were surprisingly noncompetitive with one another, too. Kenneth Rexroth knew that Judge Horn taught the Bible, and accordingly he argued that *Howl* was "Biblical"—a prophetic poem similar in style and subject matter to the books of the Old Testament—an argument that seems to have swayed Horn. Herbert Blau, a San Francisco State teacher and the co-founder and consulting director of the Actors Workshop of the San Francisco Drama Guild, testified that *Howl* was "resurrective in quality" and a "sort of paean of possible hope." Mark Linethal, who also taught at San Francisco State, explained that *Howl* was an indictment of "violence, greed, wastefulness" in language that was "violent and powerful." Walter Van Tilburg Clark—the author of two riveting, popular novels that had been made into impressive films, *The Ox-Bow Incident* and *The Track of the Cat*, and the most famous witness for the defense—argued that Ginsberg was an "honest poet" and a "highly competent technician." Leo Lowenthal, who taught at the University of California at Berkeley and was the author of *Literature and the Image of Man*, observed that *Howl* was a "genuine work of literature" and "characteristic for a period of unrest and tension"—like the period that followed World War II. From almost every critical point of view, *Howl* was dissected, analyzed, and lauded.

Luther Nichols, the book reviewer for the *San Francisco Examiner*, explained that Ginsberg was legitimately angry about the atom bomb, and he noted that people who were angry often used four-letter words like "fuck." When asked to interpret the section of *Howl* in which Ginsberg mythologizes Neal Cassady's sexuality, Nichols explained that it was about "fertility." From his perspective, one might say that the "secret hero" of the poem was meant to be a sex god who would rejuvenate the sexless wasteland of modern society—and that *Howl* itself was an invitation to a more open and healthy sexuality.

The star of the show for the defense was Mark Schorer, whom Ginsberg described as the Lionel Trilling of the West Coast. A distinguished professor in the English department at the University of California at Berkeley, Schorer had made his mark as a scholar, novelist, short story writer, editor of college textbooks, and paid consultant to the United States Army on the selection of texts for its educational programs. With all his erudition and his skills in interpreting poetry, Schorer argued that *Howl* had an "esthetic structure," that it depicted "modern life as a state of hell," and that the form, the language, and the style of the poem

were entirely appropriate—given the theme. When asked to in-
terpret the line, "with dreams, with drugs, with waking night-
mares, alcohol and cock and / endless balls," Schorer said that
"these are uprooted people wandering around the United States,
dreamy, drugged." As for the phrase "who got busted in their pu-
bic beards"—it meant "injured in their sexual beings," he noted.
It was a stunning literary performance.

### Not Guilty, Not Obscene

Judge Horn took his cues from Schorer, Ehrlich, and Supreme
Court Justice William O. Douglas, the most liberal member of the
Supreme Court. Thus, he concluded that *Howl* describes a "night-
mare world" and that it offers an indictment of "materialism, con-
formity, and mechanization leading toward war." It wasn't just a
boatload of insensitive obscenities. Horn echoed Justice Douglas
when he noted that the American people ought to be their own
"self-guardians" and not allow the government to decide for
them what was "noxious literature." Freedom of expression was
essential to a democratic society, he argued, and creative writers
could not be expected, nor should they be compelled, to use a vo-
cabulary made up of "vapid innocuous euphemism." Nor could
writers of adult books be expected to use the standards set for
children's literature. With all the evidence in hand, Judge Horn
ruled that *Howl* had "some redeeming social importance," that it
was not obscene, and that Ferlinghetti was not guilty of the
charges against him. In the course of the trial, the spectators had
variously expressed pleasure and displeasure at the testimony.
Now they screamed with joy. The *San Francisco Chronicle* added
to the joy when it reported that the "judge's decision was hailed

with applause and cheers from a packed audience that offered the most fantastic collection of beards, turtlenecked shirts and Italian hairdos ever to grace the grimy precincts of the Hall of Justice."

## A Venerable Classic

When he delivered his verdict, Judge Horn did not discuss at length the artistic merits of *Howl*, nor did he assess its overall place in the body of American literature. During the trial itself, however, there was considerable testimony about great literature, the classics, and literary tradition. Vincent Hugh—a science-fiction writer and an assistant to Clifton Fadiman at the *New Yorker*—noted that *Howl* belonged to a tradition of literature about hell that went back to Ezra Pound (especially Cantos 14 and 15), Dante's *Inferno*, Homer's *Ulysses*, and all the ancient "mythologies of the world." Rexroth argued that *Howl* was "great literature" because it exhibited great technical competence and because—despite its dark vision of fragmented lives—it posited the "possibility of being a whole man." Ehrlich suggested that *Howl* belonged in the pantheon of major American literature. Like many "great works and classics of literature," *Howl* had been "condemned by those who see destruction in everything . . . and find pornographic skeletons in every closet," he noted. He suggested that like many of the "suppressed books" of the past, it too would become a "venerable classic."

Ever since the trial of *Howl*, Ginsberg's poem has grown in stature—though now and then it has also gone through periods of neglect. Marjorie Perloff, who has written insightfully about Ginsberg and about *Howl*, noted that she once "tended to ignore Ginsberg's achievement, perhaps in reaction to the journalistic overkill devoted to the Beat Generation." Other critics have been less candid, though they, too, have ignored *Howl*. Half a century after its initial publication, *Howl* is widely recognized as an American classic and, in the words of Perloff, as the "most harrowing as well as the funniest of autobiographies."

*Howl* also seems to meet most of the criteria for a classic that T. S. Eliot—whose authority Ginsberg both respected and railed against—mentions in his incisive 1944 essay, "What Is a Classic?" "The perfect classic must be one in which the whole genius of a people will be latent," Eliot wrote. "The classic must, within its formal limitations, express the maximum possible of the whole range of feeling which represents the character of the people who speak that language." And, within its own unique formal structure, *Howl* expresses the extremes of American feeling and the extremes of the American character. In *Howl*, Ginsberg moves from futility to ecstasy, paranoia to inner peace, and from a sense of terror to a sense of holiness. He captures the feelings of doom and despair that many Americans experienced in the wake of World War II. And he records the American sense of renewal and rebirth. Ginsberg's America is both hell and paradise. It's a land of the open road and the dead end of civilization. In *Howl*, America is Alcatraz and Los Alamos, lonely streets and crowded asylums. There are echoes of the comedy of Charlie Chaplin and the blues of Charlie Parker, the world weariness of T. S. Eliot and the innocent wildness of Walt Whitman. *Howl* is a quintessentially American poem of the mid-twentieth century. It is a scream that woke the country, shocked it, and reminded it of its dreams, possibilities, and joys. It still has the power to provoke profound emotional responses, to make readers think about their own secrets, their own nakedness, their own madness.

In his 1957 review of *Howl*, James Dickey dismissed Ginsberg's poem as the work of an "American adolescent." And there is a uniquely American adolescent energy about *Howl*. There's a boyish delight in obscenity and a prankish joy in provoking and poking fun at authority figures. Ginsberg admitted the adolescent quality of his poem when he explained that in writing *Howl* he hoped that he might smuggle the word "fuck"—a "clean Saxon four-letter word," he called it—into "high school anthologies permanently and deflate tendencies toward authoritarian strong-arming." An adolescent view of august authorities can be refreshing—as in J. D. Salinger's *Catcher in the Rye* (1951). The American adolescent energy of *Howl*—like the adolescent energy of *Catcher in the Rye*—seems to add to rather than diminish its appeal.

When we read a classic, Eliot observed, we do not say that "'this is a man of genius using the language' but 'this realizes the genius of the language.'" In *Howl*, Ginsberg realized a great deal of the genius of the American language. Like *Leaves of Grass*, *Howl* was an experiment with language. Ginsberg combined the vernacular with the lexicon of holy men, mixed obscenities with sacred oaths, linked the slang of the day with the rhetorical flourishes of the founding fathers of the Republic. He spoke the language of immigrants, natives, New Yorkers, hipsters, and transcendentalists; he borrowed from Latin and broke new verbal ground. Ginsberg honored the language of dead poets, but also the language of the living street. As he wrote *Howl*, he became intoxicated with words and the sounds of words—"boxcars boxcars boxcars racketing through snow toward / lonesome farms." Even today, reading the poem yields a feeling of intoxication. The words produce an electrical charge that is exhilarating.

Eliot noted, too, that a classic "will find its response among all classes and conditions of men." *Howl* has been read and appreciated all around the world—by men in overalls and women in academic gowns, by African American intellectuals and immigrants from Europe and Asia. *Howl* has been embraced by bohemians, hipsters, beats, hippies—by nonconformists in Prague and Peking, existentialists in Paris, and poets in provincial towns. The Nobel Prize poet Czeslaw Milosz—who endured the Cold War on the communist side of the Iron Curtain before moving to the United States—praised *Howl* as a visionary scream against a century of murder, and he lauded Ginsberg, too, as a poet of global sanity. Bob Dylan was inspired by the vision and the language of *Howl*, as were John Lennon and the Beatles. A great many poets and writers—Christopher Buckley, Paul Slansky, and Louis Simpson, Allen's classmate from Columbia College—have parodied *Howl*, but no one has equaled it. "Every great work of poetry tends to make impossible the production of equally great works of the same kind," Eliot wrote. "Every supreme poet, classic or not, tends to exhaust the ground he cultivates." In *Howl* Ginsberg exhausted the ground he cultivated.

### Death and Fame

Ginsberg went on writing poetry for forty years after he wrote *Howl*, and Ferlinghetti continued to publish Ginsberg's work long after *Howl and Other Poems* appeared in 1956, even though he felt that Ginsberg declined as a poet. "There was a shocking deterioration," Ferlinghetti said. Ginsberg himself didn't see it that way. From his point of view there were "peaks of inspiration" over the years as well as "valleys and plateaus." His own creativity came and went in cycles, he felt. There was certainly no diminution in the years immediately after *Howl*. *Kaddish* (1956–1959) is a masterful work in which he expressed his grief for his mother, memorializing her and her generation of European immigrants. In *Kaddish*, he transcended his misogyny, put himself in the background, and put Naomi in the foreground, emphasizing her life and times, not his own. He also learned to allow his deepest feelings to come to the surface, and at the same time to compose a poem with complex form and intricate movement back and forth in time—like a surreal movie.

Ginsberg tried repeatedly to write another big, bold poem for his generation and about his generation—but he didn't just try to imitate *Howl*. For forty years, he experimented, changed direction, and recycled himself. He wrote short poems, lyrical poems, humorous poems, poems with rhyme, and poems set to music, as well as long political poems like *Wichita Vortex Sutra* (1966) and *Plutonian Ode* (1978), in which he wanted language to have all the force of direct action. In *Wichita Vortex Sutra*, he wrote an impassioned antiwar poem from the American heartland, a poem inspired by the peace movement of the mid-1960s that amplified the chorus of voices opposed to the war in Vietnam. In "Put Down Your Cigarette Rag" (1971, 1992) and "C'mon Pigs of Western Civilization Eat More Grease" (1993), he used poetry not to try to alter the political and economic foundations of the world, but to invite readers to change their own individual, age-old habits of consumption, of eating and smoking. Using irony and sarcasm and pouring forth invective, he ranted and raved about the dangers of nicotine and fat.

Poet laureate Billy Collins has described poetry as an antidote to the "noise of public life," and while Ginsberg often wrote a noisy kind of poetry for public life, he also managed to have a sense of humor about himself and the world. Ferlinghetti complained that Ginsberg's "Buddhist practice really harmed his poetry," and while harm may be too strong a word, it may not have helped, either. Ginsberg's Buddhist beliefs may have given him too easy an access to ready-made mythologies, beliefs, and phrases. Still, there are deeply moving poems like "On Cremation of Chögyam Trungpa, Vidyadhara" (1987), which was informed by Buddhism. Here Ginsberg notices the absence of Trungpa, the Buddhist teacher who encouraged him, as did Kerouac, to be more spontaneous and to trust his first thoughts. In "On Cremation of Chögyam Trungpa, Vidyadhara," the poet observes himself and his own breathing. He observes that he forgets, and he notices the particulars of the world around him. That ability to observe himself and his immediate surroundings gives the poem a sense of majesty. Of course, before he officially called himself a Buddhist, Ginsberg was already meditating, practicing detachment, and paying attention to his own breath. Buddhism accentuated these habits, but it didn't make him a better poet, anymore than joining the Church of England made T. S. Eliot a better poet. Of course, he had read Buddhist texts while he was writing *Howl*, and with Kerouac as a spiritual guide he took on the persona of the Buddhist holy man, a persona that helped to infuse the poem with a sense of the suffering of life.

Perhaps Ginsberg's best poems in the last two decades of his life were about himself, and his personae, his friends, and his family. In "Garden State" (1979), he describes memories of his youth in New Jersey. In "Brooklyn College Brain" (1979), he depicts himself as a middle-aged academic on campus. In 1984, when *Collected Poems* was published, Helen Vendler hoped that he might go on to write poems of old age that would be as good as the late work of W. B. Yeats and Wallace Stevens. There are, indeed, moving poems about aging, loneliness, dying, and death, including "Personal Ads" (1987) and "Autumn Leaves" (1992), a near-perfect eight-line poem of precise images, a poem that's wistful, sorrowful, and yet energetic. As Charles McGrath noted in the *New York Times Book Review*, Ginsberg wrote "his best, most impassioned poetry as a young man"; yet there were also late poems, McGrath recognized, in which the author took "radical pleasure in the deeply ordinary," thereby delighting the ordinary reader. In "Death and Fame" (1997), written shortly before his death, Ginsberg returned one last time to the themes that had preoccupied him his entire life—fame and death, immortality and mortality. Here he imagines his own funeral, writes his own obituary, sums up his career, and bids farewell to the world. "Death and Fame" shows how sharp he was as a poet—how vivid his imagination—until the very end.

It seems likely that in years to come, as students, teachers, and scholars read and assess Ginsberg's work, they will find gems throughout his career—from the 1940s to the 1990s. Indeed, the poems in *Empty Mirror* show how poignant a poet he was before he wrote *Howl*, much as the poems in *White Shroud* and *Cosmopolitan Greetings* show how seductive and candid a poet he could be long after he wrote *Howl*. Still, it seems likely that *Howl* will occupy a singular place in his body of work, not only for its pivotal role in the making of the Beat Generation and the counterculture of the 1960s and the 1970s but also for the poet's own explosive language and his innovative sense of form. In *Howl*, Ginsberg was at his most original. In *Howl*, he moved American poetry forward, forging a global tradition of poetry that included

Whitman, Eliot, Rimbaud, Williams, and a bit of García Lorca and Mayakovsky, too. Then, too, in *Howl*, he finally wrote a poem to match the immense persona that he had had in mind for himself for years—the persona of an American prophet. From bits and pieces of his own life and from the bits and pieces of the nation itself, he created a work that was "beautiful in an ugly graceful way," to borrow a phrase of Jack Kerouac's. With passion and precision—and from a sense of anomie and terror—Allen Ginsberg told the truth, as best he could, about himself, the world, and the cosmos. In *Howl*, he owed no allegiance to any cause, party, or movement in poetry. By following his own muse he found his own voice and by expressing his own madness he disclosed much of the madness of America.

# Notes and Sources

## Abbreviations Used

AGCP    Allen Ginsberg. *Collected Poems: 1947–1980.* New York: Harper & Row, 1984. Rpt. New York: Perennial Library, 1988.

AGHO    Allen Ginsberg. *Howl: Original Draft Facsimile, Transcript & Variant Versions, Fully Annotated by Author, with Contemporary Correspondence, Account of First Public Reading, Legal Skirmishes, Precursor Texts & Bibliography.* Edited by Barry Miles. New York: Harper & Row, 1986. Rpt. New York: HarperPerennial, 1995.

AGIA    Jane Kramer. *Allen Ginsberg in America.* New York: Random House, 1969. Rpt. with a new introduction by the author. New York: Fromm, 1997.

AGJEF    Allen Ginsberg. *Journals: Early Fifties, Early Sixties.* Edited by Gordon Ball. New York: Grove, 1977.

AGJMF    Allen Ginsberg. *Journals: Mid-Fifties, 1954–1958.* Edited by Gordon Ball. New York: HarperCollins, 1995.

AGSM    Allen Ginsberg. *Spontaneous Mind: Selected Interviews, 1958–1996.* Edited by David Carter. Preface by Vaclav

Havel. Introduction by Edmund White. New York: HarperCollins, 2001.

Bancroft    The Bancroft Library, University of California, Berkeley.

BBG    Steven Watson. *The Birth of the Beat Generation: Visionaries, Rebels, and Hipsters, 1944–1960*. New York: Pantheon, 1995.

BD    *Beat Down to Your Soul: What Was the Beat Generation?* Edited and introduced by Ann Charters. New York: Penguin, 2001.

Berg    Berg Collection, New York Public Library.

Columbia    Rare Book and Manuscript Library, Columbia University.

DA    Jack Kerouac. *Desolation Angels*. New York: Riverhead, 1995.

DB    Jack Kerouac. *The Dharma Bums*. New York: Penguin, 1986.

DP    Allen Ginsberg. *Deliberate Prose: Selected Essays, 1952–1995*. Edited by Bill Morgan. Foreword by Edward Sanders. New York: HarperCollins, 2000.

Fales    Fales Library, New York University.

FB    Allen Ginsberg and Louis Ginsberg. *Family Business: Selected Letters between a Father and Son*. Edited by Michael Schumacher. New York: Bloomsbury, 2001.

JKSLI    Jack Kerouac. *Selected Letters, 1940–1956*. Edited and introduced by Ann Charters. New York: Viking, 1995.

JKSLII    Jack Kerouac. *Selected Letters, 1957–1969*. Edited and introduced by Ann Charters. New York: Viking, 1999.

LGCP    Louis Ginsberg. *Collected Poems*. Edited by Michael Fournier. Introduction by Eugene Brooks. Afterword by Allen Ginsberg. Orono: Northern Lights, 1992.

LGMSP    Louis Ginsberg. "Allen Ginsberg: My Son the Poet." *Chicago Sun-Times Book Week*, Jan. 12, 1969, 2.

LWB    William Burroughs. *The Letters of William Burroughs, 1945–1959*. Edited and introduced by Oliver Harris. New York: Penguin, 1994.

OPAG    Louis Hyde, ed. *On the Poetry of Allen Ginsberg*. Ann Arbor: University of Michigan, 1984.

OTR    Jack Kerouac. *On the Road*. New York: Viking, 1957. Rpt. New York: Viking, 1972.

PBR Ann Charters, ed. *The Portable Beat Reader.* New York: Viking, 1992.

PJK Jack Kerouac. *The Portable Jack Kerouac.* Edited by Ann Charters. New York: Viking, 1995.

Stanford Department of Special Collections, Stanford University Libraries.

TC Jack Kerouac. *The Town and the City.* New York: Harcourt Brace Jovanovich, 1978.

Texas Harry Ransom Humanities Research Center, the University of Texas at Austin.

TSESP T. S. Eliot. *Selected Prose.* Edited and introduced by Frank Kermode. New York: Harcourt, Brace, 1975.

WAW *Writers at Work: The "Paris Review" Interviews.* Third series. Edited by George Plimpton. Introduction by Alfred Kazin. New York: Viking, 1967.

## Preface: Allen Ginsberg's Genius

xi **Allen Ginsberg's genius.** Robert Pinsky, "Defiant America," *Village Voice,* Apr. 15, 1997, 36.

xii **to the secret or hermetic.** AGHO, xi.

xii **Oh, yes, the Cold War** & related comments. Ginsberg read at College of Marin on Mar. 15, 1985, when this interview took place. Notes in possession of the author.

xiii **Frances Stonor Saunders,** *The Cultural Cold War: The CIA and the World of Arts and Letters* (New York: New Press, 1999).

xv **candor, accurate candor.** Ginsberg performed at Sonoma State University on Apr. 5, 1986. Notes on his two-day stay at SSU in possession of the author.

xviii **long karmic connection.** The San Francisco memorial for Ginsberg, which I attended, took place on Apr. 20, 1997, two weeks after his death. The remarks from speakers are from my notes.

xviii **cultural busybody** & related quotations. Charles McGrath, "Street Singer," *New York Times Book Review,* Apr. 27, 1997, 43.

xix      **gave me.** AGIA, 42.

xix      **Allen brought his poems.** Interview with Dr. Philip Hicks, San Rafael, Calif., Mar. 6, 2001.

xix      **false ... self-deprecating & angels.** BD, 211.

xx      **really an homage.** WAW, 295.

xx      **coming out of the closet.** AGSM, 313.

xx      **really about my mother.** Allen Ginsberg, "More Explanations Twenty Years Later," in *A Letter about Howl 1956* (Lincoln: Penmaen Press, 1976), 11.

xx      **emotional time bomb.** "Author's Preface: Reader's Guide," AGHO, xii.

xxi      **point of stress.** Adrienne Rich, quoted in Bill Moyers, *The Language of Life: A Festival of Poets* (New York: Doubleday, 1995), 338.

xxi      **The artist is extremely.** John Haffenden, *The Life of John Berryman* (London: Ark, 1983), 7.

xxii      **What do you have & A little glimpse of death.** Kenneth Koch, "Allen Ginsberg Talks about Poetry," *New York Times Book Review*, Oct. 23, 1977, 44.

xxiv      **Ginsberg's 'Howl,' the single poem.** Cynthia Ozick, "T. S. Eliot at 101," *New Yorker*, Nov. 20, 1989, 153.

xxiv      **Do I contradict?** Walt Whitman, *Leaves of Grass* (New York: Bantam, 1983), 72.

xxiv      **scream from.** William Everson, *Archetype West: The Pacific Coast as a Literary Region* (Berkeley: Oyez, 1976), 15.

xxiv      **I occasionally scream.** DP, 251.

xxv      **Almost all times & historical product.** Octavio Paz, *The Bow and the Lyre* (Austin: University of Texas Press, 1973), 33, 169.

## 1. Poetickall Bomshell

1–2      **poetickall Bomshell, deal, certain subterranean celebration,** & related quotations. Gary Snyder to Phil Whalen, Sept. 1955, *The Gary Snyder Reader: Prose, Poetry, and Translations 1952–1998*, introduction by Jim Dodge (Washington, D.C.: Counterpoint, 1999), 159.

4    **Reactionary opinion & we are all.** Tennessee Williams, "On the Art of Being a True Non-Conformist," *New York Star*, Nov. 7, 1948, 5.

5    **were leading us.** Louise Levitas, "To Norman Mailer War Is a Four-Letter Word," *New York Star*, Aug. 22, 1948, 3.

5    **Babylonian plutocracy, grossly affluent, & should have exhibited.** Tennessee Williams, *Memoirs* (Garden City: Doubleday, 1975), 3.

5    **last remnants.** Stephen Spender, "The Situation of the American Writer," *New Directions 11* (New York: New Directions, 1949), 123.

5–6   **revolutionary artists, significant novelty, & cultural revolution.** W. H. Auden, foreword to Adrienne Rich, *A Change of World* (New Haven: Yale University Press, 1951), 125, 126.

6    **conservative business suits, brave and honest.** Williams, "On the Art of Being a True Non-Conformist," 5.

6    **I need to practice.** Sylvia Plath, *Letters Home: Correspondence, 1950–1963*, selected and edited with commentary by Aurelia Schafer Plath (New York: Harper & Row), 1975, 144.

7    **that event launched.** Telephone interview with Gary Snyder, May 17, 1999.

7    **I was twenty-two.** Interview with Michael McClure, Aug. 10, 2003.

8    **I was the one.** DB, 13.

9    **San Francisco is a mad city** & related quotations about San Francisco. George Rathmell, *Realms of Gold: The Colorful Writers of San Francisco 1850–1950* (Berkeley: Creative Arts, 1998), 131, 161, 240.

9    **San Francisco . . . always gives you.** DA, 130.

10   **The only people for me.** OTR, 8.

10   **ideology of fear & sworn oaths.** E. L. Doctorow, *Jack London, Hemingway and the Constitution: Selected Essays, 1977–1992* (New York: Random House, 1993), xi.

12   **run down.** DP, 239.

12          **fucking mind.** Berg, Ginsberg to John Allen Ryan, Sept. 9,
            1955.

12          **There is more of.** Lewis Ellingham and Kevin Killian, *Poet
            Be like God: Jack Spicer and the San Francisco Renaissance*
            (Hanover: University of New England Press, 1998), 23.

13          **defy the system.** DP, 239.

13          **6 poets at 6 Gallery.** AGHO, 165.

14          **first scraps.** Berg, Ginsberg to Ryan, Sept. 9, 1955.

15          **This was no.** AGHO, 165.

15          **rather stiff.** DB, 14.

15          **glug a slug.** DB, 15.

15          **they got drunk.** AGHO, 165.

15          **little wows.** DB, 15.

16–17       **reading was such.** AGHO, 165.

17          **to the original.** Allen Ginsberg, "Improvised Poetics," in
            *Composed on the Tongue* (San Francisco: Grey Fox, 1980), 59.

17          **elegy in itself.** DB, 15.

18          **small and intensely.** PBR, 274.

18          **Scores of people.** DB, 15.

18          **strange ecstatic intensity.** AGHO, 165.

18          **Everyone was yelling** & **wiping his tears.** DB, 14.

18          **Berry Feast.** PBR, 279.

19          **This poem.** Michael Schumacher, *Dharma Lion: A Biogra-
            phy of Allen Ginsberg* (New York: Norton, 1992), 216.

19          **for a big.** DB, 16.

19          **square bookstore owner.** Paul Iorio, "A 'Howl' That Still
            Echoes," *San Francisco Chronicle*, Oct. 28, 2000, D1.

19          **I greet you.** Iorio, "A 'Howl' That Still Echoes," D1.

19          **most extraordinary** & **I greet you.** Gay Wilson Allen, *Walt
            Whitman* (New York: Grove, 1961), 58.

20          **better than Pound.** Berg, Ginsberg to John Allen Ryan.
            Dec. 8, 1955.

20          **barbaric yawp** & **over the roofs.** Whitman, *Leaves of
            Grass*, 73.

20          **across the tops.** AGCP, 126.

21          **One's-Self.** Whitman, *Leaves of Grass*, 1.

21      **Democracy is** & **America is not.** William Burroughs, *Naked Lunch* (New York: Grove, 1959; rpt. New York, Grove, 1990), 121, 12.

21      **end of America, dregs of America, washed out bottom,** & **whole mad thing.** OTR, 78, 274, 234, 82.

21      **green and wondrous, end of the continent,** & **loneliness of San Francisco.** Ibid., 168, 170, 73.

22      **locked in the Cold War.** Michael McClure, *Scratching the Beat Surface: Essays on New Vision from Blake to Kerouac* (San Francisco: North Point, 1982; rpt., New York: Penguin, 1994), 12.

22      **had the feeling** & **there was no.** Ibid., 12.

22      **cheering** & **a barrier.** Ibid., 15.

22      **primary good.** AGJMF, 178.

23      **The solitary and haunted.** Ibid., 178–79.

23      **surface, littered, rusty machinery,** & **energetic** & **healthy.** AGHO, 158.

23–24   **positive redemptive catalogue.** Schumacher, *Dharma Lion*, 605.

24      **be a genius.** Stanford, Journals, Box 1.

24      **God! How great** & **I am the greatest.** AGJMF, 248.

## 2. Family Business

25      **Family Business.** Ginsberg quoted in Harvey Blum, "Allen Ginsberg: Anxious Dreams of Eliot," *Boston Book Review* (Aug. 1995), 4.

26      **What can I say?** JKSLI, 200.

27      **local poet-hero.** FB, 37.

27      **It's a wild, rhapsodic.** Ibid., 35.

28      **Do tell me.** Ibid., 50.

28      **Russian émigré.** AGCP, 814.

29      **My mother got.** Stanford, Journals, Box 1.

29      **Her sickness is.** Ibid.

29      **Mommy came home.** Ibid.

29      **Lou should have known.** Ibid.

29–30   **human individuality** & **modern, mechanical.** Quoted in

Elenore Lester, "Allen Ginsberg Remembers Mama," *New York Times*, Sec. 2, Feb. 6, 1972, 5.

30    **A lot of madness, She had a great grasp, & She was no madder.** Ibid.

30    **She / reads the Bible.** AGCP, 219.

30    **I saw God & When we die.** Ibid.

31    **I waited for that day.** Ibid., 217.

31    **Take out ... references.** FB, 140.

31    **beard about the vagina, It's bad taste, Too obscene, & an archetypal experience.** FB, 118, 140, 122.

31–32   **My mother locked & she also.** Stanford, Journals, Box 1.

32    **The boys stood there.** LGMSP, 2.

32    **saw what he never.** Edith Ginsberg in Jerry Aronson's 1983 documentary film *Life and Times of Allen Ginsberg*.

32    **With his own mother.** AGHO, 18.

32    **with mother finally.** AGCP, 130.

32    **One time I thought.** Ibid., 219.

33    **Ride 3 hours.** Ibid., 213.

33–34   **I'm an atheist, killing all the Jews, the world is now, & fascists are winning.** Stanford, Journals, Box 1.

34    **"To Aunt Rose."** AGCP, 184.

35    **It is the poet.** Ibid., 811.

35    **I'm the smallest, fragile, baser emotions, & I'm capable of almost anything.** Stanford, Journals, Box 1.

35    **Do what you want.** Barry Miles, *Ginsberg: A Biography* (New York: Simon & Schuster, 1989), 27.

35    **naked victims.** AGCP, 303.

36    **When I loved.** FB, 99.

36    **There is no joy.** LGMSP, 2.

37    **You are the Spirit.** LGCP, 84.

37–38   **anachronism & XX Century.** Ibid., 418–19.

38    **"Buttercups."** Louis Untermeyer, *Yesterday and Today: A Comparative Anthology of Poetry* (New York: Harcourt, Brace & World), 1926, 168.

38    **"On Reading."** AGCP, 6.

| | |
|---|---|
| 38–39 | **contemporary prophetic.** LGCP, 419. |
| 39 | **My sons, watch out.** Ibid., 245–46. |
| 39 | **"The Revolt of the Machines."** Ibid., 146–48. |
| 39 | **I grew up** & **Poetry . . . was a.** Quoted in Blum, "Allen Ginsberg," 4. |
| 39 | **Would that all.** LGCP, 423. |
| 40 | **Tradition . . . cannot be.** TSESP, 38. |
| 40 | **the most individual.** Ibid., 38. |
| 40 | **If some future.** Stanford, Journals, Box 1. |
| 40 | **"Walt Whitman and Carl Sandburg."** Stanford, Memorabilia, Box 1. |

## 3. Trilling-esque Sense of "Civilization"

| | |
|---|---|
| 44 | **Trilling-esque sense of "civilization."** BD, 209. |
| 44 | **ten years' animal.** AGCP, 132. |
| 44–45 | **American adolescent** & **meaningless.** James Dickey, "From Babel to Byzantium," *Sewanee Review*, July–Sept. 1957, 509. |
| 45 | **leaping** *out* **of a.** BD, 209. |
| 45 | **Allen holds you.** FB, 6. |
| 46 | **I read each.** Stanford, Journals, Box 2. |
| 46 | **who studied Plotinus.** AGCP, 127. |
| 47 | **whole syndrome.** AGIA, 119. |
| 48 | **salvation of American art.** Quoted in Alexander Bloom, *The New York Intellectuals and Their World* (New York: Oxford, 1986), 58. |
| 48 | **more he studied.** Stephen L. Tanner, *Lionel Trilling* (Boston: Twayne, 1988), 14. |
| 48 | **I want to learn.** Ibid., 19. |
| 49 | **liberal progressive** & **when a man does.** "From the Notebooks of Lionel Trilling," *Partisan Review* 51, 1984, 505, 506. |
| 49 | **liberal ideology.** Lionel Trilling, *The Liberal Imagination: Essays on Literature and Society* (New York: Harcourt Brace Jovanovich, 1978), 94. |

50    **Kafka . . . decadent.** Stanford, Memorabilia, Box 2. See for example Ginsberg's unpublished college papers "A Sane View of Kafka" and "*The Castle:* Franz Kafka."

51    **best minds.** AGCP, 126.

51    **madmen and artists.** Columbia, Ginsberg to Eugene Brooks, 1944.

51    **he couldn't take** & **discharged as.** Ibid.

52    **Allen, as classwork,** & **He is making.** FB, 5.

53    **what I call.** Columbia, Ginsberg to Brooks, 1944.

54    **to be in on.** Jack Kerouac, *Vanity of Duluoz: An Adventurous Education, 1935–46* (New York: Penguin, 1994), 230.

54    **I think I'll start.** Columbia, Ginsberg to Eugene Brooks, 1944.

54    **My multitudes.** The unpublished draft of the novel is at Stanford, Journals, Box 2.

55    **There is only.** Stanford, Memorabilia, Box 2. From a college essay on Max Nomad's *Apostle of Revolution.*

55    **A criminal is** & **marvelous experiment.** Columbia, Ginsberg to Eugene Brooks, Sept. 1944.

55    **great prophetic** & **tremendous book.** Stanford, "Spengler as Prophet," Memorabilia, Box 1.

56    **back alleys.** DP, 458.

56    **where is your former** & **the homosexual.** FB, 6.

56    **Polonius-like.** Ibid., 23.

56    **Whee!** Stanford, Journals, Box 2.

56    **In our day.** Stanford, college essay, "Dante," Memorabilia, Box 1.

56    **The poet is the creature.** Stanford, Letters, Box 1, Ginsberg to Lucien Carr, Mar. 8, 1945.

57    **phallus.** Stanford, Journals, Box 2.

58    **"The Bloodsong."** Stanford, Manuscripts, Box 17.

58    **I don't want you** & **I do feel.** LGMSP, 2.

59    **Paisley scarf.** TC, 376, 365.

60    **Fuck the Jews.** Miles, *Ginsberg,* 59.

60    **who were expelled.** AGCP, 126.

60      **"A Violent Ballad"** & **"Times Square."** Stanford, Memorabilia, Box 2.

61      **Reaction rather than reform** & **Each howl.** From unpublished essay entitled "The Road We Are Traveling," Stanford, Memorabilia, Box 2.

62      **They keep telling me.** Texas, Ginsberg to Kerouac, Aug. 12, 1945.

63      **I am alien.** Ibid.

63      **all-inclusive indictment.** Stanford, Memorabilia, Box 2, college essay on *Season in Hell.*

63      *Season in Hell.* Columbia, Ginsberg to Trilling, Sept. 4, 1945.

63      **Unscrew the locks.** Whitman, *Leaves of Grass*, 41.

64      **Misfortune was my.** Arthur Rimbaud, *A Season in Hell and the Drunken Boat*, trans. Louise Varese (New York: New Directions, 1961), 3.

## 4. Juvenescent Savagery

65      **Juvenescent Savagery.** Allen Ginsberg, ". . . This Is the Abomination," *Columbia Review*, May 1946, 163.

66      **Boba' s Birthday.** Ibid., 138–40.

66–68      **". . . This Is the Abomination."** Ibid., 159–63.

69      **telescoping of images** & **amalgamating disparate.** TSESP, 60, 64.

69      **It appears likely that.** Ibid., 65.

69      **I smiled to.** Allen Ginsberg, "A Night in the Village," *Jester-Review* 42, 1944, 2.

70      **poet who lives.** Paul Mariani, *William Carlos Williams: A New World Naked* (New York: McGraw-Hill, 1981), 490.

70      **doing it on.** Neal Cassady, *The First Third* (San Francisco: City Lights, 1971; rpt. San Francisco: City Lights, 1981), 153.

71      **The Mover.** LWB, 37.

71      **A tremendous thing.** OTR, 7.

71–72    **I ripped into** & **to have a cunt.** Cassady, *The First Third*, 152, 202.

72    **You know you, I am lonely,** & **What must I do.** Columbia, Ginsberg to Cassady, n.d.

72    **Exorcise Neal.** FB, 19.

73    **Art is a secret.** Columbia, Ginsberg to Trilling, circa Dec. 1948.

74    **Birthday Ode.** Stanford, Manuscripts, Box 1.

74    **irritation & ennui.** FB, 15.

74–75    **I am insane.** Texas, Ginsberg to Kerouac, 1947.

75    **suffered a series.** Stanford, Letters, Box 1, Ginsberg to Wilhelm Reich, 1947.

76    **various anti-romantic.** Stanford, Manuscripts, Box 3.

76    **poetry is not.** TSESP, 43.

76    **Love's gender was.** AGCP, 813.

76–77    **"Dakar Doldrums."** Ibid., 752–53.

77    **"Many Loves."** Ibid., 156–58.

78    **"Please Master."** Ibid., 494–95.

78    **auditory hallucination.** WAW, 303.

78    **One of the.** Paul Berman in OPAG, 342.

78    **I cooked it.** Jack Foley, *O Powerful Western Star* (Oakland: Pantograph, 2000), 145.

78    **leap blindly** & related quotations. John Clellon Holmes, *Go* (New York: Ace, 1952; rpt. New York: Thunder's Mouth, 1997), 87–88.

79    **"Vision 1948"** & **"On Reading William Blake's 'The Sick Rose.'"** AGCP, 8, 6.

79–80    **dull** & **I don't like.** AGHO, 156.

80    **he was an** & **his life was.** David Lehman, "'Kaddish' for Allen Ginsberg '48," *Columbia College Today*, Fall 1997, 21.

## 5. Just like Russia

81    **Just like Russia.** Texas, Ginsberg to Kerouac, July 3, 1949.

81    **sinister symbols, big secret mystic,** & **didn't know if.** WAW, 293, 292, 294.

81    **mad author** & related quotations. Ginsberg's review of Cé-

line's *Death on the Installment Plan* appeared in *Halycon*, Spring 1948, 51.

83 **a sense of disgust** & **at last slipping.** Benjamin G. Schafer, ed., *The Herbert Huncke Reader* (New York: Morrow, 1997), 51.

83 **wondrous personal prose** & **like an older.** Texas, Ginsberg to Kerouac, Apr. 15, 1948.

83–84 **I really will, losing control, haunting queer bars, more actively queer,** & **in the most.** Texas, Ginsberg to Kerouac, Apr. 15, 1948.

84 **artificial, thru other men's voices, I have let,** & **find a style.** Texas, Ginsberg to Kerouac, 1948.

84 **forties were a.** Robert Creeley, *The Poetics of the New American Poetry*, ed. Donald Allen and Warren Tallman (New York: Grove, 1973), 254.

85 **We cannot.** Eliot quoted in Mariani, *William Carlos Williams*, 570.

85 **so shrill and** & **passion and vigor.** Stanford, Manuscripts, Box 1.

85 **the clearest expression.** Schumacher, *Dharma Lion*, 100.

86 **No more movements.** W. H. Auden, "Squares and Oblongs," in *Poets at Work*, ed. Charles D. Abbott (New York: Harcourt, Brace, 1948), 176.

86 **New Vision.** BBG, 39.

86 **vision or madness** & **knowledge of form.** Karl Shapiro, "The Meaning of the Discarded Poem," in *Poets at Work*, 92.

86 **limit their audience** & **seemed to be written.** Selden Rodman, "Introduction," *One Hundred Modern Poems* (New York: Mentor, 1949), viii, xxi.

87 **The resistance to poetry, poetry is foreign, poetry as an art,** & **almost any man.** Muriel Rukeyser, *The Life of Poetry* (New York: A. A. Wyn, 1949), 5, 6, 7.

87 **wanted to be.** Stanford, Journals, Box 3.

87 **I haven't even.** Ibid.

88 **mythologizing.** Ibid., "The Fall."

88 **crazed and confused.** Ibid.

89  **tied-in.** "Wrong-Way Turn Clears Up Robbery," *New York Times*, Apr. 23, 1949, 30.

89–90 **a shit, father confessor, stop fiddling, I am sick, to be cured, & stable, serene, secure.** Stanford, Journals, Box 3, "The Fall."

90  **mighty cricket.** Texas, Ginsberg to Kerouac, June 15, 1949.

90  **The punishment literally.** Stanford, Journals, Box 3.

90  **crazyhouse.** Texas, Ginsberg to Kerouac, June 15, 1949.

91  **I got so hung up, made up a lot, hidden invocations, under the surface, & themselves under.** Ibid.

92  **the hero is a madman.** Stanford, Journals, Box 3.

92  **a nation of.** Ibid.

92  **destroyed by madness, madman bum, armed madhouse, madtowns, visible madman, & invincible madhouses!** AGCP, 126, 131, 133, 139, 132.

92  **It is just like Russia.** Texas, Ginsberg to Kerouac, July 3, 1949.

93  **machine men, the doctors, seersucker liberals, & apoetic bourgeoisie.** Ibid.

94  **finish . . . my father.** Stanford, Journals, Box 3.

94  **the proletariat.** Ibid.

95  **"A Poem on America."** AGCP, 64.

95  **Moloch whose name.** AGHO, 64.

95  **It seems to me.** Quoted in Richard Kostelanetz, "Ginsberg Makes the World Scene," *New York Times Sunday Magazine*, July 11, 1965, 32.

95  **police states & both dig.** *Playboy*, Apr. 1969, 238.

95  **Franco has murdered.** AGCP, 167.

96  **The communists have nothing.** Ibid., 353.

96  **Birdbrain.** Ibid., 738.

96  **I'm Kirilov.** AGHO, 114.

96  **The cadence & Not one of.** Ibid.

97  **Because of Solomon.** Texas, Ginsberg to Kerouac, July 3, 1949.

97        **a perfect opportunity.** Ibid.

97        **statism, abstract capitalism, & the writer's duty.** Jean-
          Paul Sartre, *What Is Literature?* trans. Bernard Frechtman
          (New York: Philosophical Library, 1949; rpt. New York:
          Harper & Row, 1965), 241, 280.

97–98     **there is no.** AGHO, 118.

98        **homosexual hipster & huge apocalyptic.** Texas, Ginsberg
          to Kerouac, July 3, 1949.

98        **masters & on our lips.** Email from Richard Howard to the
          author, Jan. 22, 1999.

98–99     **it gave me, batty, insecure, & patronizing.** Documents
          from the New York State Psychiatric Institute.

99        **self-expression & antisocial activity.** Ibid.

99        **laughed all over the ward, Palm Beach suit, Jesus Gins-
          berg, & Christ comments.** Ibid.

100       **"Paterson."** AGCP, 40.

101       **disappointed in.** Documents from the New York State Psy-
          chiatric Institute.

101       **It's the best.** Ibid.

101–2     **In spite of.** Williams included Ginsberg's letter in *Paterson*
          (New York: New Directions, 1963), 204.

102       **old Englishmen.** Ibid., 205.

102       **I believe that.** Schumacher, *Dharma Lion*, 700.

102       **actual talk rhythms.** Ibid., 125.

103       **No ideas but, no ideas, & things are.** Allen Ginsberg, "An
          Exposition of William Carlos Williams's Poetic Practice,"
          *The Teachers & Writers Guide to William Carlos Williams*, ed.
          Gary Lenhart (New York: Teachers & Writers Collabora-
          tive, 1998), 132.

103       **prophetic sort of.** Ibid., 145.

103       **absolute freedom & the past.** William Carlos Williams,
          "A Letter, Touching the Comintern, upon Censorship in
          the Arts," in *A Recognizable Image: On Art and Artists*, edited
          and introduced by Bram Dijkstra (New York: New Direc-
          tions, 1978), 186, 187.

## 6. Ladies, We Are Going through Hell

104 **Ladies, we are going through hell.** William Carlos Williams, introduction to *Howl*, AGCP, 812.

104–5 **an introvert, an atheist,** & related quotations about the novel. AGJEF, 17.

105 **I remember when.** AGCP, 141.

105 **archive** & **relentless.** DP, 380, 381.

105–6 **This young Jewish.** AGCP, 809.

107 **Russia whose avowed.** Mariani, *William Carlos Williams*, 652.

107 **unadulterated hell** & **mental derangement.** Ibid., 669.

107 **instinctively drawn** & related comments to Moore. Ibid., 647.

107 **I walk around.** Stanford, Journals, Box 4.

108 **I don't like.** Ibid.

108 **I never thought, ability to survive,** & **to see the truth.** AGCP, 811.

108 **through hell.** Ibid.

108 **a howl, not defeat,** & **in spite of.** Ibid.

109 **I feel like.** Stanford, Journals, Box 4.

109 **All of the time.** Ibid.

109 **a prison** & **I may have.** Ibid.

109 **to put naked.** Ibid.

109 **tip my mitt.** Ibid.

109 **had put himself.** Ibid.

110 **mysteries** & **beauty.** Ibid.

110 **agonist with.** Ibid.

110 **spy from.** Ibid., Box 6.

110–11 **stabbed and aghast, hanging in the,** & **in the windows.** Ibid., Box 4.

111 **Jack is.** Ibid.

111 **They have totally, They gamble,** & **But they have.** Ibid.

111 **I have had.** JKSLI, 239.

111 **curse of.** Ibid.

112 **It is a decade.** Ibid., 229.

112 **gather in one.** Ibid., 292.

112     **cruds of New York.** Ibid., 378.

112     **millionaire jews.** Ibid.

112     **unbearably lonely.** Ibid., 386.

112     **long, dark & thoughts of suicide.** Ibid., 389.

112     **I've been in.** Ibid., 391.

112     **Wandering WASP.** Ted Morgan, *Literary Outlaw: The Life
        and Times of William S. Burroughs* (New York: Henry Holt,
        1988; rpt. New York: Avon, 1990), 149.

113     **blocks of ruined buildings.** Sylvere Lotringer, ed., *Bur-
        roughs Live: The Collected Interviews of William S. Burroughs,
        1960–1997* (Los Angeles: Semiotext(e), 2001), 23.

113     **All of my.** WAW, 174.

114     **anyone who doesn't.** Brenda Knight, *Women of the Beat
        Generation: The Writers, Artists and Muses at the Heart of a
        Revolution,* foreword by Anne Waldman, afterword by Ann
        Charters (Berkeley: Conari, 1996), 56.

114     **in the bleachers.** Stanford, Journals, Box 5.

114     **ruffians.** Ibid.

114     **Should I go.** Ibid.

115     **It's a shallow.** JKSLI, 131.

115     **San Francisco.** Ibid., 157.

115     **We will go.** AGCP, 86.

115     **"In Hospital Visiting Naomi."** Stanford, Journals, Box 5.

115     **I feel that.** Ibid., Box 3.

116     **I am beginning.** Texas, Ginsberg to Kerouac, July 3,
        1949.

116     **Don't be mad, I want you.** Fales, *Kaddish,* 16–17.

117     **Rosenbergs are.** Dennis McNally, *Desolate Angel: Jack Ker-
        ouac, the Beat Generation, and America* (New York: Random
        House, 1979), 171.

117     **burnings & burning.** Stanford, Journals, Box 5.

117     **dream of rich.** Ibid., Box 6.

117     **drumming / . . . whistling.** AGCP, 92.

117     **intrepid American & great explorer.** Texas, Ginsberg to
        Kerouac, June 18, 1954.

118     **White Goddess & Mayan secrets.** Stanford, Letters, Box 3.

118     **sweet brown man's.** Ibid., Box 6.
118     **deathshead, own mad mind,** & **crucial words.** AGCP, 97–110.
118     **alone naked.** Stanford, Journals, Box 6.
118     **tanned and bearded** & related quotations. AGCP, 110.
118–19  **nation over.** Ibid.
119     **America . . . inundated.** Federico García Lorca, *Ode to Walt Whitman and Other Poems* (San Francisco: City Lights, 1988), 47.
119     **"A Supermarket in California."** AGCP, 136.
119     **"America."** AGJMF, 36.
120     **reveal in shorthand.** Ibid., 36.

## 7. Another Coast's Apple for the Eye

121     **Another Coast's Apple for the Eye.** AGJMF, 63.
121     **God damn.** Ibid., 116.
121     **America is new.** Stanford, Journals, Box 5.
122     **I occasionally scream.** DP, 251.
122     **limitation** & **strength.** Richard Wilbur, quoted in X. J. Kennedy, ed., *An Introduction to Poetry* (Boston: Little, Brown, 1966), 172.
122     **opened his mind.** Everson, *Archetype West*, 116.
122     **dread Frisco.** AGJMF, 49.
123     **Athens-like.** Ibid., 132.
123     **"In the Baggage Room at Greyhound."** AGCP, 153.
123     **"Sunflower Sutra."** Ibid., 138–39.
124     **valley floor.** AGJMF, 149.
124     **terribly straight-laced, islands of freedom,** & **whole underground.** Quoted in Nancy J. Peters, "The Beat Generation and San Francisco's Culture of Dissent," *Reclaiming San Francisco: History, Politics, Culture*, ed. James Brook, Chris Carlsson, and Nancy J. Peters (San Francisco: City Lights, 1998), 203.
125     **all but incomprehensible, uncarpeted rooms, mustachioed papas,** & **approximation to a primitive.** Mildred

Edie Brady, "The New Cult of Sex and Anarchy," *Harper's*, Apr. 1947, 313, 320, 316.

| | |
|---|---|
| 126 | **Marlon Brando.** AGHO, 127. |
| 126 | **saintly motorcyclists.** AGCP, 128. |
| 126 | **all night rocking.** Ibid., 129. |
| 126 | **the vast lamb.** Ibid., 134. |
| 127 | **sukiyaki joints.** AGJMF, 64. |
| 127 | **art is a community.** Ibid., 78. |
| 128 | **dear shadows.** Ibid., 65. |
| 128 | **This is my body.** Ibid., 105. |
| 128 | **"Thou Shalt Not Kill."** PBR, 233–41. |
| 128 | **Rexroth is.** Texas, Ginsberg to Kerouac, Apr. 22, 1955. |
| 129 | **Rexroth's face.** AGCP, 152. |
| 129 | **dug it** & **conception of spontaneity.** Texas, Ginsberg to Kerouac, Sept. 7, 1954. |
| 129 | **scribbled secret, The unspeakable visions,** & **composing wild.** AGHO, 137. |
| 129 | **Bookmovie.** Ibid. |
| 129 | **Writer-Director.** Ibid. |
| 130 | **"In Vesuvio's Waiting for Sheila."** AGJMF, 60. |
| 131 | **"Notes Written on Finally Recording *Howl*."** DP, 230. |
| 131 | **Another's coast's apple.** AGJMF, 63. |
| 131 | **Fixed eye** & **A N.Y. Gotham.** Ibid. |
| 131 | **Found suddenly.** Ibid. |
| 132 | **I came to.** Ibid., 62. |
| 132 | **Golem waiting.** Ibid., 63. |
| 132 | **"Two Sonnets."** AGCP, 5. |
| 133 | **given up on New York.** On-line interview: gwu.edu/ ~nsarchiv/coldwar/interviews/episode-13/Ginsberg1 .html. Accessed 1996. |
| 134 | **drear light, submarine light,** & **darkness under.** AGCP, 126, 129. |
| 134 | **noise of wheels** & **ashcan rantings.** Ibid., 126. |
| 134 | **wars, wartime,** & **scholars of war.** Ibid., 127, 128, 126. |
| 135 | **eternal / war.** Ibid., 133. |

| | |
|---|---|
| 135 | **winter midnight.** Ibid., 127. |
| 135 | **waking nightmares.** Ibid., 126. |
| 135 | **themselves through.** Ibid. |
| 135 | **stale beer.** Ibid. |
| 135 | **great suicidal.** Ibid., 128. |
| 135 | **off fire / escapes.** Ibid., 127. |
| 136 | **themselves under** & **cut their wrists.** Ibid., 129. |
| 136 | **lament for the Lamb.** DP, 230. |
| 136 | **burned alive.** AGCP, 129. |
| 136 | **battered bleak** & **drunken taxicabs.** Ibid., 126, 129. |
| 136 | **their watches off** & **on the West Coast.** Ibid., 129, 127. |
| 137 | **tragic custard-pie.** DP, 229. |
| 137 | **around and around** & **themselves to subways.** AGCP, 127, 126. |
| 137 | **who retired to Mexico.** Ibid., 130. |
| 137 | **out whoring.** Ibid., 128. |
| 137–38 | **through the icy.** Ibid., 130. |
| 138 | **confessing out.** Ibid., 131. |
| 138 | **suffering of America's.** Ibid. |
| 138 | **Drake Monster.** Texas, Ginsberg to Kerouac, Nov. 1954. |
| 138 | **We wandered on peyote.** Texas, Ginsberg to Kerouac, Aug. 1955. |
| 138 | **children screaming.** AGHO, 58–59. |
| 139 | **Rockefeller Center tons.** Ibid., 59. |
| 139 | **Hitler! Stalin!** Ibid. |
| 139 | **Heaven which exists.** Ibid. |
| 139 | **campustown.** AGJMF, 186. |
| 139 | **cottage in the Western.** AGCP, 133. |
| 139–40 | **sex mad.** DB, 28. |
| 140 | **"A Strange New Cottage in Berkeley."** AGCP, 135. |
| 140 | **last fantastic book, last door,** & **last telephone.** Ibid., 130. |
| 140 | **Shakespearean Arden cottage.** Texas, Ginsberg to Kerouac, circa 1955. |
| 141 | **little rose-covered** & related descriptions. DB, 17. |
| 141 | **jazz mass** & **Bach fugue.** AGIA, 167, and DP, 241. |
| 141 | **vast stone.** AGCP, 131. |

141    **Robot apartments** & **demonic industries.** Ibid., 131–32.

141    **who broke down.** Ibid., 127.

141    **Moloch who entered** & **Moloch who frightened.** Ibid., 131.

142    **key phrase.** Ginsberg, "More Explanations Twenty Years Later," 14.

142    **lamb-like youths.** DP, 230.

142    **chained themselves.** AGCP, 126.

142    **negative capability.** Ginsberg's discussion of Keats's concept is in Jack Foley, *O Powerful Western Star*, 140, and AGHO, 124.

## 8. Mythological References

143    **Mythological References.** JKSLI, 372.

144    **"On Burroughs' Work."** AGCP, 114.

144    **"Dream Record: June 8, 1955."** Ibid., 124.

144    **It's crazy** & **it's so personal.** JKSLI, 373, 372.

144    **Confessions.** Ibid., 356.

145    **Who are Allen and I.** Ibid., 212.

146    **freely to whom / ever.** AGCP, 128.

146    **human seraphim** & **caresses.** Ibid.

146    **empty lots** & **diner / backyards.** Ibid.

146    **Adonis of Denver** & **joy to / the memory.** Ibid.

146    **flashing buttocks.** Ibid.

146    **Nowheresville.** BD, 69.

146    **morbid pathology** & **The main theme.** Robert Graves, *The White Goddess: A Historical Grammar of Poetic Myth* (London: Farber & Farber, 1948; rpt. New York: Farrar, Straus & Giroux, 1994), 446, 447.

147    **that familiar American.** JKSLI, 381.

147    **I dream beautiful.** AGJMF, 41.

147    **legendary Calif[ornia.]** AGJEF, 71.

147    **I want to be.** AGJMF, 25.

147    **Neal has been.** Ibid., 51.

147    **He makes me.** Ibid., 52.

148    **unbearable horror.** Ibid., 48.

148    **nagging** & **violent.** Ibid., 49.

148      *charnel.* Ibid., 50.

148      **How I hate women.** Texas, Ginsberg to Kerouac, Dec. 29, 1954.

148      **three old shrews** & related quotations. AGCP, 128.

149      **"Love Poem on Theme by Whitman."** Ibid., 115.

149      **female form** & **divine nimbus.** Whitman, *Leaves of Grass.* 79.

149      **I'm changed.** Texas, Ginsberg to Kerouac, Dec. 29, 1954.

149      **something great.** Ibid., Jan. 12, 1955.

149      **living in splendor.** Ibid., Nov. 9, 1954.

150      **I want to be.** AGJMF, 81.

150      **erotic imagination, sexual ecstasy,** & **mystical Sanctity union.** Ibid.

150      **master in bed** & **master in book.** Ibid., 82.

150      **I'm happy, Kerouac.** AGCP, 123.

151      **lost sex kid.** Stanford, Journals, Box 5.

151      **I hardly do know** & **The two of us.** AGJMF, 73.

151      **alone in San Fran[cisco]** & **empty days.** Ibid., 115.

152      **Madness! Madness!** Ibid., 64.

152      **inspired crazy** & **unrelated crazy.** JKSLI, 373.

152      **money? or more love?** AGJMF, 208.

152      **North Beach talking.** Stanford, Journals, Box 5.

152      **Neal's madness.** Ibid.

152      **There's something good.** Ibid.

152      **My mind is crazed.** AGJMF, 198.

153      **"In the Baggage Room at Greyhound."** AGCP, 153–54.

153      **I was a naive.** Interview with Dr. Philip Hicks, San Rafael, Calif., Oct. 15, 2002.

153      **For the first.** Interview with Dr. Hicks, San Rafael, Calif., Mar. 6, 2001.

153      **to overcome a block** & **greater acceptance of himself.** Dr. Hicks's report on Allen Ginsberg, Langley Porter, Oct. 11, 1955.

154      **He actually liked.** AGIA, 42.

154      **He loved his mother.** Interview with Dr. Hicks, San Rafael, Calif., Mar. 6, 2001.

155     **Carl Solomon!** AGCP, 132.

155     **unlicensed poetic version.** AGHO, 111.

155     **I was never.** Ibid., 143.

155     **This section.** Ibid., 131.

155     **who threw.** AGCP, 130.

155     **insulin Metrazol.** Ibid.

155     **No Metrazol.** AGHO, 131.

156     **Although I do.** Allen Ginsberg interview with Ellen Pearlman, "Biography, Mythology and Interpretation," *Vajradhatu Sun*, Apr.–May 1990, 17.

156     **gesture of wild.** AGHO, 111.

156     **I'm with you.** AGCP, 132.

156     **you're madder than I am.** Ibid.

156     **mistaken in my.** AGHO, 111.

156     **endurance, familial fidelity.** Ibid.

156     **you imitate.** AGCP, 132.

156     **Holy my mother.** Ibid., 134.

157–58     **I'd used Mr. Solomon's.** AGHO, 111.

## 9. Famous Authorhood

158     **Famous Authorhood.** Ginsberg to Kerouac, Fall 1956, AGHO, 159.

159     **telescoping of images.** TSESP, 60.

159     **to find the.** Ibid., 65.

159     **These fragments.** AGJMF, 118.

159     **Join images.** Ibid., 142.

159     **Do away with symbols.** Ibid.

159     **hydrogen jukebox.** AGCP, 126.

160     **incarnate gaps.** Ibid., 130.

160     **hydrogen jukebox.** AGJMF, 212.

160     **apt relation.** Ibid.

160     **evil brilliance.** Ibid., 124.

160     **apocalypse is here.** Ibid.

160     **Ripeness is all.** Texas, Ginsberg to Kerouac, 1947.

160     **The time seems.** AGJMF, 96.

| | |
|---|---|
| 161 | **"Blessed be the Muses."** AGCP, 125. |
| 161 | **I suppose I'll.** AGJMF, 186. |
| 161 | **I fill'd with woes.** Ibid., 135. |
| 161 | **to run on** & **Standardization and mechanization.** Ibid., 54. |
| 161 | **futuristic television.** Ibid., 58. |
| 161 | **television treetop.** AGHO, 15. |
| 161–62 | **Moloch whose.** AGCP, 131. |
| 162 | **"About the Beat Generation."** PJK, 560. |
| 162 | **a generation of, characters of a, subterranean heroes,** & **turned from.** Ibid., 559. |
| 163 | **I was alone.** AGHO, xii. |
| 163 | **sat idly.** Ibid. |
| 163 | **cheap scratch paper.** Ibid. |
| 164 | **would hear.** DP, 229. |
| 164 | **Each line.** Ibid., 230. |
| 164 | **just getting.** Robert Hass, "The Howl Heard round the World," *Image*, Dec. 21, 1986, 28. |
| 164 | **Who poverty.** AGCP, 126. |
| 165 | **on the word.** DP, 229. |
| 165 | **verbal orgy.** AGHO, 132. |
| 165 | **I saw.** AGCP, 126. |
| 165 | **truth of the reporting.** DP, 173. |
| 165 | **East Coast chauvinism.** Hass, "The Howl Heard round the World," 26. |
| 166 | **Started a poem.** Stanford, Manuscripts, Box 6. |
| 166 | **SF 1955** & STROPHES. Ibid. |
| 167 | **The typewriter imagination.** Lotringer, *Burroughs Live*, XX, 809. |
| 167 | **These long lines.** BD, 218. |
| 167 | **A** CRAFT & **experience writing.** Ibid., 212. |
| 168 | **mystical, hysterical, anarchy,** & **Arkansas.** AGHO, 12. |
| 168 | **I typed it up.** Ibid., 149. |
| 168 | **very powerful, with a vision,** & **waving genitals.** JKSLI, 508–9. |
| 168 | **secondary emendations** & **lingual** SPONTANEITY. Ibid., 508. |

169     **On visits to.** Philip Whalen, "Allen Ginsberg Remembered," *Wind Bell*, Summer 1997, 3.
169     **crucial revision.** AGHO, 124.
169     **tone of the poem.** Ibid.
169     **comic realism & humorous hyperbole.** Ibid.
169     **angelheaded.** Ibid., 26.
169     **negro fix, angry fix, angry streets, & negro streets.** Ibid., 12, 26.
169     **nigger radio & nigger whore.** Stanford, Journals, Box 5.
170     **I walked with.** OTR, 180.
170     **looking, exploring, & burning.** AGHO, 26, 28, 3.
171     **I am with you & cottage in the.** Ibid., 90.
172     **Moloch! Moloch! & Carl Solomon!** AGCP, 131, 132.
172     **censored & who let themselves.** James Campbell, *This Is the Beat Generation: New York—San Francisco—Paris* (Berkeley: University of California, 2001), 189.
172–73  **The beginning of the reading.** *Holy Soul Jelly Roll*, CD booklet (Los Angeles: Rino, 1994), 10, 13.
173     **I disrobed finally.** Schumacher, *Dharma Lion*, 242.
173     **Why am I & For years.** DP, 207.
174     **messiah of a sort & outside the particular.** Deirdre Bair, *Anaïs Nin: A Biography* (New York: Putnam, 1995), 402.
174     **great long & at times.** Anaïs Nin, *The Diary of Anaïs Nin: 1955–1966* (New York: Harcourt Brace Jovanovich, 1976), 64.
174     ***cannot* be associated.** Mel Weisburd, "The Merchant of Venice," *Coastlines*, Autumn 1957, 40.
175     **harder to get things.** Kenneth Rexroth, "Disengagement: The Art of the Beat Generation," in *World Outside the Window: Selected Essays of Kenneth Rexroth*, ed. Bradford Morrow (New York; New Directions, 1987), 55.
175     **I do nothing & So life.** Berg, Ginsberg to Ryan, Dec. 8, 1955.
175     ***There's* something.** *The Letters of Denise Levertov and William Carlos Williams*, ed. Christopher MacGowan (New York: New Directions, 1998), 54.

175–76    **It seems Allen & He will damage.** Ibid., 62.

176       **He is a Jew & He can walk.** Ibid., 64.

176       **I don't think.** FB, 76.

177       **"Death News."** AGCP, 297.

177       **considerable departure & keep it up.** AGHO, 150.

177–78    **type of poetry & were many mansions.** FB, 49.

178       **a little too, I hope you, I hope you behave, & beautiful.** Ibid., 50–51.

178       **My mother Naomi & My heart is.** Stanford, Journals, Box 6.

178       ***Kaddish or the Sea Power.*** Ibid.

178       **We all die.** Stanford, Box 3, Ginsberg to Eugene Brooks, July 10, 1956.

179       **voice ringing.** AGHO, 159.

179       **bombs.** Ibid.

179       **famous authorhood.** Ibid.

179       **new source of loot.** FB, 71.

179       **incredible logical revolutions.** Texas, Ginsberg to Kerouac, July 3, 1949.

180       **I'm with you.** AGCP, 133.

180       **You have no.** FB, 38.

180       **chair of guest.** Ibid., 37.

181       **actually express.** Ibid.

181       **I practically.** Ibid.

181       **precipitate great.** Ibid.

181       **actually succeed.** Ibid.

181–82    **When we interviewed.** Telephone interview with Ellen Belton, May 15, 2003.

182       **sort of surrealist anarchist tract.** FB, 37.

182       **I am wondering.** LWB, 315.

182–83    **"America."** AGCP, 146–48.

183       **I Allen Ginsberg.** AGJMF, 207.

183       **America when will ... angelic?** AGCP, 146.

183       **America when will ... mother?** AGJMF, 207.

183       **queer.** AGCP, 148.

183       **not sorry.** Ibid., 146.

184     **America it's them.** Ibid., 147.

184     **America I'm putting.** Ibid., 148.

185     **[I] hate.** AGHO, 158.

185     **a negative howl & affirmation.** BD, 290, 217.

185     **smelly shits, angels, & forgive and love.** Ibid., 211.

185     **what seems "mad"** Ibid., 209.

186     **nihilistic rebellion & enlightenment of mystical.** Ibid., 217.

186     **most remarkable.** Richard Eberhart, "West Coast Rhythms," *New York Times Book Review*, Sept. 2, 1956, 7.

186     **years of & brave new.** Ibid., 18.

187     **my first reaction.** Ibid.

187     **positive force & redemptive quality.** Ibid.

187     **Nobody I know.** Bancroft, Ginsberg to Ferlinghetti, Dec. 7, 1956.

188     **one review.** Ibid., Dec. 20, 1956.

## 10. This Fiction Named Allen Ginsberg

189     **This fiction named Allen Ginsberg.** Ginsberg quoted in Barry Miles, *The Beat Hotel: Ginsberg, Burroughs, and Corso in Paris, 1957–1963* (New York: Grove, 2000), 47.

189     **I'm a square.** Israel Shenker, "The Life and Rhymes of Ginsberg," *New York Times*, Feb. 13, 1972, 87.

189     **high school.** LGMSP, 3.

190     **While our methods.** FB, 127.

190     **"To Allen Ginsberg."** Louis Hyde, ed., *On the Poetry of Allen Ginsberg*, 84.

190     **I'm not really.** Miles, *The Beat Hotel*, 47.

191     **So finally.** Ibid.

192     **greatest story.** FB, 77.

192     **The future is not.** Ibid.

192     **Neither side.** Ibid., 91.

193     **mad dictatorial.** Ibid., 89.

193     **mass hypnosis.** Ibid., 92.

193     **great nation & communism had.** Ibid., 85, 81.

194     **shift to cooperative.** Ibid., 88.

194    **The masses are wrong & world is going.** Bancroft, Ginsberg to Ferlinghetti, circa Oct. 1957.

194    **old line socialists.** FB, 89.

194    **American democracy.** Stanford, Letters, Box 3, Allen Ginsberg to Louis Ginsberg, Feb. 2, 1958.

194    **great experience & like going.** FB, 72.

195    **beautiful & to expatriate.** Ibid., 73.

195    **hard, closed.** Stanford, Letters, Box 3, Allen Ginsberg to Louis Ginsberg, n.d.

195    **Europeans have & big black.** FB, 77.

196    **naked idealized.** Stanford, Letters, Box 3, Allen Ginsberg to Louis Ginsberg, Aug. 10, 1957.

196    **mad Shelley's.** FB, 65.

197    **no vitality & full of the author.** Ibid., 70.

197    **republic of poetry.** Ibid.

197    **spiritual democracy & indestructible.** Ibid.

197    **Last nite I dreamed** & related quotations. AGJMF, 427.

198    **"T. S. Eliot Entered My Dreams."** Allen Ginsberg, *Poems All over the Place, Mostly Seventies* (Cherry Valley: Cherry Valley Editions, 1978), 47.

199    **poetic mentor & I showed him.** John Hollander, "Allen Ginsberg: 1926–1997," *Proceedings of the American Academy of Arts and Letters*, 2d series, 48, 1998, 73.

199    **dreadful little volume** & related quotations. John Hollander, "Poetry Chronicle," *Partisan Review*, Spring 1957, 297–98.

200    **nasty.** Stanford, Letters, Box 3, Ginsberg to Eugene Brooks, June 1957.

200    **exhibitionist welter, comic talent, & passion for values.** James Dickey, "From Babel to Byzantium," *Sewanee Review*, July–Sept. 1957, 510.

200    **Attitude & really not.** Ibid., 509.

200    **hysteria & dope-addicts.** Norman Podhoretz, "A Howl of Protest in San Francisco," *New Republic*, Sept. 16, 1957, 20.

200    **homosexuality.** Ibid., 20.

201     **enormous antipathy** & **vested centers.** Bruce Cook, *The Beat Generation* (New York: Charles Scribner's Sons, 1971), 97.

201     **Suzuki rhythm boys.** James Baldwin, "The Black Boy Looks at the White Boy," *Nobody Knows My Name* (New York: Dell, 1961), 180.

201     **Beatsville** & **Squaresville.** *Life*, Sept. 21, 1959, 30.

202     **history of modern.** Norman Podhoretz, "The Know-Nothing Bohemians," *Partisan Review*, Spring 1958, 316.

202     **There were people.** Cook, *The Beat Generation*, 97.

202     **little volume.** Podhoretz, "The Know-Nothing Bohemians," 305.

203     **homosexuality, preserve,** & **darker side.** Ibid., 308, 309.

203     **violence and criminality.** Ibid., 308.

203     **more idyllic.** Ibid., 311.

204     **worships primitivism.** Ibid., 307–8.

204     **The spirit of hipsterism.** Ibid., 318.

204     **The Beat Generation is no.** PJK, 562.

204     **a Beat Generation all** & **most sensitive.** Ibid., 564.

205     **Dear John, Yours in the,** & **Nella Grebsnig.** AGIA, 163, 177.

205     **Well what's all** & **I don't know.** Ibid., 173.

205     **whole horror** & **who is absolutely.** Ibid., 166, 167.

205     **American Egghead, Podhoretz** & **jerks who.** Ibid., 175, 174, 168.

205–6   *wrong* **(unscientific)** & **ridiculous provincial.** Ibid., 165.

206     THEY CAN TAKE. Ibid., 168.

206     **Poetry is what.** Ibid., 170.

206     **I am sick.** Ibid.

206     FORM FORM FORM. Ibid., 169.

206     **John, heart and,** & **take me.** Ibid., 165.

207     **outright vicious.** Stanford, Journals, Box 7.

207     **They should treat** & **after all.** Ibid.

207     **in 20 years.** Ibid.

207     **too familiarly** & **accepted in.** Ibid.

207        **Kerouac opened.** BD, 67.

207–8      **The only pattern** & **discovered in.** Stanford, Journals, Box 7.

208        **Any poem I.** AGIA, 173.

208        **"I'm a Prisoner of Allen Ginsberg."** *White Shroud: Poems 1980–1985* (New York: Perennial Library, 1987), 40.

## 11. Best Minds

209        **Best Minds.** AGCP, 126.

209        **gang** & **up to 400.** Mariani, *William Carlos Williams*, 730.

210        **bored** & **real horror.** JKSLII, 36, 43.

210        *ROCK AND ROLL* & **double the sales.** Ibid., 27.

210        **chickenshit** & **put off.** Ibid., 46.

210        **I'm introduced as.** Ibid., 42.

210–11     **dirty, ugly, entangle, in trouble,** & **cut them.** FB, 35.

211        **who let themselves.** Allen Ginsberg, *Howl and Other Poems* (San Francisco: City Lights, 1956), 12.

211        **selling like.** Stanford, Letters, Box 3, Ginsberg to Eugene Brooks, June 20, 1957.

211        **you wouldn't want.** OPAG, 43.

212        **most advanced.** DP, 242.

212        **I almost hope** & **I am almost.** AGHO, 151.

212        **great classic.** Ibid.

213        **I guess the seizure.** FB, 60.

213–14     **finest Catholic** & **international avant-garde.** Kenneth Rexroth, "San Francisco Letter," *Evergreen Review* 1, no. 2, 1957, 9–10.

214        **one of the** & **the most sensational.** Ibid., 12, 11.

214        **It is Hollywood.** Ibid., 11.

214        **first genuinely.** Ibid., 12.

214        **to reading only** & related quotations. William Hogan, "Between the Lines," *San Francisco Chronicle*, Apr. 7, 1957, 26.

214        **most significant single.** OPAG, 43.

214        **sad wastes.** Ibid., 43–44.

215        **It was Ginsberg's.** William Everson, *Archetype West*, 116.

215        **Let me report.** JKSLII, 40–41.

216    **like Germany.** Ibid., 41.

216    **So Allen.** Ibid.

216    **sorry to miss** & related quotations. Stanford, Letters, Box 3, Ginsberg to Eugene Brooks, June 20, 1957.

217    **redeeming social importance.** Edward de Grazia, *Girls Lean Back Everywhere: The Law of Obscenity and the Assault on Genius* (New York: Random House, 1992), 430.

217    **salacious** & **noble.** OPAG, 46.

217    **one of the most.** Ibid., 46.

218    **a significant modern.** Ibid., 47.

218    **It may or may not.** Ibid.

218    **every citizen.** J. W. Ehrlich, ed., *Howl of the Censor* (San Carlos, Calif.: Nourse, 1961), 117.

219    **whole boatload.** AGCP, 132.

219    **understand it** & **I think it is.** Ehrlich, *Howl of the Censor*, 96.

219    **It has no.** Ibid., 93–94.

219    **weak imitation** & **to a long-dead.** Ibid., 77, 91.

220    **The desire to censor.** Ibid., 111.

220    **crystal, transparent,** & **skin.** Ibid., 106.

220    **I love thee not** & **zounds.** Ibid., 105.

220    **Biblical.** Ibid., 63.

220    **resurrective** & **sort of paean.** Ibid., 68.

220    **violence, greed** & **violent and powerful.** Ibid., 66.

221    **honest poet** & **highly competent.** Ibid., 54.

221    **genuine work** & **characteristic.** Ibid., 60.

221    **fertility.** Ibid., 44.

221    **esthetic structure** & **modern life as.** Ibid., 26, 33.

222    **with dreams, with drugs,** & **these are.** Ibid., 31–32.

222    **who got busted** & **injured in.** Ibid., 31.

222    **nightmare world** & **materialism, conformity.** Ibid., 119.

222    **self-guardians** & **noxious literature.** Ibid., 126, 127.

222    **vapid innocuous.** Ibid., 122.

222    **some redeeming, not obscene,** & **not guilty.** Ibid., 127.

222–23    **judge's decision.** OPAG, 53.

223    **mythologies.** Ehrlich, *Howl of the Censor*, 72.

223    **great literature** & **possibility.** Ibid., 64.

223     **great works and classics** & **condemned.** Ibid., 110.

223     **suppressed books** & **venerable classic.** Ibid., xii.

223–24  **tended to ignore** & **most harrowing.** Marjorie Perloff, "A Lion in Our Living Room," *American Poetry Review*, Mar.–Apr. 1985, 35.

224     **The perfect classic** & **classic must.** TSESP, 127–28.

225     **American adolescent.** James Dickey, "From Babel to Byzantium," 509.

225     **clean Saxon four-letter.** AGHO, xii.

225     **this is.** TSESP, 124.

225     **boxcars.** AGCP, 127.

226     **will find its.** TSESP, 128.

226     **Every great work** & **Every supreme poet.** Ibid., 125.

226     **There was a shocking.** David Meltzer, ed., *San Francisco Beat: Talking with the Poets* (San Francisco: City Lights, 2001), 101.

226     **peaks of inspiration** & **valleys and plateaus.** AGCP, xx.

227     **noise of public life.** Billy Collins, poetry reading, Santa Rosa, Calif., Nov. 1, 2002.

228     **Buddhist practice.** Meltzer, *San Francisco Beat*, 104.

229     **his best** & **radical pleasure.** Charles McGrath, "Street Singer," *New York Times Book Review*, Apr. 27, 1997, 43.

230     **beautiful in an ugly graceful way.** PJK, 559.

# Index

abnormality: homosexuality as, 41, 52; poetry-writing as, 59. *See also* madness

academia, 5–6, 80, 84–85; Black Mountain College, 47–48, 206; Brooklyn College, 181–82, 228; culture war with bohemia, 44–51, 198–208; Ginsberg as teacher, 46, 180–82, 228–29; language, 102; and obscenity trial, 216–17, 220, 221; poetry readings vs., 12, 14, 15, 21–22; San Francisco State College, 13, 180, 216, 220; Sonoma State University, xv–xvii; Stanford's Ginsberg archive, 80; University of California, Berkeley, 180, 221; Whitman not included, 20, 47; William Carlos Williams not included, 106. *See also* Columbia College

Adams, Joan. *See* Burroughs, Joan Adams

Adams, Walter, 82, 144

adolescence: *Howl*, 44–45, 225; Rimbaud, 63. *See also* teens

adversarial culture, 49, 50, 80, 207–8. *See also* Beat Generation; bohemianism; culture war; non-conformists; underground

advertising, 113, 176; Gap, 176; Ginsberg for friends, 184; Ginsberg for *Howl*, 174–76, 187–88, 197; Ginsberg jobs, 114, 130; hell, 136

Africa: Dakar, 75–77, 137, 170. *See also* Morocco

African Americans: writers in culture war, 201. *See also* blacks

allegory, 91, 144

Allen, Donald M., 213, 217–18; *The New American Poetry*, 206

Allen, Gay Wilson, 20

ambivalence: about blacks, 169–70; about everything, 152; *Howl*, 142; about madness, 152; respectability/underground, 130

Clark, Walter Van Tilburg, 220;
*Ox-Bow Incident*, 221; *The Track
of the Cat*, 221
Cleophas, Sister Mary, *Between
Fixity and Flux*, 180
Clinton, Bill, 208
Coit Tower murals, 125
Cold War, xii–xv, 3–6, 11; Gins-
berg politics, xii–xv, 93–96,
183–84; *Howl* and, xii–xv, xx,
xxv, 3, 21, 182; "ideology of
fear," 10; Milosz, 226; San Fran-
cisco, 10–11; Six Gallery
poetry reading, 9, 22; Solomon
politics, 97–98; William Carlos
Williams and, 70. *See also* anti-
communism
Coleridge, Samuel Taylor, 59, 86;
"The Rime of the Ancient
Mariner," 75–76
collage, art of, 174
College of Marin, xii, xiii–xiv
Collins, Billy, 227
Colorado, Ginsberg travels, 137
Columbia College, xiii–xiv, 44–
60; Adams, 82; Boar's Head
competition (1948), 76; Butler,
60; Carr, 43, 52; culture war,
44–51, 198–201, 205, 207;
Dakar trip and, 75–77; Gins-
berg arrest, 89; Ginsberg and
Auden, 59, 61, 66–67, 72, 119,
196; Ginsberg contradictory
feelings about, 62; Ginsberg
expulsion, 61; Ginsberg labor
lawyer aspirations, 42–43;
Ginsberg last semester, 77–80;
Ginsberg prizes, 102; Ginsberg
reinstatement, 65–70; Ginsberg
secrecy, 58; Ginsberg sexuality,

48, 57–60, 87; Ginsberg and
violence, 204; Ginsberg and
Whitman, 46, 47, 50, 102, 119;
vs. homosexuality, 48, 52; Rich-
ard Howard, 98; *Howl* influence,
xxi, xxv, 22, 44, 45, 46, 60, 65,
80; *Howl* reading, 177–78; *King
Lear*, 160; literary magazine, 58;
Simpson, 114, 226. *See also*
Trilling, Lionel
*Columbia College Today*, 80
*Columbia Review*, 66, 68, 69, 199
comedy, 200; "America," 183;
*Howl*, xiv, 137, 169, 180, 183,
224
*Commentary*, 202
commercialism, 5, 111, 175–76,
198, 207–8; *Howl* sales, xx, 174–
76, 179, 187–88, 197, 213. *See
also* advertising; money
communism, 33–34, 53, 93–98,
153, 170, 193–94; Beats as
bigger threat than, 202; Colum-
bia, 55; Communist Party, 28,
68, 94, 97, 98, 116, 180, 193;
Naomi Ginsberg, 26, 28, 68,
116, 154; Hay, 10–11; in *Howl*,
180, 183; San Francisco, 10;
Trilling and, 49. *See also* anti-
communism; Cold War;
Marxism
concentration camps, 4, 33, 92
conformity: Cold War and, 5;
San Francisco culture vs., 15;
"silent," 162. *See also* non-
conformists
Congress, U.S., 5, 42. *See also* Mc-
Carthy, Joseph/McCarthyism
Congress for Cultural Freedom,
xiii

Whitman, 20, 40–41, 109–10.
*See also* Orlovsky, Peter
Ginsberg, Allen (journals), xxii, 25,
35, 109; "apt relation of dissimi-
lars," 160; on art, 56; on Bur-
roughs as "spy from the future,"
110; on California, 114–15; on
cities, 132–33; on Columbia
years, 46; on Eliot, 159, 197–98;
"A Few Notes on Composition,"
159; on genius, 40; on hell, 132–
33; on homosexuality, 152;
howl/howling in, 117; on
Huncke, 83; list of madmen and
suicides, 110–11; on madness,
152; Mexico, 118–19; on mirror
image, 108; on Naomi, 29, 31–
33, 115–16, 178; at New York
State Psychiatric Institute, 93–
94; on original poetry, 207–8;
on politics, 33–34, 92–95; on
San Francisco, 131, 132; suicidal
thoughts, 111; twenty-ninth
birthday, 161; on walking
around, 107
Ginsberg, Allen (poems), 8, 20–
21; "After All, What Else Is
There to Say?," 106; "After
Lalon," 208; "Airplane Blues,"
xvii; "America," xiv–xv, 119,
172, 182–84, 194; "At Apolli-
naire's Grave," 191; "Autumn
Leaves," 229; Berkeley, xxiii,
140; "Birdbrain!," xii, 96;
"Birthday Ode"/"Surrealist
Ode," 74; "Black Shroud," 157;
"Blessed be the Muses," 161; *A
Book of Doldrums*, 74, 100–101;
"Brooklyn College Brain," 228;
"Capitol Air," xii; *The Character*

*of the Happy Warrior/Death in
Violence*, 76; "C'mon Pigs of
Western Civilization Eat More
Grease," 227; *Collected Poems:
1947-1980*, xv, 77, 182, 228–29;
"Confrontation with Louis
Ginsberg's Poems," 37; *Cos-
mopolitan Greetings*, 229; "Dakar
Doldrums," 76–77; "Death and
Fame," 229; "Death News," 177;
death theme, xxii, 105, 114, 118,
177, 229; "Death to Van Gogh's
Ear!," 95–96, 191; "The Denver
Doldrums: Suicide Waltzes for
the Denver Birds," 72–74;
"Doom," 79; "Dream Record:
June 8, 1955," 144; *Empty Mir-
ror*, 100, 105–6, 108, 109, 118,
229; following *Howl*, 172, 182,
191; "A Further Proposal," 76–
77; "Garden State," 228; "The
Green Automobile," 115; "Hart
Crane," 69; after *Howl*, 226–30;
howl/howling in (pre-*Howl*),
117; *Howl and Other Poems*, xi,
77, 79–80, 177, 179, 181, 185,
199–200, 226; "I'm a Prisoner
of Allen Ginsberg," 208; "In
Death, Cannot Reach What Is
Most Near," 105; influences
claimed by Ginsberg, xvi, 184,
190; "In Hospital Visiting
Naomi," 115; "In the Baggage
Room at Greyhound," 123, 153;
"In Vesuvio's Waiting for
Sheila," 130; "Kral Majales," 96;
"The Last Voyage," 76; "The
Lion for Real," 79; "Long Live
the Spiderweb," 106; "Love Let-
ter," 76–77; "Love Poem on

Williams, 27, 102–3. *See also* father figures
merchant marine (U.S. Maritime Service), 61–62, 65
metaphysical poetry, 69, 76
Mexico: Burroughs, 113; Ginsberg, 117–19; *Howl*, 137; Kerouac, 112, 139
Miami, 117
Michaux, Henri, 97
Michelangelo Buonarroti, 196
Mike's Place, 127
Miles, Barry, 25, 137
Miles, Josephine, 127
military-industrial complex, xx, 11, 193. *See also* war
Military Sea Transportation Service, *Sgt. Jack J. Pendleton*, 178–79
Mill, John Stuart, 47
Miller, Arthur, 5; *The Death of a Salesman*, 4; *A View from the Bridge*, 11
Miller, Henry, 5, 97, 125, 212–13; *The Tropic of Cancer*, 145, 212–13; *The Tropic of Capricorn*, 145
millionaires: American, 5; Jews, 112
Milosz, Czeslaw, 226
Milvia Street cottage (Berkeley), 13, 139–42, 168–69, 171
mimeograph revolution, 177
mind: mind/body, 29, 35; modern, 105–6; movements, 159
misogyny, Ginsberg's, 61–62, 148–49, 227
modernism, 49, 50–51, 62; "robotic," 198

modernity, Ginsberg on, 67–68, 82, 105–6
Moloch, 138; *Howl*, 30, 95, 130–33, 138–39, 141–42, 161–62, 170; like Louis's "fierce Behemoths," 39; Rexroth's "Thou Shalt Not Kill" and, 128
money: America and, 193–94, 195, 205; Louis Ginsberg, 36, 42; Ginsberg advertising *Howl*, 176; *Howl* sales, xx, 179; *Howl* theme, 42; millionaires, 5, 112; writers, 5, 42. *See also* commercialism
Monroe, Marilyn, 115
Moore, Marianne, 102, 107
Morocco, 209–10, 216. *See also* Tangiers
Moscow, 95, 132
mother figures: Joan Burroughs, 37, 62, 113. *See also* Ginsberg, Edith Cohen (stepmother); Ginsberg, Naomi Levy (mother)
movies, 11; *An American in Paris*, 110; *The Blackboard Jungle*, 203; bookmovie, 129; Charlie Chaplin, 114, 180, 224; *East of Eden*, 126; *Kaddish* and, 227; Marx Brothers, 136–37, 180; *Metropolis*, 131; *Rashamon*, 110; *Rebel without a Cause*, 11, 126; *The Wild One*, 126. *See also* Hollywood
murals, WPA, 125
Murao, Shigeyoshi, 215, 218, 219
murder: Kammerer, 53–54. *See also* killing

*tor*, 75; Columbia and, 47; grave, 196; revolutionary, 59
Shields, Karen, 118
Shilling, Andrew, xviii
Simpson, Louis, 114, 226
Six Gallery, poetry reading, 1–3, 6–9, 12–23, 141, 154, 171–72, 174
Slansky, Paul, 226
Snyder, Gary, xviii, 13, 173, 187; "Berry Feast," 18; City Lights *Howl* edition, 179; in *Evergreen Review*, 213; *Howl* as "Strophes," 167; Japan, 16; *Myths and Texts*, 18; Six Gallery poetry reading, 1–3, 7, 8–9, 16, 18, 179; as Thoreau successor, 110; William Carlos Williams and, 102
socialism, 10, 33–34, 43, 98, 193–94
Socialist Party, 34, 98
Solomon, Carl, xxiii, 96–99; *Howl*, 42, 96, 145, 154–57, 166; madness, 97, 145, 154–57, 165; marriage, 101; New York State Psychiatric Institute, 96–99, 155, 157; Pilgrim State Hospital, 154–57; "verbal orgy," 165
Sonoma State University, xv–xvii
South, civil rights movement, 11, 169–70, 203–4
Soviet Union, 4, 204, 226; CIA and, xiii; Czechoslovakia invaded by, 95; "Destalinization," 184; Ginsberg assessments, 33–34, 193–94; nuclear age, 183–84; Solomon and, 97; William Carlos Williams and, 70, 103. *See also* Cold War; Russia

Spanish Civil War, 34
Speiser, Lawrence, 217
Spender, Stephen, 5, 166
Spengler, Oswald, 46, 67; *Decline of the West*, 55–56
Spicer, Jack, 12, 14, 211–12
spontaneity, xv; "America" and, 182–83; Buddhism and, 228; *Howl* and, xix, 167–68, 170–71; *Howl* review and, 186; Kerouac and, 129, 167–68, 228
Sputnik, 192
squareness, 19, 133, 189, 201
Stanford, Ginsberg archive, 80
Starkie, Enid, 49
State Department, U.S., 5
Steinbeck, John, 9
St. Elizabeth's Hospital, Washington, D.C., 91, 101, 117, 151
Stevens, Wallace, 102, 229
Stevenson, Adlai, 114, 162
Stofsky, David, 78
Styron, William, 52
Sublette, Al, 158
subterranean world: Ginsberg's, 27; Kerouac's heroes, 162–63; Six Gallery poetry reading, 8
suburbia, xi, 67
suicide, 110, 135; Adams attempt, 82; Berryman, xxi–xxii; Carr attempt, 52; Crane, 95; Allen Ginsberg and, xxii, 77, 83–84, 111, 135; Naomi Ginsberg attempt, 31–32; *Howl* and, 135–37; Natalie Jackson, 37, 152; Kerouac thoughts, 112, 135; Mayakovsky, 95, 193; Phil White, 110–11
Superman comic books, 47

|  |  |
|---|---|
| Designer: | Nola Burger |
| Compositor: | G & S Typesetters, Inc. |
| Indexer: | Barbara Roos |
| Text: | 10/15 Janson |
| Display: | Janson |
| Printer and Binder: | Maple-Vail Manufacturing Group |